WITHDRAWN
HARVARD LIBRARY
WITHDRAWN

Loving beyond Your Theology
The Life and Ministry of Jimmy Raymond Allen

Endowed by
TOM WATSON BROWN
and
THE WATSON-BROWN FOUNDATION, INC.

Loving beyond Your Theology
The Life and Ministry of Jimmy Raymond Allen

Larry L. McSwain

MERCER UNIVERSITY PRESS
Macon, Georgia USA

MUP/H805

Loving beyond Your Theology.
The Life and Ministry of Jimmy Raymond Allen.
Copyright ©2010
Mercer University Press, Macon GA USA
All rights reserved
Printed in the United States of America
First edition

Mercer University Press
is a member of Green Press Initiative
<greenpressinitiatige.org>, a nonprofit organization
working to help publishers and printers increase their use
of recycled paper and decrease their use of fiber
derived from endangered forests. This book is printed
on recycled paper and meets the minimum requirements
of American National Standard for Information Sciences—
Permanence of Paper for Printed Library Materials,
ANSI Z39.48-1984.

Library of Congress Cataloging-in-Publication Data

[CIP data on file at the Library of Congress.]

Isbn 978-0-88146-205-0

BX
6495
.A435
M37
2010

Contents

List of Tables 8

Abbreviations 9

Foreword
Jimmy Allen: Personification of the Christian Leader,
by Jimmy Carter 11

A Jimmy Allen Album 13

Acknowledgments 22

1. Introduction: The Story of a Prophetic Priest 24

2. Early Narratives: A Scripted Child 32
   The Allen Genogram, 32
   From Providence to Detroit, 35
   An Itinerant Preacher in One State, 37

3. Faith and Education Journeys 42
   Elementary Schools, 43
   Profession of Faith and Baptism, 45
   High Schools, 47
   Call to Preach, 49
   Howard Payne College, Brownwood, Texas, 52
   Youth Revival Movement, 59
   Conclusion, 63

4. Young Adulthood and Foundational Leadership 66
   Royal Ambassadors, 66
   Love and Marriage, 70
   Southwestern Baptist Theological Seminary, 73
       Student pastorates, 77
       Dissertation, 80
       Thomas Buford Maston, 81
   Conclusion, 83

5. The Mandate for Applied Christianity 85
   Christian Life Commission, 86

A New Vocation, 88
Continuity and Change in the Christian Life Commission, 92
  Alliances in Austin, 95
  Racial Crises, 97
The Kennedy Assassination, 100
CLC Staff, 102
Conclusion, 105

6. San Antonio Beckons: Visionary Pastoral Leadership 106
An Unofficial Interim, 107
First Steps in a New Pastorate, 111
Distinctive Programs, 113
Outreach to the Military, 119
Connecting Through Media, 120
Results, 125
  Buildings, Budgets, and Baptisms, 125
  Qualitative Measures, 127

7. Denominational Leadership: Enlarging the Vision 132
President of the Baptist General Convention of Texas, 132
President of the Southern Baptist Convention, 137
Bold Mission Thrust, 138
Year One, 141
  Mission Service Corps, 142
  The Atlanta Convention, 13-15 June 1978, 145
Year Two, 149
  Allen and the Carter White House, 150
  The Houston Convention, 12-14 June 1979, 152

8. Ventures in International Relations 157
Religious Liberty in Israel, 157
  Meetings in Israel 1978–1979, 159
  Meetings in Israel 1980, 161
The Iranian Hostage Crisis, 164
  From Prayer to Travel, 166
  Activities in Iran, 169

9. Kingdom Communication in a Television Age 175
   Continuity and Discontinuity at the RTVC, 176
      National Awards, 179
      Change in the Air, 179
   The ACTS Satellite Network, 181
   Money, Money, Money, 185
   The CenturyMen in China, 190
   Conclusions, 195

10. Loving Past Your Theology:
    The Pain of a Prophetic Priest 200
    Darkness in the Allen Household, 201
    HIV/AIDS in the Allen Family, 203
    "Granddad! I don't have a secret anymore. I've gone public," 206
    Jimmy Allen the Advocate for HIV/AIDS Ministry, 207
    Theology from the Pain Down, 211

11. Transitions: New Geography,
       New Ministries, New Leadership 213
    The Chapel at Big Canoe, 215
    Religion and the News Media, 219
    Organizing the Cooperative Baptist Fellowship, 222
    Celebration of a New Baptist Covenant, 225

12. Postscript
    The Measure of the Man and His Ministry 228

    Appendix 236

    Bibliography 238

    Index 249

List of Tables

Table 1.
RTVC Annual Budgets, 1980–1989 187

Table 2.
Debt Accumulation and Interest Expense, 1980–1989 188

Abbreviations

The denominational and national context in which Jimmy Allen served connected him to multiple agencies and organization. Rather than use the full title of each organization or group and for the reader's benefit, the following abbreviations are used.

BC Baptists Committed to the SBC, later named Mainstream Baptists

BGCT Baptist General Convention of Texas, Dallas

BJC Baptist Joint Committee, Washington DC,
formerly Baptist Joint Committee for Public Affairs

BWA Baptist World Alliance

CBF Cooperative Baptist Fellowship

CP Cooperative Program,
the unified giving program for Southern Baptists

CLC Christian Life Commission, Texas

FBC First Baptist Church.
(The city follows to identify which FBC where necessary.)

FMB Foreign Mission Board of the SBC,
later named the International Mission Board

GAs Girls' Auxiliary, the mission education program
of the Women's Missionary Union for young girls

HMB Home Mission Board of the SBC,
later named the North American Mission Board

IMB International Mission Board, SBC

NABF North American Baptist Fellowship, the members
of the Baptist World Alliance in Canada and the U.S.

NAMB North American Mission Board, SBC

OEO   Office of Economic Opportunity,
a part of the War Against Poverty in the 1960s

RAs   Royal Ambassadors, the mission education program
of the Brotherhood Commission for boys

RTVC   Radio and Television Commission, SBC

SBC   Southern Baptist Convention

CLC   Christian Life Commission
of the Southern Baptist Convention

SBTS   Southern Baptist Theological Seminary

SWBTS   Southwestern Baptist Theological Seminary

WMU   Woman's Missionary Union,
an auxiliary of the Southern Baptist Convention

Foreword
Jimmy Allen: Personification of the Christian Leader

I cannot think of any other Baptist leader who has had more of a beneficial effect on my life than Jimmy Allen. There are many Baptists leaders for whom I have great admiration and who may be more famous on a global basis. Billy Graham immediately comes to mind. But as far as my personal career as a Baptist, Jimmy would be preeminent in his constant, persistent, and dependable inspiration and guidance for me.

We first met during my campaign for president of the United States while he was pastor of the First Baptist Church in San Antonio, Texas. I became acquainted more personally with him and his energy, vision, and effectiveness as a leader while I was a member of the Brotherhood Commission of the Southern Baptist Convention when the investment of laypersons was more valued in my denomination. When he became president of the Southern Baptist Convention, I was especially taken with his vision for a global mission advance by Southern Baptists with the gospel as a message for salvation and a force for justice and human dignity in our world. When I was president and he wanted to magnify greatly the involvement of Baptist men in short-term missionary efforts, he called on me, and I helped all I could. I remember well his focus on the Mission Service Corps, the Southern Baptist Convention effort to challenge all laypersons to commit themselves to short-term mission appointments. When he asked for our assistance in building support for this idea, Rosalynn and I supported the effort financially and with our influence in a major fund-raising event at the Mayflower Hotel in Washington, D.C., in 1977, and at the Southern Baptist Convention meeting in Atlanta in 1978.

He offered significant support to my efforts to bring national and international policies of human justice in the work of our government, for which I am grateful. Through our frequent contacts he has become a valued friend and spiritual advisor to whom I look for encouragement, prayer, and work together.

Jimmy Allen is the personification of what a Christian should be. To me, that is the highest accolade that can be given to anyone. He is a man of great capability, a natural leader, kind, gentle, benevolent, humble, forceful, and an idealist who has the strength to turn his dreams into reality. He is innovative and has clear concepts of what Christian life ought to be. Jimmy is diverse in his interests, not only as head of the Southern Baptist Convention, but in his life since then. He has been very much involved in our family, for instance in the Friendship Force, of which Rosalynn was a board member. When I have had challenges in my life, I have always felt that I could turn to him for advice because I trust his judgment.

I think Jimmy's legacy is still being formulated. There would be unanimity among those Christian brothers and sisters in being grateful to Jimmy Allen for his achievements within the moderate Baptist movement, including his leadership role and his willingness to participate in efforts to promote reconciliation, even among people with whom we may have been in disagreement. In fact, I had a meeting of Baptist leaders at the Carter Center in the 1980s, seven of whom have been president of the Southern Baptist Convention. Jimmy Allen was one. He had already served and was the only moderate there. He joined me in trying to heal the wounds that divided the Baptists in this country. In every way he has been the foundation and inspiration for those who have made that kind of effort.

Jimmy and I are still working together. We are still trying to have a forum, if not organization, in which Baptists can cooperate in a non-exclusive way that might be more ambitious than what was done in the past, particularly in breaking down the racial divide. We are trying to bring all Baptists together. We are not trying to exclude anyone, whatever their theological commitments, if they are willing to accept certain concepts of freedom in the framework of historic Baptist beliefs. Jimmy will continue to serve a very important role in my life and in the future of Christianity in this country.

I am delighted to see this biography of his life written and distributed within the Baptist family. His life is a compelling story of God's call and the exercise of that call in making the world a better place in which all God's children can live together.

Jimmy Carter
Thirty-ninth president of the United States

A Jimmy Allen Album

Earl Allen

Edna Allen

Jimmy and his mother at her seminary graduation

Pastor and Mrs. Earl Allen

Jimmy Allen

*James Dunn, Jimmy Allen,
Phil Strickland, Foy Valentine*

With Menachem Begin

*In the Oval Office
with President Jimmy Carter*

Best wishes to Jimmy Allen, our good friend!
Rosalynn Carter Jimmy Carter

With President Carter
at the White House

*In the Ready Room,
Waiting to Preach at the SBC*

Preaching at the Southern Baptist Convention

At Abe Lincoln Awards

At Radio and Television Commission Office with Emmy Award

Astrodome, Southern Baptist Convention 1979

Jimmy and Linda Allen

Acknowledgments

My gratitude for assistance in this work is for many individuals. Most important is Jimmy Allen for hours of interview time, making his personal files available, and answering every question asked of him over four years of work. Without his cooperation and encouragement, this book would never have come to fruition.

Deep appreciation must be expressed to Jim Newton, journalist par excellence, who has been a long-time friend, coworker, and supporter of Allen. Jim has insider knowledge and connection with Southern Baptist leaders over forty years of ministry as a journalist, and has published scores of articles and interviews about them and their work, including Jimmy Allen. Jim and I began this venture with the intention of serving as coauthors of this book, but his health prevented that. He gave many hours of helpful interview time and editorial counsel, however, and the book is more readable and interesting because of his skill as a writer.

Most of the source material found here is from interviews conducted over the years and file collections of materials in a variety of libraries. The work of the Oral History Project at Baylor University provided archival material of essential interviews from the past. I am grateful for access to the transcriptions of all of the interviews conducted with Allen by Baylor faculty and students as well as permission of the Oral History Project staff to quote extensively from the interviews identified in the bibliography. Beth Perry, theological librarian of the Monroe Swilley Library, Mercer University (Atlanta campus), was a patient and encyclopedic guide in assisting in the location of archival material from multiple sources. Bill Sumner and Tammy Hall at the Southern Baptist Historical Library and Archives in Nashville were gracious and helpful in securing files on Allen's SBC presidency and Radio and Television Commission leadership. Laura Botts provided access to archives of early Baptists Committed to the SBC and Cooperative Baptist Fellowship meeting files located in the Baptist Archives of the Jack Tarver Library of Mercer University in Macon. Chelsea Clarke, my student assistant at McAfee School of Theology, assisted with locating and copying materials, transcribing interviews, and reading multiple drafts.

I am also grateful to the *Houston Chronicle* for granting permission to reproduce the photograph from their files of the mass gathering of Baptists in the Astrodome during the 1979 Southern Baptist Convention meeting. Permission to quote materials from Bruce McIver, *Riding the Wind*, has also been granted by Smyth & Helwys Publishers. Jimmy Allen granted permission to quote materials from Jimmy Allen, *Burden of a Secret*.

A special thank you is due to the several individuals who provided insights into Jimmy Allen through interviews, e-mail correspondence, and telephone contact. They are identified in the interviews section of the bibliography. Clay Price in the research department of the Baptist General Convention of Texas collected data for each of the congregations served by Allen. James Dunn at the Wake Forest Divinity School was helpful with his reading of the chapter on the work of the Christian Life Commission of the Baptist General Convention of Texas. Prior to his death in 2009, Richard T. McCartney, former executive vice president of the Radio and Television Commission, offered suggested details from his reading of the chapter on the work of the Commission.

I thank John Dunaway, director of the Mercer Commons, for the provision of expense resources from the Lilly Endowment, Inc. grant for the project. Most especially, Alan Culpepper, dean of the McAfee School of Theology, has provided the environment of encouragement and research funds to stimulate the completion of this project.

Appreciation is due to Marc Jolley and the entire staff of Mercer University Press for patient reviews, editorial improvements, and support in all aspects of the publication of this work. Edd Rowell was especially helpful in careful editing of the manuscript.

Finally, I thank my wife, Sue, who waited patiently during many months of writing as I finished another page before giving needed attention to her.

1 June 2009 *Larry L. McSwain*

Chapter 1
The Story of a Prophetic Priest

> The Celebration for a New Baptist Covenant would not have happened without Jimmy Allen. It just would not have happened. He was the person who energized it.
>
> —Daniel Vestal

A remarkable gathering of Baptists assembled in the Georgia World Congress Center in Atlanta, Georgia, 30 January–1 February 2008. Former President Jimmy Carter and William D. Underwood, president of Mercer University, spearheaded the celebration of what had been a year-long effort to unify a diverse gathering of Baptists in North America. They came together beyond the differences of race, gender, geography, and Baptist denominational affiliation to focus on the gospel mandate of Luke 4:18-19 in a "New Baptist Covenant." Some 15,000 participants gathered, representing thirty denominations and Baptist organizations, to form the most inclusive gathering of North American Baptists in their long history.

Carter and Underwood enlisted the consummate networker and organizer of mass meetings of this kind—Jimmy Raymond Allen—to chair the program committee of the celebration event. Though eighty years old, Allen worked tirelessly for a year to bring together this unique collection of Baptists in what Baptist historian, Walter Shurden, said, "It's the most significant Baptist meeting in my life, after playing in the Baptist yard 55 years or so. I've never been to a Baptist meeting where there was the equality as well as the presence of multiracial, multigender participation."[1] One could also add "multigenerational."

The two cochairs spoke at the first plenary session to present inspiring and informative introductions to the "Celebration for a New Baptist Covenant." Then a vintage Jimmy Allen approached the podium. The black, wavy hair of his youth was thinner and greyer and the black-rimmed glasses of his earlier years were replaced with metal ones. But the voice was the same—a staccato blend of emotion and thought with a summary challenge to the gathering. He raised the rhetorical question in the program of the event and on the platform that became the mantra of the meeting. "Have we gathered for a moment or a movement?"

---

[1]Marv Knox, "New Baptist Covenant: Unity, Harmony. Now, What Comes Next?" <http://www.newbaptistcelebration.org/news> (accessed 7 July 2008).

It will take decades before the answer to the question can be given. But that event was a culmination of the skills and connections developed in the years of the life and ministry of Jimmy Allen. It is a story of a hardscrabble existence in the Depression era in a family devoted to following the will of God without reservations. It is the account of a man who reflected the theology of his conservative upbringing in the white-hot atmosphere of Texas revivalism and evangelism in the 1940s and 1950s. It is also the saga of a man of enormous intellect and energy who grew beyond his environment and culture to develop a lifelong commitment to the blending of his inherited theology with an ethical progressivism of the Social Gospel. It is a story of a man with a pastor's heart and a prophet's passion who believed with all that was in him in a call from God to change the world.

Baptists in the South and Southwest have not been generally noted for their ethical progressivism. The dual burdens of slavery and poverty with generally inadequate levels of education consigned them too often to the backwaters of American social thought and action. It was the Northern branch of the family in the person of Walter Rauschenbusch and others who would take up the mantle of the new theology of the Social Gospel in the late nineteenth and early twentieth centuries in the United States. It was the African-American branch of the family that would awaken the nation to the cause of civil rights while too many white Southerners resisted or observed with neutrality.

Yet, in the midst of those antiprogressive stereotypes, there has been a cadre of white Baptists in the South who rubbed against the grain of culture to raise prophetic voices for change. Many are well known—Carlyle Marney, T. B. Maston, the brothers Poteat, Henlee Barnette, Clarence Jordan, W. W. Finlator, Foy Valentine, Phil Strickland, Will Campbell, Joe Trull, and James Dunn. Others like Walter Nathan Johnson are less well known.[2]

Most are overlooked because they did not write books or attract media attention. Yet, there are hundreds of stories of pastors of churches large and small who preached and served, often at the cost of the loss of their pulpits—Thomas Holmes, Paul Turner, and Herbert Gilmore, among them.

---

[2]David Stricklin, *A Genealogy of Dissent: Southern Baptist Protest in the Twentieth Century* (Lexington KY: University Press of Kentucky, 1999) provides an extensive historical account of these and many other prophets of the South.

They are difficult stories to tell because the records are scant, the names often unknown, and their ministries often dissolved into oblivion.

The story of Jimmy Allen is one of those stories that can be told because of the public visibility of his ministry and the remarkable nature of his accomplishments. This account is one based on personal interviews stretching over nearly forty years, a full-length book on family crisis and multiple articles written by him, dozens of press interviews and articles written about him, and personal files made available to this writer. It is as much an oral biography as one documented by letters, articles, and books. Given the expanse of history covered by this account, the original conceptions and language used by Allen and others of his time have been maintained. The reader will notice a decidedly masculine framework for the understandings of ministry and God documented in these pages.

Jimmy's life parallels in many respects the cultural story of America as it passed from the Great Depression through World War II to the social upheavals of the 1960s, into nearly four decades of technological innovation, economic expansion, and postmodern pluralism. Allen's life was both a reflection of that cultural change and a response to apply the gospel in multiple ways to it. But beyond that, his life is also an example, even a model, of how a man of humble, Southern beginnings can break through the chains of culture that enslave most of society to provide leadership in a progressive movement seeking to change what is ethically and morally wrong within that culture.

His life also parallels the story of Baptists in the South as he lived immersed in the theology and structures of the Southern Baptist Convention. He affirmed a traditional Baptist identity as a denominational employee, first as the director of Royal Ambassadors for the Baptist General Convention of Texas, then executive director of the Christian Life Commission for that same entity, and as president of the Radio and Television Commission of the Southern Baptist Convention.

He supported that tradition as a pastor of typical Texas Baptist churches during his student days and then modeled innovation in social ministry and media communication as pastor of the First Baptist Church in San Antonio. He proclaimed historic Baptist principles in elected leadership roles as vice-president and president of the Baptist General Convention of Texas and then as president of the Southern Baptist Convention. He became identified as a leading spokesperson for the denomination's emphases on Bold Mission Thrust and Mission Service Corps in the 1970s.

Allen always dreamed big dreams about the conventions he served. At the conclusion of his second term as the Texas convention president, he organized a mass meeting of all but one of the six African-American Baptist conventions in Texas with the annual meeting of the state convention in the Astrodome in Houston. More than 41,000 people attended that rally, making it the largest meeting of Baptists in American in history at that point in time. It also established a pattern for Allen's future leadership with a similar rally at the conclusion of his term as president of the Southern Baptist Convention attended by 50,000 people. In January 2008, he replicated the same ideas as program chairman of the "Celebration of a New Baptist Covenant" meeting in Atlanta. It is little wonder he was chosen in a poll of *Baptist Standard* readers one of the ten most influential Texas Baptist leaders of the twentieth century.

Allen affirmed Baptist ideals in working with fellow Baptist Jimmy Carter as he supported and advised the thirty-ninth President of the United States on social policy and international diplomacy. Such a relationship thrust him into at least two efforts at international relations in both Israel and Iran.

Jimmy Allen demonstrated his commitment to Baptist creativity with a visionary effort to form a new delivery system for communicating the Baptist message through television with the formation of the ACTS satellite network at the Radio and Television Commission. There he attempted to implement his vision of Bold Mission Thrust, especially with creative television programming of musical events in China. One of the programs he produced in that effort brought a daytime Emmy award to him and the Radio and Television Commission for "China: Walls and Bridges." The ACTS network was a costly venture doomed to limited success when the financial resources were never developed to match the size of the vision.

Though he affirmed the essential character of Southern Baptists, to some he was also an irritating agent of change among them. He made enemies. He took on the mantle of racial equality inherited from his teacher, T. B. Maston, only to have crosses burned in the front lawn of his home and death threats communicated by telephone to his family. He worked in the arena of public policy for religious liberty, economic justice, and protections for children and families. He sought to present a public face of Baptist intelligence and civility through the media to counter what he considered limited stereotypes. He spoke vigorously against right-wing political activities and for religious liberty, even to the point of challenging his friend in the White House, Jimmy Carter, when efforts were made to appoint an ambassador to the Vatican. He has often spoken and acted with little regard for popularity because he is a champion of truth as he understands it.

Among his deepest commitments is his uncompromising support for the First Amendment. He advocated its guarantees of both freedom of religion and its corollary, separation of church and state, as a member of the Baptist Joint Committee and Americans United for the Separation of Church and State, which he served as chairman. He is a staunch defender of the freedom of the press, believing freedom of religion is so closely attached to freedom of the press that the two cannot be separated: they are two sides of the same coin. This he demonstrated as a researcher at the First Amendment Center at Vanderbilt University and as one of its representatives as a trustee of the Freedom Foundation. He is a board member and has served as chairman of *Baptists Today*.

Jimmy also became the victim of that affirmation of traditional Southern Baptist life when the most wrenching controversy in Southern Baptist life erupted in the last year of his presidency of the Southern Baptist Convention. The traditional synthesis of unity through missions and evangelism was broken by a concerted turn to biblical inerrancy and denominational imposition of that theology led by Paul Pressler and Paige Patterson.[3] Allen is known to many as the last "moderate" or "traditional" president of the SBC. By the end of the 1980s, that new direction was fully in place and Allen's leadership of the Radio and Television Commission

---

[3]The resources available for study of the SBC controversy are sizable. I have chosen not to make it the focus of this story except at specific points where Jimmy Allen was involved personally. Readers interested in the controversy will find the best information from persons directly involved in it. Cf. Paul Pressler, *A Hill on Which to Die: One Southern Baptist's Journey* (Nashville: B and H Publishing Group, 1999) and Jerry Sutton, *The Baptist Reformation: The Conservative Resurgence in the Southern Baptist Convention* (Nashville: Broadman and Holman Publishers, 2000) for the fundamentalist perspective. Cf. Walter B. Shurden, editor, *The Struggle for the Soul of the SBC* (Macon GA: Mercer University Press, 1993) and Cecil Sherman, *By My Own Reckoning* (Macon GA: Smyth & Helwys, 2008) for moderate Baptist viewpoints. Barry Hankins, *Unease in Babylon: Southern Baptist Conservatives and American Culture* (Tuscaloosa AL: University of Alabama Press, 2002) takes a more mediating position between the polar camps in the controversy.

was concluded by his resignation before the new forces of leadership could terminate him.

But Allen was not to be deterred. Resigning from the commission in 1989, he attempted to keep the dream alive with his own resources, a step that brought personal financial bankruptcy. But the pain of that experience was incomparable to another pain that was closer to home. Allen lived much of his adult life with grief and pain from the effects of mental illness in his family. His wife, Wanda, experienced deep depression in her life while they were still in Dallas during the Texas Christian Life Commission days. She was hospitalized for several months during his transition to First Baptist Church, San Antonio, a burden he carried with frequent trips to visit her in the hospital, while maintaining his rigorous pastoral and denominational leadership schedule. Their eldest son, Michael, was born with several limitations that were eventually diagnosed as paranoia and schizophrenia. He struggles to this day with the effects of his illness, but functions with effective medications. His sons Stephen (Skip) and Scott rebelled against the dysfunctions in their family with alcohol and drug use in their teen and young-adult years, to overcome them by the grace of God and with the help of Alcoholics Anonymous. Jimmy faced those challenges with public openness and renewal in his faith journey as he sought to care for a congregation and speak healing words through his preaching. Yet, he often struggled to balance the need for attention with these family issues and frequent absences from them.

But nothing proved more challenging than the story of Scott, Jimmy and Wanda's youngest son, and his family. Scott was in seminary at Golden Gate Baptist Theological Seminary in Mill Valley, California and pastor of a nearby church when his wife, Lydia, required a blood transfusion as a result of difficulties during her first pregnancy. Unknown to any of them, the blood used in the transfusion was infected with the HIV/AIDS virus. Eventually, both of their sons and Lydia herself would die from the ravages of this disease few understood at the time. Rejection from church after church followed and Wanda and Jimmy Allen suffered through the heartache of that horrendous experience with their children and grandchildren. His book, *Burden of a Secret*, became his public manifesto of a theology of love in the face of pain and suffering. The theme of his chapter on God's response to suffering in that book is the title of this biography.

Allen's newfound freedom outside denominational structures after leaving the Radio and Television Commission resulted in his use of his networking skills to work toward alternative futures for the Baptist family. He became chairman of Baptists Committed to the SBC, the Texas organization committed to the election of moderate forces within that convention and the Southern Baptist Convention. He worked to coordinate efforts to elect another moderate to the SBC presidency, Daniel Vestal. When that strategy failed at the SBC meeting in New Orleans in 1990, the moderate wing of the convention gave up its political efforts to change it. So, he participated with Vestal, Cecil Sherman, and many others in the formation of new mission efforts and eventually the Cooperative Baptist Fellowship.

The next chapter in this man's journey is a beautiful story of redemption and renewal. After a short stint as a fundraising consultant, interim pastor, and itinerant preacher, Allen was called to become the chaplain of the Chapel at Big Canoe, Georgia. A move to North Georgia created a new environment in which the beauty of the mountains and the love of a warm, ecumenical congregation brought healing. As it was a small congregation, Allen took on an additional challenge of using his connections and knowledge of the media. He became a member of the board of trustees of the Freedom Foundation, a think tank supported by *USA Today*, after his participation in a Freedom Forum-funded research project at Vanderbilt University in Nashville, Tennessee. Jimmy cooperated with media researchers and editors/writers to study the use of news resources for addressing the religious context of the nation in the media.

Allen's final chapter is still being written. He retired from his role at Big Canoe in 2002. Wanda succumbed to her long journey in the darkness and later cancer in 2003. Now remarried to Linda Greer Allen, Jimmy continues to work as a consultant to several organizations, gives support to emerging regional meetings of the New Baptist Covenant, and serves on the board of *Baptists Today*.

This book is a rather detailed review of his life and ministry. It is a fascinating story because it is filled with so many twists and turns of providence that include an ambitious calling to make a difference in the world. And what a difference he did make. He made a difference not only in Texas and Southern Baptist life, but in the life of our world, our nation, and our civil society. Perhaps as important, he made a difference in the lives of countless individuals whose stories intersected with Jimmy Allen's story, and their lives were changed forever. By the time you finish reading this book, your life may be one of them.

Now in his eighties, Allen works as energetically as ever, seeking to fulfill the calling of God that is captured by his central verse of Scripture:

> You did not choose me, but I chose you and appointed you that you should go and bear fruit and that your fruit should abide; so that whatever you ask the Father in my name, he may give it to you. —John 15:16 RSV

Chapter 2

Early Narratives: A Scripted Child

> My grandpaw and grandmother were a great influence on me and the whole family when we were growing up. I thought he was God. He had a full head of grey hair, and he spoke with a deep, booming, commanding voice that never needed electronic amplification. When he spoke, it sounded to me like the voice of God.
>
> —Skip Allen

Jimmy Raymond Allen was born October 26, 1927 in the farmhouse of his grandparents in the Providence community near Hope, Arkansas. The area, a few miles northeast of Hope, is reminiscent of much of the South and eastern Southwest with acres of pine and native timber. The tree lines are broken with parcels of small pastureland and fields of cotton and various grain crops. Both the environment of his childhood and the hardiness of his family had significant influences on the life, ministry, pain, and leadership that have characterized the story of Jimmy Allen.

The Allen Genogram

Family-systems theorists suggest that three generations of family structure provide all of the genetic and environmental influences necessary to understand how an individual is likely to function in a given situation.[1] You cannot really understand the drama of Jimmy Allen's life without taking into consideration the genetics and social context in which he, his parents, and his grandparents lived.

His family inheritance contributed significantly to Jimmy's personality, hopes, and dreams, and patterned reactions to events. But, you can hardly find in this family all of the elements necessary to understand his complex holy ambition, insatiable curiosity, and boundless energy.

The two family systems that came together in the marriage of Jimmy's parents, Earl Lester Allen and Edna May Ray, were similar in their backgrounds and deprivations. The Allen clan, like most Anglo-Saxon Southern families, was one branch of a group of Allens who emigrated from England, beginning in the sixteenth century. Three major waves of the Allen family found their way into the colonies. One wave settled in Vermont, from which

---

[1] For most useful resources for understanding the importance of family in shaping identity see Ronald W. Richardson, *Becoming a Healthier Pastor* (Minneapolis: Fortress Press, 2005) and *Family Ties That Bind*, 3rd ed. (North Vancouver BC: International Self-Counsel Press, 2007).

the Revolutionary War leader Ethan Allen of the "Green Mountain Boys" descended. Another branch found its way into America via Virginia, and still a third made its way from Bristol, England to Charleston, South Carolina. With successive decades, this latter group grew and spread across the South.

When Jimmy's great-grandfather, Charles Allen, reached the Ozarks of Arkansas, the rolling hills of trees and valley meadows attracted him enough that he planted his life in that geographic and cultural soil. He settled on a large acreage of land near Mount Ida, Arkansas, some forty miles west of Hot Springs. Charles Allen was relatively successful economically. In addition to the land, he owned a hotel in Hot Springs as well as a number of slaves. Charles was the father of several sons, included Jimmy's grandfather, William O. Allen, born circa 1858. Jimmy's grandfather told him stories about his older brothers, Charlie and Andy, joining General Nathan Bedford Forrest to fight for the Confederacy in the Civil War.

W. O. Allen made his way from the Hot Springs area to a poor farm at Providence. There he married Amanda Jane Flowers, his fourth wife, with whom he fathered eight children, five boys and three girls. One of the sons was Earl, Jimmy's father. Grandfather Allen was a gentle and irenic Methodist known to his neighbors as "Uncle Billy."

Amanda Jane Flowers, Jimmy's grandmother, was a rough and hard-headed Baptist with no formal education. Her father was an educated man who was tutored in both Latin and Greek, but came home from the Civil War shell-shocked and incapacitated. He refused to teach his daughters to read, giving such attention only to his sons. Amanda was sufficiently driven that she taught herself to read using the Bible as her textbook. Her grammar was poor, an embarrassment to Jimmy as a child. Only when he was older did he appreciate her determination and intelligence. This family heritage also made Jimmy realize later the importance of education in trying to break free from Southern culture when addressing complex moral and ethical issues, including race relations.

Grandmother Allen was argumentative when it came to her religion. She was a "hard-shelled" Baptist in the Landmark tradition. Her strong religious views influenced all of the Allen children, except for one who became a Presbyterian, as they made their way from an initial Methodist upbringing to a pilgrimage of embracing the Baptist perspectives of their mother.

Earl Allen, born in 1901, was an outstanding basketball and baseball player. Six feet one inch tall, Earl became a basketball star in high school and was the first of his family to finish high school. At that time, a high school diploma was all that was required for one to teach. After working on his father's farm through high school, he took a job as a high school coach and teacher in the Providence School.

Earl had experienced a call to preach at the age of fourteen. On one occasion during their summer visits to the family farm in Arkansas, he took son Jimmy to the place he had felt that call and told him the story of his experience. During a revival meeting one evening, Earl felt that God was calling him to preach. The next day, while using a cornstalk cutter on the farm, he pondered the preacher's message. Then he got on his knees and asked God to help him overcome his problem of stuttering so he could become a preacher. Yet, he continued to teach school and coach at the Providence School for several years.

One of the students in his classes was a diminutive young woman of four feet, eleven inches named Edna May Ray. Her father, J. W. Ray, and her mother, a member of the Cullins family, had moved to Arkansas from Missouri. Mr. Cullins was a timberman and had massive farms and a tree-cutting operation in Missouri. J. W. Ray went to work for him, and when he met Cullins's daughter, Ida, they married. She was fifteen at the time. Jimmy's mother was born in Bourney, Missouri, on August 27, 1908. When the Ray family moved from Missouri to Hope, Arkansas, J. W. Ray opened a butcher shop. He earned enough to buy a farm in the Providence community.

The community had a Baptist church where Rev. Arthur Fox, pastor of the First Baptist Church in Hope, would come to preach on Sunday afternoons. Shortly after Edna became a Christian as a preteen, she walked down the church aisle saying she felt God was calling her to be a missionary. Edna's brother, Leo, walked the aisle at the same time. When asked if he was going to be missionary too, he responded, "I'm going to have to because Edna is too little to be one on her own. I have to protect her if she's going to China."[2]

Because of his height, Earl earned the nickname "Big Jim." His success as a coach became legendary with a series of undefeated basketball seasons.

---

[2] Jimmy Allen, "Early Life Experiences," interview no. 1 with Larry L. McSwain, Big Canoe GA, 1 November 2004, 6.

Edna Ray never finished high school, though she did take some classes, at least with the tall and successful coach. They were in love and married January 10, 1926. "Big Jim" Allen continued to coach and to teach. Edna would pursue her own learning in more informal than formal ways. An avid reader, she became a life-long student with largely self-taught discipline; she earned her high school equivalency and an associate college degree in her sixties.

Edna and Earl, who towered fourteen inches taller than his bride, were told by their doctor that they would never to be able to have children. Edna was so petite and small framed such a possibility was ruled out. But for this newlywed couple such pronouncements were less powerful than the providence of God, because they were blessed with a son, their only child.

His mother regaled Jimmy early in his childhood with the uniqueness of his birth. The doctor who was supposed to deliver him was not able to come to the family farm in Providence when needed. So his new assistant, a young doctor who delivered Jimmy Raymond Allen, brought his first baby into the world. According to Mrs. Allen, the doctor was so nervous he put the wrong date on the birth certificate, recording October 25, 1927; she insisted it was October 26, 1927. Evidently there was some difference of opinion of how he should be named. In the original birth certificate the name Earl Allen, Jr. is entered, but the Earl Jr. is marked through with "Jimmy Raymond" written in its place. In an interview in 1972, Allen reflected:

> The name Jimmy—J-I-M-M-Y—is actually my birth certificate name. This is rather difficult in a formal kind of world to maintain a relationship with yourself in the name of a nickname. It became a crisis for me in my life later, but it was a kind of liberating experience when I decided not to try to be James Allen but to be Jimmy Allen. I was simply named by the name that they wanted to use. My mother's name, [her] family name, was Ray, so the name, Raymond, may have had some relationship with that. But I really was named for no one.[3]

---

[3] Jimmy Allen, Allen interview no. 1 with Thomas L. Charlton, Baylor University Program for Oral History, San Antonio, 15 September 1972, 2.

From Providence to Detroit

Ten years of teaching and coaching evidently brought Earl to a plateau in his ambition. Like thousands of other Southerners of his generation, the lure of economic prosperity in the industrializing North proved magnetic to his spirit. Roy Haggard, Earl's brother-in-law, had taken a correspondence course in electronics from a school in Chicago. With that training, he made the pilgrimage to Detroit, Michigan, and got a job with Ford Motor Company where he worked for forty years. Roy spread the word back to Arkansas of the jobs available and Earl and Edna decided they would go. In the spring of 1929, the Allen household loaded their eighteen-month-old baby and all they could pack into their DeVeaux sedan and traveled to Detroit. Earl was able to secure a job as a coach for a basketball team supported by a pipeline company. When the company failed, he went to work on an automobile assembly line, but he hated the work. When pushed by the foreman to do more, Earl replied he was doing all a mule could do. His boss quickly responded: "I know about mules. They can always do more than they let you know they can do."[4]

The Allens spent about three and one half years in Detroit. Within months of their arrival the stock market crash of 1929 occurred, and the nation moved into the depths of the Great Depression. Earl did not survive the assembly-line work and began working instead as a door-to-door insurance salesman selling "nickel insurance." The premium was five cents per week; he would sell the policy and then collect the premiums weekly. This man who was self-conscious about his speech now had to talk to earn a living. He gradually overcame his stuttering. Each Christmas, the family would pack the DeVeaux sedan for a visit back home with Arkansas family.

Jimmy Allen recalls unusual early memories of his childhood in Detroit which are probably a mixture of remembered experiences and frequent stories of their experiences from his mother. He remembers a snow that was so deep it was over his head, his daily meetings of his daddy when he came home from work, and travel to the Detroit Public Library when he was age four to secure his own library card, the youngest person to have one.

The most dramatic event of that sojourn happened in 1931. An outbreak of scarlet fever had reached epidemic proportions in the city. Jimmy con-

---

[4]Allen, "Early Life and Experiences," 7.

tracted the disease and was quarantined in his house with a yellow notice posted at the entrance to their house. Five children died from the disease on the same block the Allen family lived. The door and window to Jimmy's room were nailed shut preventing his father from entering. His mother rubbed his hands because of the fear the fever would settle in them and he would lose use of them. Jimmy recounts, "In the next room, we could hear my dad praying, pleading for the life of his only child. Dad had been running away from God's call to preach the gospel. . . . Dad promised God that if he would spare my life, Dad would return south and preach God's Word. God did and Dad did."[5]

The Reinhart Baptist Church was the first Southern Baptist church in Detroit and Louie B. Newton, noted pastor of the Druid Hills Baptist Church in Atlanta, Georgia, was preaching a revival at the church. Earl Allen sought out Newton and asked his advice about what he should do next. The venerable pastor said he should go to seminary in Louisville, Kentucky. When Earl responded he had family in Texas, Newton suggested he go to Texas and go to seminary there.

So, a truck bed apparatus was attached to the DeVeux, and all of the possessions accumulated in Detroit were loaded. In 1932, the family moved to Dallas, Texas where a new chapter in their family saga would be written. Jimmy celebrated his fifth birthday as a Texan.

An Itinerant Preacher in One State

In Dallas during the 1930's, Earl Allen became a prototypical pastor in the free church tradition that emphasizes the importance of calling over mandated educational requirements. Like hundreds of pastors before and after him, he struck out like Abraham of old to serve God as best he knew how with little expectation for reward. He walked by faith, trusting that God would both lead and provide. Most of the churches he served were small; none was affluent. Yet he went wherever he sensed a need and gave of himself with little regard for the outcome. Such ministry is the essence of faithful and committed service. It is a model Jimmy Allen never forgot in his own pilgrimage of faith and service.

Earl and Edna Allen left the adventure of Detroit with a four-year-old son and a few possessions during the growing economic desperation of the

---

[5]Jimmy Allen, *Burden of a Secret* (Nashville: Moorings, 1995) 8.

Great Depression. Earl went to work for the Rio Grande Insurance Company in Dallas. Because they asked him to live in the neighborhoods he was working as a door-to-door salesman, the family moved frequently. They first moved in with relatives and then to an apartment near the Gaston Avenue Baptist Church. Edna got a job at a small cafe down the street for one-fourth of each day's net income. A lady at the house where they lived cared for Jimmy while Edna and Earl worked. Soon they found a church home at the Gaston Avenue Baptist Church where Dr. Marshall Craig was the pastor.

Life took a series of up and down moves for them with a succession of events. During the summer of 1933 the banks across the nation failed and Earl Allen's few savings were lost completely. Until late in his life, Earl never trusted a bank again, relying on cash transactions for all of his business. Jimmy later recalled his lack of awareness of their poverty, except in retrospect. On the day the banks failed, he said, "We had only oatmeal in the house and no money. And so I ate that day; neither of them ate."[6]

After two years of worship at Gaston Avenue Baptist Church, Craig encouraged Earl Allen to consider working at the Munger Place Baptist Church. The pastor of the church was Earl Anderson, a red-headed, freckle-faced man with a strong personality. A former ally with J. Frank Norris, Anderson had broken with the fundamentalist and affiliated his church with the Dallas Baptist Association. The Allens joined the church and began working there as Earl continued to sell insurance. They actually lived in the church building for a couple of months until they could become more stable, and the church employed Earl to be a paid superintendent of the Sunday school, a position equivalent to today's minister of education in Southern Baptist churches.

Soon Edna was employed part-time as church secretary at Munger Place. They continued working there through Jimmy's first year of elementary school. It was there that Jimmy publicly accepted Jesus Christ as his Savior and was baptized.

In 1935, Earl had the itch to preach. He discovered a need for ministry in the neighborhood where they had first lived in Dallas. The congregation meeting in the McKinney Avenue Baptist Church was relocating to the Oaklawn area near Highland Park. Hispanics had moved into the neighbor-

---

[6]Allen, "Allen interview no. 1" with Charlton, 6.

hood in such numbers the church was not able to minister effectively. The congregation relocated to form the Highland Baptist Church. They left a vacuum and Earl felt led to move there. Allen recalls:

> So we started a Sunday school when I was in third grade. In that process he rented a building, a house about the next block from the empty church for fifty-five dollars a month. He quit his job. He had three cents in his pocket and no salary and no church to sponsor him. I remember as an eight-year-old as a new believer my dad and my mother and I began taking a census (to discover people who were unchurched)—I took census on one side of the street and he took it on the other. . . . I remember one lady who came to the door, Stella Sims. She said to me: "Do they send babies out from that church?" And I said, "Well if you come help then we won't have to do that." She came and joined the church. When I was elected president of the Southern Baptist Convention, I got a letter from Stella. She was living in a trailer camp in Tucson and said, "I never had a time since that I have not been a part of a mission church." It blew my mind. Here was this woman who responded to an eight-year-old. Stella was my example about going house to house and calling on folks and God using that.
>
> We moved into that house and lived there. We got some chairs and a piano, and began holding worship service in our home. We had thirty-six people the first Sunday, most of them children. We stayed there and organized the Memorial Baptist Church. Meanwhile the McKinney Avenue Baptist Church building could not be sold. Dad kept talking to the pastor and they decided that it was just sitting there empty so the mission could use it. . . . The old kitchen in the back of the auditorium became my bedroom. The old parlor became their bedroom. So half of my bedroom was our kitchen and half was where I slept. We lived in that facility almost four years. . . . That building at McKinney is now the Hard Rock Café. [Subsequent to this interview it was demolished.] So I lived in the Hard Rock Café. I went up and told the manager I'd like to see my old house and he took me around. I like to tell folks that I was the only kid in the ghetto to live in a three and one-half-million-dollar house and have his own swimming pool. When Dad would baptize they'd have to bring the candidates through my bedroom. I swam there; it was a five stroke swim and it was a big baptistery. I had a built-in swimming pool. It was an adventurous life.[7]

---

[7]Jimmy Allen, "Faith and Education Journey," interview no. 2 with Larry L. McSwain, Alpharetta GA: 13 November 2004, 23.

On Pearl Harbor Day, December 7, 1941, Earl Allen began his ministry as pastor of the Pine Street Baptist Church in south Dallas. After five years at Pine Street, Earl started the Inwood Baptist Church in the Kenwood area near Love Field. They bought a house and started the church while Jimmy was in college. Jimmy recalls a major change for his father at that time:

> He got sick. He had tuberculosis as a young man and did not know it. He lost the sight in his eye and went through a crisis where it looked like he was not going to be able to preach. At that time he went down to Martin Springs Baptist Church in Sulpher Springs, Texas. . . . The first day he was there I counted thirty-nine 'dirt dobbers' and thirty people in the building. I could not see how God could be doing this to my dad. . . . They built a church building. He became the *Progressive Farmer* "Rural Pastor of the Year" while he was there at that place. He went from there to pastor down in Lufkin at Providence Baptist Church. Then he went to First Baptist Church of Celeste which is outside of Greenville and then back to Martin Springs. . . . After that he started the Texas Baptist Historical Center of Independence—which is where Baylor University was born, where the Baptist General Convention of Texas was born, and where Sam Houston (the first president of the Republic of Texas), was baptized. They asked daddy if he would come and pastor that little church and be a host for the tourists that would come to the Historical Center. That's where he ended his ministry. He was there doing that when he had his heart attack. I have a letter from Lyndon B. Johnson when he was president as the Baptist Historical Center was started, talking about his grandfather, George Washington Baines, who was pastor there. Dad became very active in the historical circles. I got the call when Scott and I were in Glorietta for a Christian Life Commission conference that he was out in the garden by the church and died instantaneously of a heart attack. My mother stayed two years holding things together and got things organized for a new director. Then my mother moved to San Antonio.[8]

Earl Allen seemed to relish his service at the Independence Baptist Church at Brendan, the birthplace of much of Texas Baptist life. The church building was owned by the Baptist General Convention of Texas, the only such church in the state. The state convention built a new building housing the Texas Baptist Historical Center, and the Allens organized the building and dedication effort. The new building also provided classroom space for

---

[8]"Faith and Education Journey," interview no. 2 with Larry L. McSwain, 16-17.

the church and they served as hosts to the many visitors who came to the site of the baptism of Sam Houston.[9]

Jimmy's father became the pastor in Independence in 1965 and served there until his death in 1973 at the age of seventy-two. Earl Allen was buried in the Snell Cemetery in Emmett, Arkansas. When Mrs. Allen moved to San Antonio in 1975, where Jimmy was then pastor of the First Baptist Church, she decided to go to college. She enrolled at San Antonio College at the age of sixty-four after taking a high school equivalency test. She earned an associate degree and became a student volunteer in the library. Soon the library staff employed her to work there, which she did until reaching the mandatory retirement age of seventy. When she could not continue to work she declared she would become a student volunteer again. So they worked out an arrangement for her to work one more year until she was seventy-one years old.

Edna May Allen was her son's strongest cheerleader. After the Allen family relocated to Fort Worth in 1980, she moved from San Antonio to Dallas and lived at the Buckner Homes until her death at age ninety-two. Her son preached her funeral at the Wilshire Baptist Church on 11 September 2001. She was interned next to her husband in Emmett, Arkansas.

---

[9]Bert Tucker, "Independence Church Still Making History," *Baptist Standard*, 15 March 1967, 8-9.

Chapter 3

Faith and Education Journeys

> We can't help you much but we will make sure you don't drown.
> —Earl Allen to Jimmy in college

On close examination of Jimmy Allen's early years of education, spiritual formation, and intellectual development, three qualities emerge that continue to this day. First, he is a high extrovert. Allen's energy flows from people. The more people, the more complex the gathering, the greater is the flow of energy. He is at his best interacting with a group in a "think tank" to solve a problem or imagine a new direction.

Second, Allen is highly adaptable. New situations that would frighten many people seem to strengthen his courage and resolve. He lives fearlessly in the moment of new and challenging realities. His mind seems to "kick into high gear" when confronted with new, large, and seemingly difficult situations.

Third, he sees a visionary quality in almost every situation. He enjoys walking into what most view as a challenge, an insurmountable obstacle, or a problem beyond solution. He faces such situations with an almost quixotic notion that here is an opportunity for change that must be addressed.

One reason for this is his spiritual sensitivity. Another is seeing up-close-and-personal as a child and as a teenager the willingness of his own father and mother to venture repeatedly into the unknown in seemingly impossible situations. Like his mother and father, Jimmy strongly believes in the capacities of God as Father to transform the most unlikely of circumstances into opportunities.

Such a pattern of aggressiveness toward new people, his adaptability, and visionary quality of life seem rooted in the life experiences of his earliest learning and faith ventures. The challenges of his childhood were for him opportunities to grow and enjoy what life was offering. Jimmy's intellectual and spiritual capacities were developed in both formal and informal ways. Much of what he learned, both academically and in the realm of ministry, was by "osmosis." As the only child of parents who viewed him a special gift of God, he was encouraged, nurtured, prodded, and supported in becoming an inquisitive, social, and learned person. Their resources were few, but these were showered upon him in abundance.

While his family was not highly educated, they prized learning. His mother read constantly and encouraged the habit in her son. Allen recalls finding a trunk of books in the basement of the McKinney Avenue Church where they lived. The trunk was a treasure chest filled with Junior Classics which Jimmy read for personal pleasure. *King Arthur and the Knights of the Roundtable* captured his imagination at age eleven.[1] Those books were like gold nuggets found by a young boy searching for hidden treasure.

One of the most obvious patterns in his early pilgrimage was "movement." By his own count, Allen declares, "I've lived in thirteen different places in Dallas and thirty different houses because of being a preacher's son and an insurance salesman's son."[2] During the nine years it took him to finish school from grade one through twelve, he attended three elementary schools, one junior high school, and two high schools.

A pattern clearly emerged. He had choices to make about how he would respond to the constancy of change in his life, and he chose to maximize the opportunities presented by each situation.

Elementary Schools

Jimmy Allen began his formal education at the age of six in the fall of 1934 by enrolling at the Ascher Silberstein Elementary School on Hollis Avenue in Dallas. His first-grade teacher was Ms. Ducey about whom he has fond memories.

His innate social-justice sensibilities were evident at that early time. One of his neighborhood friends in a grade ahead of him had a bicycle and offered him a ride home from school. Since the first-grade classes concluded earlier than others, Jimmy made his way to the bicycle stand where he waited to meet his friend.

When the principal asked what he was doing there, Jimmy responded that he was waiting for his friend to go home. She did not believe him and smacked him on the back side with her hand. This incensed the young prophet to be. So he marched home to announce to his mother he would not be returning to school. He became a school dropout on day three!

Jimmy's mother immediately called the principal. After they talked, his mother encouraged Jimmy to return to school and said she thought the principal might be nicer to him. The next day, the principal summoned Jimmy to her office. When he arrived she was listening to the Detroit Tigers

---

[1] Jimmy Allen, Allen interview no. 1 with Thomas L. Charlton, Baylor University Program for Oral History, San Antonio, 15 September 1972, 8.

[2] Jimmy Allen, "Early Life and Ministry," interview no. 1 with Larry L. McSwain, Big Canoe GA, 1 November 2004, 11.

baseball game on the radio. They listened and talked about the Arkansas pitcher who had joined the Detroit Tigers the previous year, Lynwood "Schoolboy" Rowe.³ Coincidentally, it was the last week in August 1934 that Rowe tied an American League record of winning sixteen games in a row.⁴ All was well and Jimmy returned to school.⁵

In the summer following his first year of study at Silberstein School, he began a pattern that would continue each summer for the next several years. He traveled to Arkansas where he lived most of the summer with his grandparents, J. W. and Ida Ray, on their farm near the small community of Providence. There he would work in the fields with his aunt and uncle who were his age, listen to family stories told by Grandfather Allen, and connect with the rural heritage which had shaped his parents.

His first trip at age seven was a great adventure. He met the train in Dallas and traveled alone to Texarkana where he changed trains to travel to Hope. What he did not know was that his parents had talked with the conductor on the train about watching over him as he made the transfer in Texarkana. He thought he had done it all on his own.⁶

Since the school calendar was different in Arkansas, the young Allen got a month of summer school study which assisted him in making several "double promotions" through elementary school. The little school at Providence started classes during the month of August and then dismissed classes for the month of October, allowing the children to pick cotton and other crops in the fall. Each August, Jimmy went to the five-grade, one-room schoolhouse in Providence, with cousins and siblings of his mother. Here he was exposed to what was being taught at several grade levels. Always inquisitive, he often listened to the lessons taught to the older students which advanced him in his own grade level in Dallas.

Allen returned to Dallas in September to be enrolled in the Davy Crockett Elementary School. Based on the level of his skills, he was shortly promoted to the third grade. Allen recalls, "They did intellectual promotions

---

³Jimmy Allen, "Faith and Education Journey," interview no. 2 with Larry L. McSwain, Alpharetta GA, 13 November 2004, 22. The accuracy of Allen's memory is rather phenomenal given the fact this interview was conducted seventy years after the event!

⁴"Schoolboy's Triumph", *Time*, 3 September 1934. <http://www.time.com/time/magazine/article/0,9171,747859,00.html> (accessed 28 May 2007).

⁵Allen, "Faith and Education Journey," 23.

⁶Allen, "Faith and Education Journey," 23.

instead of social promotions at that time."[7] In the course of that school year the family moved once again and he transferred to William B. Travis Elementary School. They were behind the level he had been studying at Davy Crockett, so he was promoted once again to the fourth grade. He remained at Travis through the seventh grade and then completed junior high at Alex Spence School. Because of the reconfiguration of the junior-high system, he would advance another grade in the transfer process.

The years of 1939 and 1940 were significant educationally for the Allen family in another way. Both Earl and Edna Allen enrolled in the Diploma in Theology program at Southwestern Baptist Theological Seminary in Fort Worth. Jimmy was now old enough to be left alone after school, and they commuted for two years to complete the program there, both graduating 9 May 1941. It was the family pattern for Jimmy to come home from school, keep the house clean, and prepare the family meal for the evening as his parents drove home from study at the seminary. He was paid one dollar and twenty cents per week for performing such chores. Jimmy bought his first bicycle on the installment plan with his allowance. He paid one dollar down and one dollar per week for nineteen weeks until the payments were complete. He often used the story to teach his own children the importance of paying one's debts.

Profession of Faith and Baptism

The elementary school years were also significant for Jimmy from a faith perspective. He made his profession of faith at the age of eight at the Munger Place Baptist Church where his parents were staff members.

Hyman Appleman, one of the more colorful evangelists of the twentieth century, was preaching a revival at the church. Born in Russia in 1902 to Orthodox Jewish parents, Appleman was a skilled linguist and knew Hebrew, German, Russian, Yiddish, Polish, and English. After immigrating to the United States with his family, he graduated from DePaul University with a law degree in 1921. He practiced law in Chicago until 1924 when a vocational crisis and physical breakdown led him to leave Chicago and travel for a time. As a result of multiple encounters with Christians at YMCA centers where he stayed during his travels, he was converted and baptized at the Central Christian Church of Denver, Colorado. He joined the

---

[7]Allen, "Faith and Education Journey," 24.

Army after being rejected by his family and fiancé for his newfound faith. He was stationed at Fort Sill in Lawton Oklahoma where he began preaching through the Central Baptist Church in 1928. In 1930, he married Verna Cook and both became students at Southwestern Seminary from 1930 to 1933. As a student at Southwestern Seminary in Fort Worth, he served briefly as pastor of two Texas Baptist congregations. In December 1933, he was appointed as an official evangelist for Texas Baptists. Jimmy Allen was one of the early converts under the influence of a man who became quite notable in the history of evangelism in America.[8] The message of this colorful evangelist made an impact on the young Allen. He describes the experience:

> We had a revival meeting at the church led by the Jewish evangelist Hyman Appleman who was quite popular across the country at that time. During one of the services I felt a very strong sense of conviction. Later that is what I called it; I did not know what to call it at the time. . . . I was listening to the sermon and during the invitation I felt a strong urge to do something. I didn't know what to do. When I got to our car I told my dad and mother I felt like going down to the front but did not know why. Mother turned to me in the car and began talking with me about those feelings. She went through John 3:16 with me and got me to put my name in the text. She asked me if I really believed that and if I believed in Jesus. That meant if I believed in him I could ask him to save me. I did that on the way home. When I got home I was so excited about it I told the landlady. We were living in an apartment, and I will never forget how amazed I was that she was not excited about it. It was a very heavy thing from my point of view and that next night I could hardly wait for the invitation to come and I could share that I had trusted Christ as my savior.[9]

In the exuberance of his newfound faith, Allen also shared his experience with several others, including his first-grade teacher, Ms. Ducey, at Silberstein Elementary School. She was encouraging, though Jimmy said later he had no particular knowledge of her faith experience.

At the end of the revival, the church conducted baptism services and Allen joined with several others who had made commitments to Christ

---

[8]Interestingly, there is no published biography of Appleman in book form. These details of his life were compiled from an unknown author and posted as "Hyman Jedidiah Appleman, 1902–1983," <http://www.believerweb.org> (accessed 28 May 2007).

[9]Allen, "Faith and Education Journey," 19-20.

during that week. Interestingly, neither his father nor his pastor, Earl Anderson, performed the baptism. Jimmy tells the story in his own words:

> After that we had the baptism at the close of the revival series. . . . The pastor had a visiting preacher who had two sons who had made professions of faith. They wanted him to baptize them. So they came to me and asked me if I wanted him to baptize me or wait and let Earl Anderson, the pastor, baptize me. Well, I did not care who baptized me and did not want to wait. I was baptized that night by a man whose name I do not know.[10]

Even though he was only eight at the time, these events are impressed into Allen's mind in considerable detail. This is partly because of what happened the next day. When Jimmy awoke the next morning he had a full-blown case of chicken pox. At that time there was great anxiety about the effect of the disease on the person's eyes, so he was placed in bed in a darkened room for ten days. Here he was exposed to what might now be called "home schooling." Not one to waste an opportunity, Jimmy's mother prepared a collection of note cards with a scripture passage written on one side and the reference citation on the other. By the time he was able to go back to school Jimmy had memorized more than 150 passages of Scripture. They provided a core resource for his preaching through the years as he still quotes them frequently from memory. Of course they are etched in his mind in the King James Version. He laughingly suggests he often has to use more contemporary translations to explain the meaning of these memorized verses.[11]

High Schools

Allen began high school in the sophomore class at North Dallas High School at the age of thirteen in the fall, 1941. Because of advances he made through a series of double promotions, he was now among the youngest and smallest in his high school classes. After only one semester of study at North Dallas, Jimmy transferred to Forrest High School in the neighborhood of the Pine Street Baptist Church in South Dallas where his father accepted the call to pastor. While the Allens had lived in much of the central core of Dallas, the southern neighborhoods were even more

---

[10]Allen, "Faith and Education Journey," 20.
[11]Allen, "Faith and Education Journey," 21.

ethnically diverse and tougher than some of their other places of service. Jimmy Allen had another adjustment to make.

He became a fighter. Small in size, Allen began boxing as an activity after school in the armory near his home. He had considered fighting in the Golden Gloves, but his mother refused permission. Ever obedient, he chose to practice and fight in informal competitions. By the time of the move to Pine Street, his new skills proved useful. The first day at the church, the son of a deacon, Billy Ray, tried to pick a fight with him. He responded that he would not fight on the church grounds or on Sunday but would meet him after school on Monday. When asked, "Who won?" Allen quickly replied, "I did. I had learned to fight. It was a survival thing. I was quick and I knew how to box. . . . That was the way I survived in high school."[12]

Fighting was the closest Allen came to becoming identified as a rebellious preacher's kid. He remembers occasional black/white encounters on the streets of his racially mixed south Dallas neighborhood. He even carried a lead pipe to football games for protection, although he never used it. His most notable memory, however, was a fight with a teacher.

His physical education teacher at Forrest High School, Mr. Hutchinson, was particularly tough and carried a paddle with him during playground duty. He was not afraid to use it. On one occasion when it was raining he set up boxing matches indoors for the physical activity of the day. He chose a student to fight with Jimmy. After Jimmy had defeated the third challenger, Hutchinson put the gloves on himself to teach the cocky, young boy some humility. "He whipped me," Allen recalls, "but I blacked his eye and marked him up on the face so everyone could see he had been in a fight. When you do that people don't make much fun of you as a preacher's kid."[13]

These were the years of World War II, and Allen anticipated he would likely be in the Army. He signed up for Junior Reserve Officer Training Corps during high school, but his motivation was not so much the military as the fact uniforms were provided. By being in R.O.T.C. he could wear a uniform the school provided for him since his family did not have adequate income to buy him clothes. By the time he was old enough to be eligible for the draft, the war was near its end; he never had to make the choice of military service.

---

[12] Allen, "Faith and Education Journey," 27.
[13] Allen, "Faith and Education Journey," 28.

Graduation came for the sixteen-year-old Allen in the spring of 1944. He had made a clear commitment to preach, had begun preaching somewhat regularly, and was planning to attend seminary. Given those early commitments, he tended to respond best to teachers who demanded high academic performance. He did poorly, however, in practical hands-on classes such as woodshop. He barely passed shorthand. But because of the influence of Miss Laurania Miller he completed Latin each year of high school. Miss Miller even offered to teach him Greek informally so he met with her during his senior year two mornings each week before classes began to study Greek. He was unaware the biblical *koine* Greek he would learn in college and seminary was quite different from the classical Greek she was teaching. The better teachers in this somewhat inferior high school were older and more challenging. An English teacher took enough interest in him to push him to join in enough extracurricular activities he could be eligible for membership in the National Honor Society.[14] He summarizes: "I was an achiever, and I was very unhappy when I didn't do well."[15]

Call to Preach

One could hardly imagine growing up in this tightly connected preacher's family and not encounter a sense of calling to follow in the pattern set by parents who were both so involved in the work of God's kingdom through the church. Jimmy certainly did.

In addition to their own ministries in churches and study at the seminary, both Allen parents were significantly involved in the activities of the Dallas Baptist Association. Jimmy's mother was deeply involved in the Woman's Missionary Union at both the church and associational level. At that time, the WMU sponsored missions education programs called Girls' Auxiliary for young girls and Royal Ambassadors for young boys. So it was as natural as breathing for Jimmy to become involved in the boys' organization.

Royal Ambassadors consisted of weekly meetings at the local church with mission studies and advancement steps similar to the progression used by the Boy Scouts for the same age group of boys. An important part of the program was participation each week during the summer in a RA camp held at a variety of regional camp facilities operated either by Texas Baptists or

---

[14]Allen, Interview no. 1 with Charleton, 21-22.
[15]Allen, Interview no. 1 with Charleton, 25.

Baptist associations across the state. Jimmy recalls his personal experience at camp:

> I had been active in everything at church and became involved in the Royal Ambassador program. . . . During that time I was studying the various steps, . . . and that meant memorization of scriptures. So I went to RA camp at Latham Springs Baptist Assembly which is down by Hillsboro, Texas. . . . I was twelve. During that week, we had [worship] services morning and night . . . and I really had several times felt a kind of rededication and searching in my faith. There was something prodding me that I couldn't quite understand, itching where I could not scratch. God was doing something in my life and I kept trying to tell Him I would do anything He wanted me to do. The peace I had was not really there. I was under conviction but did not know why.
>
> I remember bowing my head and asking God to tell me what it was. The invitation time was going and the songs were being sung and people were making decisions. . . . A man who was not in charge of the service came forward and said "I have something I need to say." I listened to him as he said, "I have a sense there is somebody here who is being called to preach. I was twelve years old when I understood the call that God wanted me to preach. I just believe there is someone here who needs to surrender to preach." [Jimmy's voice on recorded interview full of emotion.] It was right at that time I had asked God to show me what he wanted me to do. . . . So I came to surrender to preach. . . . There were several other people who came [forward]. I don't think anyone there thought it was an unusual thing. But it was pivotal for me.[16]

It would have been customary at that time for Jimmy to share such a decision with his home church the following Sunday. Given his age, little expectation for immediate preaching would have occurred; but Jimmy began teaching in Sunday school at that time and immersed himself in RA work and study. During the summer after high school graduation, he was ambassador in chief for the Dallas Baptist Association and was chosen to represent the association with a trip to a Young Men's Mission Conference at Ridgecrest Baptist Assembly in Ridgecrest, North Carolina. He had also achieved the rank of Ambassador Plenipotentiary, the highest rank in the group. Both he and Browning Ware achieved the rank at the same time. So they divided the funds made available to them by the associational WMU.[17]

---

[16] Allen, "Early Life and Ministry," 21.

[17] James Cooper remembers Allen and Ware as close competitors for the highest rank in the organization with Allen completing the requirements an hour before Ware, making him the first boy in Dallas and probably in Texas to earn

The Life and Ministry of Jimmy Raymond Allen

At Ridgecrest he heard Clarence Jordan from Koinonia Farms in Americus, Georgia,[18] preach about racial reconciliation, only to resist the message from the perspective of the segregated tradition in which he had been raised. He claims to have argued publicly with Jordan.

> I was very angry at Clarence Jordan; I was in his class every day. We argued the whole time. I took a totally segregationist posture. I was influenced, . . . in a way that's rather interesting to me now. When I was young[er], I was at my grandfather Allen's home and found an old book on the beginnings of the Ku Klux Klan. . . . I read that novel without anybody ever having recommended it or knowing that I read it, but it colored my thinking about the Ku Klux Klan at that time so I really accepted it as being true. . . . It was, and as I look back on it, a very foolish thing because I did not discuss it with anybody. My dad never participated in the Ku Klux Klan nor did my grandparents, but this novel affected me, you know, growing up in this racial hostility of the time. My grandmother Allen didn't think a Negro had a soul . . . though she thought Caroline had a soul, who was the lady who worked with her through her life. But she had that kind of inconsistency of the slaveholding mentality. My dad was a segregationist who was gentle and kind and thought Negroes ought to stay in their place. So I came out of that background.
>
> Clarence Jordan hit me at Ridgecrest with the demands of the Christian ethic. And it was years later before I communicated with Clarence how much he helped me, but he really shook me up. And I left for home very angry about what he had said but unable to get away from the logic of it and later became convinced and convicted that this was a pattern of concern for my own life.[19]

Allen preached his first revival at the Pine Street Baptist Church at the age of fifteen. Evidently he was effective with his peers as there was an evening church baseball game on Thursday evening. He and the team showed up for the services in their baseball uniforms and six of his teammates made professions of faith that night as Jimmy preached in his uni-

---

Ambassador Plenipotentiary. Cooper also earned the rank and he and Allen dispute to this day who did so first. James Cooper, Interview with Jim Newton, Dallas, 5 July 2005, 4.

[18]Much has been written about Jordan. For a brief summary of his life and work see David L. Stricklin, "Koinonia Farm: Epicenter for Social Change, Clarence Jordan (1912–1969), Jasper Martin England (1901–1989), and Millard Fuller (1935–   )" in *Twentieth Century Shapers of Baptist Social Ethics*, ed. Larry L. McSwain, 163-87, 328-29 (Macon GA: Mercer University Press, 2008).

[19]Allen, Interview no. 1 with Charleton, 34.

form. After that, he would preach wherever the opportunity would present itself, especially as he moved into college.

Howard Payne College, Brownwood, Texas

There was never any question in his mind that Jimmy would go to college. It was a requirement to go to seminary, which was his real goal. College was a step on the way to the larger goal of fulfilling his calling and ambition to serve God in whatever ways God would lead. Where he would attend was a more pragmatic question and was answered largely through a series of experiences which made the decision relatively easy.

Baylor University was the logical choice for a bright son of a Texas Baptist preacher with high aspirations for leadership. Several Dallas friends with whom he was in school or children of pastor friends of his father did just that—Browning and Weston Ware, and Browning's wife Martha among them. There was just one problem. Jimmy knew the costs of Baylor were not affordable for his family so the possibility was never even explored. A teenager who joined Junior R.O.T.C. so he would have a uniform to wear to high school would not even raise such a hope with his parents.

Through his sophomore year in high school, he continued to make his annual summer pilgrimage to Arkansas to visit with grandparents and other relatives. There he worked in the fields picking up potatoes for ten cents per hour. In the year he was thirteen, Grandfather Allen died at the age of eighty-two. The following summer of 1941 was Jimmy's last in Arkansas. The activities of RAs and part-time summer work opportunities occupied his time and energy.

Summer camps were a part of the ritual of activity for Allen. One of the camps he attended regularly was Woodlake near Sherman and Denison. There was a street-car route close enough that Jimmy could ride the train to the camp each year. One of the Bible teachers there who made an impression on the young preacher was a faculty member from Howard Payne College, M. E. Davis. Professor Davis had limited eyesight so he had memorized much of the Bible and taught out of that memory. That positive impression brought Howard Payne College to the surface of Jimmy's thinking.

One of Allen's closest and lifelong friends from those days was James Cooper who became a notable leader among Texas Baptists in his own ministry. James's father, R. B. Cooper, was the pastor of First Baptist Church, Pleasant Grove, Texas. He hosted a group of students called the Life Service Band from Howard Payne College and Jimmy attended. Impressed by their spirit, further investigation indicated no applicant was rejected there because of money. James Cooper was there a year ahead of Allen and encouraged him to attend and offered much support to him through his first years there. "I went there by choice," Allen recalls. "I did not compare it to this university or that university. It was a path I could get to with my calling."[20]

During the summer after his high school graduation, Allen secured a job at the Goldstein Women's Hat Factory with the help of a member of Pine Street Baptist Church who worked there. He now was making fifty cents per hour blowing the dust from hat forms with an air hose. It was dirty work in a hot "sweatshop" environment. So he applied for a better position and moved to stocking the hat blocks after they had been blown clean. That job gave him a start for college. With $137 in his pocket, Jimmy enrolled at Howard Payne College in Brownwood, Texas in the Fall of 1944, at the age of sixteen.

The college was fairly typical of the smaller Baptist colleges of the South and Southwest in the aftermath of the Great Depression and during World War II. There were few male students because of the impact of the war. Most such colleges were struggling to survive. The academic quality of the student body was modest. Howard Payne College had been founded in 1889 by local Baptist church leaders and named after the benefactor of a "sizeable gift" from the brother-in-law of John D. Robnett, Edward Howard Payne. Robnett was pastor of the First Baptist Church in Brownwood and the president of the first board of trustees.[21] The longest tenured president in the history of the school, Thomas H. Taylor, serving from 1929 to 1955, was there during the four years of Allen's study. Taylor is credited with saving the school when the stock market crash of 1929 prompted Texas Baptists to decide they could no longer provide funding and would close the school. A prayer meeting with the faculty resulted in a commitment of the group to sacrifice annual contracts to keep the school open on a policy of spending only available receipts of income.[22] Even today the school, now Howard Payne University, is relatively small with fewer than

---

[20] Allen, "Faith and Education Journey," 28-29.
[21] Robert G. Mangrum, "A Brief History of Howard Payne University," 2 November 2006 <hppt://www.hputx.edu/history> (accessed 15 June 2007).
[22] Robert G. Mangrum, "Dr. Thomas H. Taylor, 1929–1955," 24 January 2005 <hppt://www.hputx.edu/history/presidents> (accessed 15 June 2007).

2,000 students. During the first two years of Jimmy's study, enrollment would average less than 400 students, but enrollment exploded during his last two years with veterans returning from military service. By 1947 enrollment had reach 775.[23]

Allen's young age was probably a determining factor in his going to college. Had he been older when he graduated from high school, military service would have been the more likely path he would have taken. Never a pacificist, Allen was committed to the involvement of the United States in World War II, had participated in Junior R.O.T.C. in high school, and considered seriously enlistment in the Navy after his eighteenth birthday. He recalls, "I remember calling my dad and telling him I'm going to get drafted anyway. And he said, 'Well, if they want you, they'll come get you, so please hold tight.'"[24] He took a military physical in January 1945, but as the end of the war was sufficiently near, he was never drafted.

It would be fair to say that Jimmy Allen's major at Howard Payne College was "extracurricular activities." Ever the high-energy extrovert, the academic demands of the college were less stringent than his Dallas high school. While he did well in school, it was the multiple activities outside the classroom that captured his memory.

He recalled in 1972:

> My favorite memory would have to be the dormitory life, the fellowship that I had there with a group of people. I felt that the strength of Howard Payne College was in its student body and the intensity of Christian commitment of the large portion of the student body. And, that really was the warmest recollection that I have.[25]

He admits his frequent involvement with pranks and hazing activities that eventually landed him in the office of President Taylor, who demanded some restraint in the kind of hazing being done in the dorms.[26]

He intended to major in Bible. When a faculty member from Hardin-Simmons College challenged him not to major in Bible because he would have three years of such in seminary, he decided to major in English

---

[23]Robert G. Mangrum, "Historical Vignettes," 24 April 2006 <hppt://www.hputx.edu/historicalvignettes> (accessed 15 June 2006).
[24]Allen, Interview no. 1 with Charleton, 29.
[25]Jimmy Allen, Interview no. 2 with Charlton, Baylor University Program for Oral History, Waco TX, 1 May 1973, 46-47.
[26]Allen, Interview no. 2 with Charlton, 55.

literature. He did minor in Bible, took Greek instead of Algebra, and almost had a double major.

Allen wanted to serve as pastor of a church, but soon discovered a sixteen-year-old boy without a car had little opportunities for such. As a freshman at Howard Payne, he participated in a number of religious activities including the Life Service Band that visited the local jail. He also worked for a time as a music leader at a small church in a poorer section of Brownwood.[27] He finally brought up the subject of a car with his father, and recalls tearfully his response: "We can't help much but we will make sure you don't drown."[28] His roommate, Lonnie Richardson, had a job at the local electrical store named Gilland's. Mr. Gilland had a car he wanted to sell, a Dodge coupe. The two young students decided to buy a car together and Jimmy's father loaned him the money to buy half a car. They worked out a schedule for sharing the car which gave him an opportunity to go out and preach. But the experiment did not work particularly well. So, out of a "disagreement of who got the car and when, dad decided I needed a car and he sold me the family car. It was a 1936 Chevrolet two-door. I named it Genevieve. I drove at almost the rest of my college days."[29] After paying on the car for a few months, the remainder of the debt on it was forgiven by his father, the only substantive financial help he received from his family to complete his education.

Allen soon discovered a car would not compensate for his youthfulness when it came to finding a church where he could preach. During the summer after his freshman year, he was able to secure a job as a replacement mailman in Dallas. He had a flexible schedule and could work summers and Christmas holidays, and it was the best-paying job he would have. Then he heard that the little church at Bee Cave near Austin was without a pastor. The associational Baptist missionary there, Olan Miles, knew Jimmy and arranged for him to preach at Bee Cave. Allen says,

> During those three Sundays I went out to visit and work and we had about thirty additions which was about two or three times as many as they had the year before. So they became very interested in what to do about me as a pastor. . . . But the last day the deacon, his name was Brown, asked me how old I was, and when I told him I was seventeen that was the end of that. So I made a

---

[27] Allen, Interview no. 2 with Charlton, 55.
[28] Allen, "Faith and Education Journey," 29.
[29] Allen, "Faith and Education Journey," 29.

resolution that from then on I would never tell anybody how old I was . . . I would always evade the question.³⁰

In spite of his youthfulness, the young preacher had impressed his father and others in the Dallas area with his preaching skills. During his sophomore year, at the age of seventeen, he was ordained to the gospel ministry. Wallace Bassett, the well-known pastor of Oak Cliff Baptist Church, preached his ordination sermon.³¹

What Allen lacked in maturity, he made up for with initiative and his ability to network with others. His friend James Cooper had learned that becoming the business manager of the college annual would earn a full-tuition scholarship. There is a friendly dispute between the two about the way the relationship worked, but Cooper's recollection is:

> In my junior year I was the business manager of the annual called *The Lasso*. It was my responsibility to get ads for the annual. And for that I got my tuition paid. The next year I was still business manager and I enlisted Jimmy as my associate by telling him that the next year he can get the job and get his tuition paid. Well he was elected the next year, but unfortunately they cut out the full tuition. I don't remember just how much he did get for that but it was far less than I had and he has held that against me ever since.³²

Allen's story affirms Cooper's role in securing the position, but suggests he did the work of securing ads for a year without compensation in order to get the job. At any rate, Allen was elected to the position his junior year and seems to have earned the full amount of the tuition that year. But in the second year, an effort was made to assign more duties to the role, so he "went in my labor-management conflict and resigned my job in protest in order to protect the integrity of the office, and somebody else took over that task."³³ Fortunately, his income from preaching was adequate by then to meet his needs, and he was able to graduate without debt.

Cooper was also the catalyst for the call to Jimmy's first pastorate. After his graduation, Cooper went to Southwestern Seminary and was soon called as pastor of the Big Spring Baptist Church in the Dallas Baptist Association. He had been serving a small, half-time congregation near

---

³⁰Allen, Interview no. 2, with Charlton, 61-62.
³¹Allen, Interview no. 2 with Charlton, 61-62.
³²Cooper, Interview with Newton, 1.
³³Allen, Interview no. 2 with Charleton, 56.

Evant in Hamilton County, the Fairview Baptist Church. He told Allen he would recommend him there as pastor if he would go with him on his last Sunday and preach there. Allen did and was called as pastor of the church. The church met in a schoolhouse building where a deacon had gone to start an afternoon Sunday school. There were about thirty members and Allen baptized six to eight persons during his time there.[34] He was preaching every other Sunday and managing *The Lasso* during his junior year. By the summer he had located an abandoned church building propped up by old telephone poles in another community some miles from Avant and he made contact there as well. He reflects:

> So I went around to the ranches and asked folks if they would come every other Sunday if we would clean up the building. I told them they did not have to pay me any money. We would just pass the plate and see what we could get for gasoline money. I did that and it was called Mountview Baptist Church. I went out and spent one summer there riding a horse from ranch to ranch inviting people to come. We had a revival and I baptized fourteen people in the Lampasas River. Most were high school kids and nobody had ministered to them.[35]

Allen's tenure was brief in this setting as he received a postcard from a member at the Duffau Baptist Church in Hico inquiring about his interest in being pastor there. "I thought it might be a joke," he says reflecting something of his prankster suspicion of fellow students,

> so I talked with the associational missionary and he said . . . the card was from the church clerk. So I went over to preach there and they called me as pastor. I would go there every other Sunday and get another student to go to Mountview when I was not there. By the end of the summer of my junior year they called me full-time and I went every Sunday. . . . I baptized thirty-five to forty people there.[36]

(Allen returned to preach at the church for a celebratory service on 5 October 2003.)

During his last year of college, he added another church experience to his resume as the youth minister and associate pastor of the First Baptist

---

[34]Allen, "Faith and Education Journey," 33, and Cooper, Interview with Newton, 2.
[35]Allen, "Faith and Education Journey," 33.
[36]Allen, "Faith and Education Journey," 33.

Church in Dublin, Texas. He preached on Sunday evenings, but decided he should conclude his service when he graduated because of some tension emerging with the pastor as a result of his popularity with the youth in the church. He describes the experience:

> I'd tried to be very helpful and supportive of him [the pastor] because he was a very warm person, very encouraging to me, but there was a very deep cleavage in the problem that he was facing. And I think what happened was that the people who were converted that year, nearly all of them came in the Sunday evening service when I was preaching, basically because many of them were young people . . . but a number of adults, too. And that added to his problem some because he was preaching in the morning service and here was this young preacher at night and everything that seemed to be happening was happening at night. So I was conscious of that. I felt . . . I needed to get out, so I did that without any place to go, really, except to go to the seminary.[37]

Three weeks later he was offered an opportunity that provided a new chapter in Allen's life. He became the RA director for the Baptist General Convention of Texas in Dallas.

In addition to these many preaching and work opportunities, Allen was given the opportunity to join the debate team at college. While it never captured his enthusiasm as preaching had, it enlarged his network of new acquaintances from other colleges and universities and afforded travel in a new way. The school began a debate program in his junior year. He took the requisite class in speech and was chosen for the team. This gave him contact with debaters from other schools, including Keith Parks from North Texas State University who would become the national debate champion. Decades later, Parks was president of the Foreign Mission Board of the Southern Baptist Convention and missions coordinator for the Cooperative Baptist Fellowship. Being on the debate team enabled Allen to travel to Washington, D.C., his first trip to the nation's capital.

Howard Payne College was a formative ministry-shaping experience for this energetic, gregarious, hardworking young man. He graduated with the second highest grades among ministerial students, but admittedly was not a disciplined student. However, many shaping influences were experienced there.

---

[37]Allen, Interview no. 2 with Charleton, 72.

Of the people he identifies who were most important in his educational journey there were Z. T. Huff, dean of the school whom Allen often drove to recruiting visits in the area; W. A. Todd, professor of Bible who was an encouragement; Miss Estelle Smith, "a very beautiful, Episcopal Christian, elderly person who taught English literature and took a strong interest in my academic life as did Miss Grace Wellborn, who taught English literature and biology and speech."[38]

Youth Revival Movement

The 1940s and 1950s were among the most dynamic decades in the twentieth century in America for a spirit of enthusiasm, growth, and expansion of churches across established denominations. Much of that enthusiasm was generated by a return from World War II of thousands of young men and women who had lived through the life-threatening experiences of war; the exposure to a world, its values, and religions previously unknown in American history; and a hunger for some return to normalcy in life. Even those who maintained the hearth and home in cities and town in anticipation of a safe return of America's armed forces were infected by this enthusiasm. The aftermath of the conflagration of both the Great Depression and the Great War produced a generation of survivors who would form new families, build houses, go to school, build institutions, and have more children than any previous generation.[39]

Beginning in 1945, educational institutions were refilled with returning veterans who could afford the cost of new learning with the benefits of the G.I. Bill. At the same time, there was a new revivalism breaking out across the country. It was the time of the inauguration of the long and effective ministry of Billy Graham. It also was a period of general uniformity in the practical theology of American churches that emphasized personal faith, nurture of children, and building of congregations. Consequently, the years from 1945 until the emergence of the ferment and fragmentation of the youthful generation of the 1960s were years of vitality and growth for almost all of the church bodies in America.[40] This was especially so for

---

[38] Allen, Interview no. 2 with Charleton, 70.
[39] Tom Brokow, *The Greatest Generation* (New York: Random House, 2004).
[40] See Jackson W. Carroll, Douglas W. Johnson, and Martin E. Marty, *Religion in America: 1950 to the Present* (San Francisco: Harper & Row, 1979)

Southern Baptists whose Sunday school campaign of "A Million More in '54" resulted in more baptisms in Southern Baptist churches in that year than any other in its history.

There is no question that history is a consequence of both events and movements. When it comes to religion, there is an unexplainable fusion of specific events with a spark of inspiration that one can only describe as phenomenal which generates movements that no one could anticipate nor engineer. Thus, a series of "great awakenings" have characterized the ebb and flow of religious vitality in the American context.

The history of revivalism in America has been one of mass movements led by popular evangelists or significant pastors.[41] But at least three revival movements were initiated on college campuses. The first was the "Haystack Prayer Meeting" of 1806, which took place at Williams College in Williamstown, Massachusetts. A group of five young men gathered weekly to pray together when in August 1806, they sought shelter from a rainstorm next to a stack of hay. Four of them focused their prayers on the spread of Christianity beyond America and the modern American mission movement was spawned from that group. The American Board of Commissioners for Foreign Missions was established by 1810. Included in the first five missionaries to be ordained by the group in 1812 were Adoniram Judson and Luther Rice who became Baptists and launched the modern Baptist mission movement in America.[42]

The second major campus movement was the holiness movement stimulated on the campus of Oberlin College in the 1840s by the evangelist

---

15, for a summary of the growth of the thirteen major Christian denominations in the United States between 1955–1965 and and 1965–1975. All but one, the United Church of Christ, grew in the first decade while only seven grew in the second decade. Only the Seventh Day Adventists grew at a faster pace in the second decade than the first.

[41]William Warren Sweet, *Revivalism in America: Its Origin, Growth and Decline* (Gloucester MA: Peter Smith, 1965) is the classic history of these movements.

[42]"The Haystack Prayer Meeting" and "America's First Protestant Missionaries," <http://wso.williams.edu/dchu/MissionPark/meeting.htm> (accessed 2 October 2007).

and educator Charles Finney.[43] The abolitionist movement was a fuel for its intensity.

The third primary movement came to be known as the "Youth Revival Movement" and had an impact primarily on Southern Baptists, shaping the denomination for a generation. In the waning months of the war, a group of Baylor University students became burdened for their campus and their nation. Students gathered on the campus for ninety straight nights to pray for a city-wide, student-led revival they were planning for the spring, 1945. Revivals were standard fare for most Baptist churches of that time. The practice was just emerging in many churches for the youth to offer leadership with music and preaching. The Waco revival was an incredible success and the enthusiasm and grandiosity of the students generated a movement to spread what had happened there to campuses and communities elsewhere. A leadership core grew out of that experience at Baylor that would impact much of Baptist life for the next generation.

Its leaders included Bruce McIver, long-time pastor of Wilshire Baptist Church in Dallas;[44] Jess Moody, founder of Palm Beach Atlantic University and pastor of multiple megachurches; Ralph Langley, noted preacher and pastor of Willow Meadows Baptist Church in Houston, Texas and First Baptist Church in Huntsville, Alabama; Howard Butt, grocery-store entrepreneur, author, radio commentator, and founder of Laity Lodge in Texas; Jack Robinson, All-American basketball player and pastor of First Baptist Church, Augusta, Georgia; Charles Wellborn, pastor of Seventh and James Baptist Church in Waco, Texas and professor of Religion at Florida State University; and Bo Baker, evangelist and long-time pastor of Plymouth Park Baptist Church in Irving, Texas.[45]

Such a movement is difficult to explain rationally. McIver summarized it in reflection on the events of the movement many years after it had dissipated:

---

[43]Timothy L. Smith, *Revivalism and Social Reform: American Protestantism on the Eve of the Civil War* (New York: Harper Torchbooks, 1957) 103-13.

[44]Bruce McIver, *Riding the Wind of God: A Personal History of the Youth Revival Movement* (Macon GA: Smyth & Helwys Publishing, 2002) is a written account of the event.

[45]Marv Knox, "Leaders of '40s Youth Revivals Gather to Reminisce, Kindle New 'Fires,' " *Baptists Today*, December 2006, 15.

How did it happen? I don't know. Really, I don't. And neither do the others who were deeply involved in the Youth Revival Movement. Of course, we could offer platitudes, but honesty says the Movement was beyond our doing. We were only spectators, only witnesses. As has been suggested, we were like the little boy who brought the loaves and fish to Jesus, then stood back and said, "Wow!"[46]

Professionalism was not the order of the day as students full of fervor preached the same sermons again and again from place to place. Some had only one or two such sermons and the repetition would sometimes result in humorous stories. Allen was the recipient of one such story from McIver:

> Jimmy Allen, a Howard Payne student and an extremely gifted speaker, preached with fervor one night on the Old Testament strong man, Samson. It was a great sermon, except Jimmy called him "Tarzan" all the way through his message.[47]

One of the results of the revival in Waco was an effort to replicate the same fervor on other campuses, especially across the state of Texas. Contacts through the Baptist Student Unions of the Baptist campuses resulted in invitations for representatives of the Baylor experience to visit the other campuses. This included Howard Payne College.

A student-led revival was scheduled for 8-12 November 1947 at Howard Payne with a rotation of preachers for each night of the revival. Allen was one of the preachers during that week. There was nothing particularly unusual about the event in his mind as he had been preaching in such meetings since he was fifteen years of age. The Baptist Student Union president that year, Joe Smith, reported in the campus newspaper, the *Yellow Jacket*, "It was the greatest Spiritual Revival that I have ever been in" with many decisions for Christ reported.[48]

The consequence of the events generated by this unique movement was the effort to institutionalize it at the denominational level. W. F. Howard was the director for years of the Baptist Student Union organization for the Texas convention. He was one of the most admired and creative leaders of the extensive Baptist involvement in campus ministry. As churches were

---

[46]McIver, *Riding the Wind*, 229.

[47]McIver, *Riding the Wind*, 209.

[48]Mangrum, "Historical Vignettes," summarizing events recorded in the 16 December 1947 edition.

touched by what began in Waco, Howard organized teams of students from the various campuses in Texas to conduct week-long, youth-led, revival services in churches across the state and eventually beyond. Each team at that time would have two preachers and two musicians who would travel together and provide the leadership for the services. Allen participated in these teams during the summers of his last year in college and even extending into Seminary.

Another consequence of the youth revival movement was the founding of Word Records by Jerrell McCracken in Waco in 1951. Allen claims with serious humor that he was responsible for the founding of the company because the first product was a McCracken production of a script written by him during his junior year for a BSU devotional at Howard Payne. The script, entitled "The Game of Life," set the Christian message in the form of a broadcast from radio station WORD of a football game between good and evil. Another Howard Payne student, Emily "Rusty" Nail, sent the script to Jess Moody at Baylor who published it in *The Shield* student magazine.[49] McCracken was a radio sportscaster in Waco and had helped organize a number of the youth-led revivals, especially those featuring Baylor student-musician Frank Boggs, who was the first artist to record for the new company. McCracken took the script, called the plays on a recording with sports sound effects that also featured testimonies of Christian athletes. The company developed into Word Entertainment, a large book and music publishing company that was sold to Warner Music in 2001 for a reported $84.1 million. The record of "The Game of Life" sold more than two million copies and Allen still laughingly bemoans the fact he was the impetus for the company's founding with never a dollar in royalty collected from it.

Conclusion

On 21 May 1948, Jimmy Allen became the first person in his extended family to graduate from college. His parents were there to celebrate with enthusiasm and pride. It was not particularly important to him because his real goal was attending seminary. He was now a college graduate at the age of twenty, established as a vibrant, evangelistic preacher with a variety of

---

[49]Jimmy Allen, *Burden of a Secret* (Nashville TN: Mooring, 1995) 75. "Rusty" Nail Lunday became a helpful supporter to the family during the HIV/AIDS crisis described in chap. 10.

experiences behind him. He was clearly focused on the future as pastor of a challenging congregation.

Among the more potent social-scientific hypotheses developed in the twentieth century is the assertion that one's essential values and perspectives on life are formed by the time one enters young adulthood. The dominant generational and contextual events occurring in the social order at that time become significant for both the individual and the generational cohort of that individual for the remainder of one's life. Thus, the years from sixteen to twenty-four are the most formative for a lifetime of leadership and service, or lack thereof.[50]

One aspect of Allen's value system and generational vibrancy was clearly formed by the time he graduated from college. He identifies it for himself specifically. That was the unswerving commitment of his father and his father's generation to the will of God and the leadership of the church. His father and George W. Truett, the iconic pastor of the First Baptist Church in Dallas, were the symbols for him of that commitment. Allen recalls two events that illustrate the commitment.

The first occurred when they were living in the church building on McKinney Avenue. There was no food in the house for lunch and Earl Allen called the family together in the bedroom.

> And he asked Mother, "Mother, do you believe in prayer?" And she said, "Yes, I do." And she said, "Jimmy, do you believe in prayer?" And I said, "Yes, I do." And [he] said, "Well, we don't have anything to eat today, and so we are going to pray and ask God to provide for us because we are here trying to do his service." And so we got on our knees and prayed for food. And actually the food came through a person who came by with a pound of pinto beans. . . . And in that kind of a milieu or atmosphere it becomes a very real thing that God does indeed deal personally with you.[51]

Allen developed a philosophy of ministry that one could live so close to God there could be a clear sense of direction of the Father's will, and one's leadership derived from that sense of intimacy.

---

[50]One such proponent of this view can be found in Warren G. Bennis and Robert J. Thomas, *Geeks and Geezers: How Era, Values, and Defining Moments Shape Leaders* (Cambridge: Harvard Business School Press, 2002).

[51]Allen, Interview no. 1 with Charleton, 13. Allen, *Burden of a Secret*, 12, identifies the woman as Evelyn Taft, who joined them for a bean dinner that evening.

The second significant influence for this commitment was Truett. The location of First Baptist Church was close enough to the places they lived that Jimmy would ride his bicycle to the church where he attended Vacation Bible School. He often heard Truett preach there and at associational events. When he returned from his trip to Ridgecrest, Allen commented to his father he was not impressed with the preaching he heard. His father retorted, "Son, your problem is you have been listening to the best preacher in the country in your own town."[52]

Even more memorable was attending a pastors' conference with his father at Southwestern Seminary when Truett preached and said that he would not give up being a pastor to be the president of the United States. "I sat there and said," Allen recalls, "that can't be true and my dad grew ten feet tall when I realized that what this man was doing was more important in that moment than being President."[53] Allen was thirteen years old at the time. Clearly formed by young adulthood was this deep commitment to ministry and the church. It manifested itself in a willingness to respond to any invitation to preach. When he did the message was a fiery, passionate evangelistic message from the traditional, conservative revivalism of his youth. It was a style that would never leave him even when the shape of the message and theology were broadened into a more socially conscious expression of the gospel.

Another dominant value would not come until seminary. Here he would encounter an intellectual environment that would shape his theology and experience in the direction of a new emphasis, the social application of the gospel to the church and the society in which he lived.

Two influences—passionate evangelism and social consciousness—remain in the heart and expression of his ministry to this day.

---

[52]Allen, "Early Life Experiences," 18.
[53]Allen, "Early Life Experiences," 17.

Chapter 4
Young Adulthood and Foundational Leadership

> Read no history; nothing but biography, for that is life without theory.
> —Benjamin Disraeli[1]

The ten years following Jimmy Allen's graduation from Howard Payne College were spent largely out of the spotlight, but they were crucial in preparing him for the attention that would be focused on him the remainder of his days. These ten years established a pattern for ministry in pastoral leadership that characterized much of his lifetime of service and ministry. They were years of continuing formation, education, marriage, and the birth of three sons.

Royal Ambassadors

In the summer of 1948, Allen was twenty years old. He had graduated from Howard Payne before two exceedingly proud parents. He had been the pastor of three small, rural Baptist churches, each of which had experienced an evangelistic revival. He had just completed a short tenure as assistant pastor and youth director of the First Baptist Church in Dublin, Texas. Three weeks after resigning that position he received a most unusual invitation for a young man who was not yet twenty-one, and therefore not yet considered an adult by the social customs of the time.

The work of Royal Ambassadors (RAs) was never far from his consciousness. Though he had completed the highest levels of rank in the organization in high school, he continued to participate and lead in RA camps during his college years. Texas Baptists had an extensive network of camps for youth located throughout the state owned by local churches, Baptist associations, and other organizations. The Baptist General Convention of Texas (BGCT) worked to provide programs for a number of these camps each summer.[2] Most of them would offer a schedule rotation that offered a week of programming for the various mission, education, and service organizations of the convention's work. These included weeks with a focus on Sunday school, Baptist Training Union, WMU, GAs, and RAs, as well as several other more specialized groups.

---

[1]Benjamin Disraeli, *Contarina Fleming*, 1832. <http://www.quotationsbook.com/quote/4266> (accessed 4 April 2009).

[2]Allen remembers seventeen camps in which work was done. Harry Leon McBeth, *Texas Baptists: A Sesquicentennial History* (Dallas: Baptistway Press, 1998) 232 identifies fourteen assemblies by 1952 recorded in the BGCT annual.

At that time the work of the RAs was the responsibility of the WMU, then later the Brotherhood (later to be called Texas Baptist Men). One of the iconic figures to emerge in Texas Baptist life was the newly elected executive secretary/treasurer of the Texas WMU, Eula Mae Henderson.[3] She served the organization from 1946 to her retirement in 1980, first for a year as the state young people's secretary and then for thirty three years in the executive leadership post. This mission organization exerted significant influence in raising funds for mission projects and coordinating the support of women across the state for convention-led priorities. One of her early decisions in her new role as the executive of the WMU was to employ Jimmy Allen, beginning in September 1948, as the director of Royal Ambassadors for Texas Baptists, succeeding C. W. Farrar.[4] Such a role made him responsible for coordinating RA camps across the state. He served in this capacity until January 1951, while also studying as a full-time student at Southwestern Baptist Theological Seminary.

The job gave him several perquisites unusual for a seminary student at the time. He had an office in the Baptist Building in Dallas which he jokingly suggests required him to remove the brooms and mops each time he used it. He was given the opportunity to establish connections and relationships with the core leadership of the convention life, including J. Howard Williams, the executive secretary of the convention from 1931 to 1936 and again 1946–1952. While the WMU was the main organization for supporting the RA work, the transition of boys' work to the leadership of the men's department, or Brotherhood, was underway. Thus, Allen was paid from the budget of the Brotherhood department and supervised by the secretary of the department, L. H. Tapscott, and by Eula Mae Henderson. Among the most influential persons he encountered during this time was J. Ivyloy Bishop, national secretary for RAs for the SBC. He offered Allen much practical guidance for his work and they became close friends.[5] As a member of the staff, he was involved in annual planning events with the

---

[3]She was chosen in a poll of *Baptist Standard* readers in 1999 among the ten most influential Texas Baptists in the twentieth century. Cf. Amelia Bishop, "Eula Mae Henderson," *Baptist Standard*, 8 December 1999, 8.

[4]McBeth, *Texas Baptists*, 235.

[5]Jimmy Allen, Interview no. 2 with Charlton, Baylor University Program for Oral History, Waco TX, Baylor University, 1 May 1973, 79. Bishop later served as a professor of religion at Wayland Baptist College.

WMU leadership of the national organization, putting him in contact with an even wider array of mission leaders. Another of the perquisites of this role was a convention "green book." The green book was the means of reporting travel expenses to the convention. Part of Allen's assignment was to promote RA work in churches across the state, and his travel expenses were paid by the convention. His typical schedule during the school year was to spend the week studying on the campus of Southwestern Seminary where he used his dormitory room as an office for the RA work. He also enlisted the help of a part-time student paid by the convention who assisted him in the administrative details of the work. Most Sundays he would be in a local church promoting RA work, providing training to RA leaders, or preaching. Revivals of a week's duration during the school year were a common part of his activities. James Dunn, Allen's successor as executive director of the CLC for the BGCT, recalls his first meeting of Allen at the Evans Avenue Baptist Church in Fort Worth. Dunn was a thirteen-year-old boy at the time. He does not recall whether Allen was the main preacher for the service or promoting the RA program, but he was impressed by the dynamic style communicated by Allen. When asked what kind of impression he made as a preacher Dunn responded, "Yes, high energy, fast talking, serious as a crutch, a little too serious perhaps. But it appealed to me as a kid and I remembered him."[6]

The summers were packed with twelve or more weeks of RA camps scattered among the several encampments or retreat centers related tangentially to the convention and managed by Baptist associations or other groups. He recruited a team of college students to bring order to the differences in approach and the often unorganized programming done by local groups for the camps. His philosophy was clear:

> The major objective was to give a boy-oriented activity that centered in the kind of things that would develop skills for him, that centered in the learning of missions, the development of his Christian convictions, and the understanding of the Scripture in the format of things that appeal to boys.[7]

This role was invaluable for Allen in a number of ways. First, it put him in contact throughout the state with pastors, lay leaders, and young boys who would become future leaders of their churches. His task was to recruit three

---

[6] James Dunn, Interview with Jim Newton, Dallas, 1 July 2005, 1.
[7] Allen, Interview no. 2 with Charlton, 75.

college or high-school students heavily involved in RA activities who would become a staff for each camp for twelve weeks of the summers. "We would go in and set up on Monday and break it up on Friday and move to the next place,"[8] says Allen. Out of that process, he met leaders and future leaders from virtually every geographic segment of the state. His natural networking abilities led to the development of a contact base that served him through his years of leadership at the CLC as well as the recognition afforded him in later convention offices to which he was elected. He often met "RA boys" later when lobbying at the state legislature, preaching in a local church, or presiding as president of the BGCT annual meeting. An important part of that networking was the contact established with the leadership and staff of the BGCT. He got a "hands-on" understanding of how the convention worked and the pockets of power within the staff that served him well in later years.

Second, this rather demanding role at an early age sharpened his organizational skills. He quickly moved in his new role to organize each camp along the lines of a similar workable organization. This often brought conflict because of the largely ad hoc and somewhat unorganized manner some of the camps had developed. He observed that when boys stayed in their local church groupings, problems of rivalry were often created because of the competition among local high schools. Allen developed a "chapter system" for each camp in which boys would be assigned to a chapter for activities and sleeping rather than their local group. This created opportunities to meet new friends and weakened existing groupings among boys prior to the camps. It also allowed for better discipline and new competitions among the RA chapters rather than existing church or school groupings.

Allen also organized a series of training events in the spring of each year for RA leaders to anticipate the summer organization. He found this often did not work because the leadership would change from the time of training until the summer experience.

This brought the third value of this early experience. The young leader soon learned to assert his authority, often with pastors and camp leaders many years older and more experienced than he. The new system did not always set well with local leaders who had their own entrenched traditions.

---

[8]Jimmy Allen, "Faith and Education Journey," Interview no. 2 with Larry L. McSwain, Alpharetta GA, 13 November 2004, 36.

On one occasion when facing strong resistance to his efforts to organize a camp, Allen threatened to leave the camp. The leaders backed down from their resistance, accepted his approach, and the camp went smoothly.

He recalled:

> I would come in, having met the leadership in training earlier in the spring, only to meet a different set of leaders on the Monday. [These leaders had always done it a different way in the past.] I was a twenty-year-old kid telling a fifty-year-old man how to run camps. Now, that didn't bother me; my ego drive was strong enough. But it seemed to bother them some, and so I found myself on nearly [every] Monday in great tension with people who came in.[9]

One of his more memorable confrontations was with Arthur Rutledge, then pastor of the First Baptist Church in Marshall, Texas and later president of the Home Mission Board of the SBC. Rutledge did not like Allen's chapter organization, largely because he had no prior knowledge of it. "I soon found out," Allen recalls, "I was not going to run the camp the way I wanted it that week because of the breakdown of communication before I got there."[10] So, Allen moved to a "modified" chapter system where the activities of the day were within his system while each of the campers returned to a home church base for sleeping. An important lesson was learned in the process, namely, "I found early in the game that when you ... can't do it all the way, you take whatever inch you can."[11]

Two and one-half years were spent in this endeavor. But marriage in the second year of seminary led toward a more settled life with growing family responsibilities. In January 1951, Allen began his service as pastor of the First Baptist Church, Van Alstyne, northeast of Dallas, and another chapter in his pilgrimage would begin.

Love and Marriage

Jimmy Allen was ever the gregarious kid involved in relationships with friends and active in church and school events. Though small in physical size through his college years, largely because he was younger than his peers in school, he made up for his size with physical prowess in the boxing

---

[9]Allen, Interview no. 2 with Charlton, 79-80.
[10]Allen, Interview no. 2 with Charlton, 81.
[11]Allen, Interview no. 2 with Charlton, 81.

ring and on the baseball diamond. His black, curly hair and infectious smile added to his attractiveness to the young girls of his schools.

During high school Allen had friendships with a number of young women but not a deeply romantic relationship with any. The closest to a "steady" girlfriend was with Joanne Fooshe, a classmate at Forrest High School who also attended Pine Street Baptist Church. They dated steadily but the relationship seemed more important to her than to him. Allen returned to Forrest High School in 2004 for a sixtieth high-school reunion; he was honored as an outstanding alumnus. Joanne returned to the school with her husband and they enjoyed a pleasant reunion when she introduced her "first love" to her "last love."[12] When the time came to go to Howard Payne College, Allen said "goodbye" to this girlfriend, not to see her again for sixty years.

Allen had a more serious romantic relationship while at Howard Payne College. He was actually engaged to be married for a time to a fellow student named Ruth Stephenson. His attentions toward Ruth during speech class prompted disapproval by Professor Grace Wellborn, who removed Jimmy from the debate team for awhile. While it is a relationship he does not discuss freely, there was obvious disappointment in their breakup.

James Cooper recalls some of their friendly rivalry with a story about Allen's fiancé:

> While he was pastor of Fairview church, I was in seminary and I got a new Nash automobile. I told Jimmy about it and he told the folks at the church I had a new Nash automobile but he was engaged and he would rather be engaged than have a new Nash. . . . It wasn't many weeks after that the girl broke the engagement and he was driving a Nash automobile.[13]

There may be some connection between the Nash automobile and the love of his life that brought him to marry Wanda Massey. During the beginning of Allen's senior year at college, Wanda moved with her family from Wichita Falls to Brownwood. Her father, Bill Massey, and his brothers were automobile businessmen. Mr. Massey sold a Nash Rambler dealership in Wichita Falls to open an auto parts business in Brownwood. It was not too long after he met Wanda before Jimmy decided to replace "Genevieve," his 1936 Chevrolet, with a Nash.

---

[12] Allen, "Faith and Education Journey," 25.
[13] James Cooper, interview with Jim Newton, Dallas, 5 July 2005, 3.

Wanda was living at home and attending Howard Payne as a concession to her father who offered to support her to attend another school if she would live at home for one year before leaving. Allen's description of their meeting was offered to me in the year after her death:

> She was a bright girl with sparkle and personality and hit the campus my senior year. . . . My first remembrance of Wanda was when in the college commissary I was getting something to eat and she was drinking a cold drink and acting silly like she was able to do. That is when I first saw who she was. Then we began dating after that and she just walked into my heart. She was a performer. She was a speech major or drama major and I was a debater and doing oratory things. We went to tournaments together. She always won and I came in second or third. I never was all that good. She was an after-dinner speaker with great skill and ability. I was very impressed with her so I dated her and when I went to seminary I would come back to see her. . . . At the end of my first year she was finishing her . . . junior year . . . and I asked her to marry me. . . . We moved to Fort Worth and she went to school because her daddy told her she would not finish her degree if she married. She was so hardheaded she went to three schools and took a correspondence course to finish her degree. She was the life of every party she ever saw—the unexpected humorist person. I had a mother who was an assistant pastor and I did not want one. . . . I had the feeling mother was always trying to do the work of the church with dad, for dad. I wanted somebody who would be my wife, let me be the pastor, and just enjoy life. Serve God but not feel the weight of the responsibility. She wanted that pattern and she did that well. She was who she was wherever she was. They always loved Wanda and respected me. It was just the pattern of our lives. Everywhere she went the people had a great affection for her and a tolerance of me.[14]

Jimmy Allen and Wanda Massey married August 26, 1949 after the last RA camp of the summer, but there was no immediate acceptance of this preacher in the Massey family. In reality, Wanda's father was evidently quite codependent on his daughter. On one occasion, Wanda's uncle, Luther Massey, who owned the Buick automobile dealership in Beaumont, showed up at a revival Jimmy was preaching in a Beaumont church. Allen recalls:

> He was a Disciples member and came out to the church to hear me preach. I found out later he called his brother Bill who was my father-in-law and reported, "Well, Bill, I went out to hear Wanda's husband, Jimmy. I'll tell you

---

[14]Allen, "Faith and Education Journey," 41-42.

what. She married a preacher but she married a damn good one!" So I got accepted, finally. It was always a tension about that for them. But they accepted it. My father-in-law had a hard time complementing people but before he died we were sitting out on the swing by our lake house down at Brownwood and he said, "You know if I had gone everywhere I could not have found two sons-in-law better for my daughters than you two were." And that was the only time he ever said anything good to me about my function in the family. He just had a hard time stroking people. In fact, when I married her and we went on our honeymoon he had a kind of an emotional breakdown and they had him in the hospital. . . . I went up to spend the night with him and he was under this anesthesia. He was saying, "Oh, my baby, my baby, she's dead, she's died, my baby's died." I spent the first night of my relationship with my father-in-law listening to him thinking I had killed his relationship to his daughter. It was a very interesting entry to the family.[15]

There were challenges of illness and pain throughout their marriage. But there was never a wavering in their love and devotion to each other and her support for the many ventures of ministry and service in which her husband engaged. He described her many years after their marriage:

At church, Wanda was the same person she always had been—candid and open, someone who followed her impulses. Nothing in her background prepared her for the hidden, unspoken ways of the church. She did not know how to be a selective friend; how to be in the public's eye, and yet maintain a strict code of privacy; how to carefully handle ticklish people and controversial issues. To Wanda, friendships were genuine, wholehearted, and cherished. She led with her heart, reaching out and responding with authentic feeling to everyone she met. Wanda was either on or off; hot or cold; she either loved something or hated it, but she was never indifferent.[16]

Southwestern Baptist Theological Seminary

Individuals are shaped by many different influences in life—the culture of which one is a part, individuals who impact life, peers, and sometimes significant institutions in which one is a part. The influence of Jimmy Allen's father and older ministerial leaders such as George W. Truett were identified in the previous chapter as significant life forces. From his father came the relentless desire to follow the will of God and from Truett and

---

[15] Allen, "Faith and Education Journey," 43.
[16] Jimmy Allen, *Burden of a Secret* (Nashville: Mooring, 1995) 19.

others a commitment to preaching and doing pastoral ministry. The third dominate shaper of his values, philosophy, and understanding of how to do the work of the church came from Southwestern Baptist Theological Seminary (SWBTS) in Fort Worth.

Southwestern Seminary had long been within the scope of Allen's personal radar from his youthful years when he would sometimes attend classes or conferences with his parents. The primary educational goal he claimed from the time of his calling to preach was to complete seminary at Southwestern. By the time he was in college, that goal included the completion of a doctorate. All other educational ventures were pragmatic steps toward that ultimate goal.

Founded by B. H. Carroll in 1908, Southwestern moved to Fort Worth in 1910, where it assumed a dominant regional influence in the training of church leadership for the Southwest. The seminary both inhaled and exhaled the exuberance, aggressiveness, and bigness of Texas Baptist life and Texas culture. Southwestern was ever focused on missions and evangelism, largely due to the influence of the second president, L. R. Scarborough, who was able to generate the ethos of a fiery style of preaching and evangelism that continues somewhat to this day.

By the time Allen began his study in 1948, the seminary had matured into a more scholarly environment with significant numbers of faculty earning advanced degrees at seminaries and universities beyond the Southern Baptist family. It vied somewhat for scholarly reputation with the Southern Baptist Theological Seminary in Louisville, but developed a different scholarly approach in that its faculty invested more fully in writing and publication for practicing church leaders and laity.

Any Southern Baptist with a call to ministry had three choices of a Southern Baptist Seminary at that time—Southern, Southwestern, or the New Orleans Baptist Theological Seminary. The adventurous could choose from a host of seminaries sponsored by American Baptists or divinity schools such as Harvard, Yale, Princeton, Union of New York, University of Chicago, Vanderbilt, or Duke.

It never occurred to Allen to go anywhere else. He was not Texas born, but was Texas raised, educated, and was alive with the vision of serving as pastor of a major church in Texas. He knew most of the faculty by reputation, having heard them speak or preach. He had employment that would provide the financial means for him to study during the week and minister on the weekends and through the summers. After all, the convention was paying him thirty-seven dollars and fifty cents per week during the school year and fifty dollars per week in the summer for his RA work. Then he had extra honoraria from his preaching and revivals. He had a rapidly developing love relationship with Wanda Massey in Brownwood. Fort Worth was his option and one he chose with enthusiasm and intention.

Southwestern proved to be an academic challenge for the twenty-year old with a vision. He found his earlier ease in making grades was tested by the inadequacies of his college education when introduced to names and concepts he was hearing for the first time. Nights were often spent in the library checking references to understand the names of scholars and influences about whom he was learning for the first time. The challenge proved exhilarating. Not only was he motivated to study, he was set on achieving the kind of academic record that would qualify him for doctoral studies. So, making an A grade in every class was now important, a goal he did not always achieve. But when he did not, he moved aggressively, sometimes brashly, to encounter the professor about his performance.

The professor who had undoubtedly the greatest influence on Allen was T. B. Maston, professor of Christian ethics. Interestingly, Allen had a negative experience in the first course he took with Maston because the professor graded on the curve. Allen thought a student should be given a grade based on performance related to specific criteria, however many A grades there might be. When he made a B on the first course he took with Maston, a course on family relationships, he avoided additional courses with him until his last year when he took philosophy of ethics and found a home.

Initially, the young theolog intended to complete his Bachelor of Divinity and then study Systematic Theology for a Doctor of Theology degree. Allen identifies Jesse Northcutt, then professor of theology and later dean of the School of Theology, as a favorite professor.[17] Others whom he found challenging included Ralph Phelps in ethics, Ray Summers in New Testament, Stuart Newman in philosophy, J. M. Price and William House in Religious Education, Robert Baker in Church History, and eventually Maston in Ethics.[18] Especially challenging was G. Earl Guinn in Preaching, whom Allen described as, "one of the most incisive and able professors and one of the most acid personalities that I've ever known."[19]

---

[17] Allen, interview no. 2 with Charlton, 85-86.
[18] Allen, interview no. 2 with Charlton, 87.
[19] Allen, "Faith and Education Journey," 38.

By the middle of his third year in seminary, he was settled into marriage. Wanda completed her college work at Howard Payne College by taking courses at Texas Wesleyan University and Texas Christian University in Fort Worth and summer courses at Howard Payne. A correspondence course was even added to ensure her graduation. With two and one-half years of living on the road as RA secretary, it was time to move into a new phase of ministry.

In January 1951, Allen became pastor of the First Baptist Church in Van Alstyne, northeast of Dallas. He commuted to the campus weekly to finish his degree. It was there he made the decision to shift the focus of his additional study from Systematic Theology to Ethics.

Two events propelled him in a new direction. He needed to concentrate his last semester of study in the spring of 1951 in as few days as possible given the long commute from Van Alstyne. He completed the application for a Doctor of Theology degree and was accepted to study with Northcutt in Systematic Theology. Allen decided he needed a break from school and an opportunity to spend more time with his church so he chose to take a year for pastoral leadership before beginning the Th.D.

During that year, Ralph Phelps came to Van Alstyne to preach and asked Allen about his major in the graduate degree. Allen remembers his response: " 'Well, you know I've majored in Systematic Theology, so I'll do that on the doctorate.' And he asked me, 'Why?' And I really could not answer him; there was no real depth of conviction there."[20]

Allen took a course on Philosophy of Ethics taught one day each week by T. B. Maston the same year. Here he encountered Maston the scholar as he tied together the fields of Philosophy, Theology, and Social Ethics into a process that captured Allen's attention and enthusiasm. He saw integration of his other studies in this class.

He also saw the impact in the study of Christian ethics on practical reality in pastoral ministry. As he served the people in the church and the community, he concluded the questions they were asking were not the intellectual questions of the theologian, but the practical questions of life with which he saw ethics dealing. He summarizes, "The things the people were dealing with were practical, ethical, oughtness decisions. And I was

---

[20] Allen, Interview no. 2 with Charlton, 88-89.

not able to tell them a whole lot about the theories of inspiration and the atoning doctrines."[21] He summarizes:

> So I went to Ft. Worth, got an appointment with Dr. Maston, told him I was coming into the graduate program and was truly convinced I needed to do something different about my major. . . . I wondered if it were possible for me to major in Ethics. And he was startled. He said, "You haven't had any courses with me." I said, "Yes sir, I had a course with you but I did not like the way you graded so I did not take any more. But this last course in the Philosophy of Ethics has been intriguing and the fact is I really need to do ethics." He said, "I won't lift my finger to try to get you to change your major to Ethics." "No sir," I said, "that was not really my question. What I am asking is it possible for me to shift to major in Ethics?" He said he would have to talk to the graduate committee about it. He went to the graduate committee and Robert Baker and Jess Northcutt on the committee decided if I wanted to do that I could do it if I would audit every course he taught. I decided that is what I would do.[22]

The next six years Allen balanced his time between service as a pastor and commuting to Fort Worth as a graduate student. He did, indeed, audit each of Maston's courses taught the following year, served as his grader during that time, completed his seminars for the Th.D., and submitted a dissertation written largely from the office of his church.

His course of study included seminars in Ethics with Maston, Ray Summers in New Testament, James Leo Garrett in Systematic Theology, and Jesse Northcutt in Theology and Preaching. C. W. Scudder also read his dissertation.

Student Pastorates. Jimmy served three churches while studying as a student at SWBTS. He served First Baptist Church in Van Alstyne from January 1951 until July 1952. It was there he made his first efforts at the local church level to address issues of race relations in the church as well as in the larger community.

He had developed warm relationships with the pastor of the Disciples of Christ congregation, a student at Brite Divinity School at Texas Christian University in Fort Worth, with whom he often commuted to Fort Worth. The pastor of the local Methodist church was an older pastor and the three

---

[21] Jimmy Allen, "Life, Ministry, and Friendships," interview with Jim Newton, Dallas, 31 July 2005, 15.1

[22] Allen, "Life, Ministry, and Friendships," 15-16.

of them agreed to support a community program around Boy Scout Day with an interracial audience, inviting the pastor of the local Negro Baptist church to preach. The plan was to meet in the Methodist church because of the greater say of the pastor in that denomination for the use of the facility. However, the church was in a building program that did not finish in time for the planned event. Allen reports:

> I had to make a decision as to how to handle that. And I went to my leadership people and laid it before them; we were in this kind of spot. It was a very interesting thing because the deacons, one of them very candidly said, "This is not the way I feel; this is not the way I think is wise. Our denomination, though, has been on record as being for this," which was the first time I learned that denominational posture really did assist a congregation, "and the community is planning it. Therefore I don't see how we can avoid doing it." So I began the salesmanship job within about four or five day's time. We had the service—packed out the place, the biggest crowd they'd ever had. It was very tense, very tight, and one or two of the deacons were very upset with me for getting us involved in it . . . but the young preacher preached a masterful, thoughtful, and beautiful message and sort of saved my skin. I told him later—we became fast friends over a period of years—if the Lord hadn't really blessed him with great power that night so that there was an obvious moving of God's Spirit, we would have all been in trouble, especially me.[23]

In reality, he did face several leaders and members of the church after the event who were quite angry with him. Ever the optimist in the face of opposition, he concluded, "I found out something in this; that if you love your people enough and you establish some things with them on that, they oftentimes will tolerate your irritating them over ethical idealism."[24]

Then he moved to First Baptist Church, Wills Point. Here he experienced an even more entrenched resistance to racial reconciliation in a community that embodied a more southern East Texas culture. He was pastor there in 1954 when the SBC dealt with the issue of the Supreme Court decision *Brown vs. Board of Education* desegregating the schools systems of America. He recalled in 1973:

> In Wills Point I had to face what to do about the 1954 Supreme Court decision because I went to the convention in St. Louis where we were voting

---

[23] Jimmy Allen, Allen interview no. 3 with Daniel B. McGee, Baylor University Program for Oral History, Waco TX, 9 June 1973, 93.
[24] Allen interview no. 3 with Daniel B. McGee, 94.

as a convention whether to back the Supreme Court or not in the school desegregation decision. And I went as a young field hog greatly convinced that we ought to politic as strongly as possible to get the convention on record behind the Supreme Court decision and worked at it among my crowd as strongly as I could. [I] was very grateful for Dr. Witherspoon [Southern Seminary Ethics professor giving leadership to the resolution] and others who saved the day for us there at that point. I think it was one of the most significant decisions that Southern Baptists made in the decade because if we had gone on record in the other direction, the robbing of the local church of what I discovered in Van Alstyne, which was denominational witness, would have devastated us.[25]

The young pastor returned from the Convention to his church and reported on the action as an effort to stimulate discussion and support. Again, some disagreed, but Allen's success in evangelism overcame criticisms of his stance on the controversial issue of race. He reported with excitement, "we were having a great number of decisions of people finding Christ. I was there about four years and baptized 235 people, and there were just 2,030 people in the city. So it's the only pastorate I've ever had where over a four-year period I was able to baptize ten percent of the population."[26]

Among the many accomplishments of his tenure in Wills Point was the expansion of the facilities of the church. A new 600-seat sanctuary was constructed at a cost of nearly $90,000 after a building fund campaign had been conducted in 1951. Ground was broken for the building in September 1954, with construction completed in time for a week of dedication and celebration 23-27 March 1955. The local newspaper was full of articles about the history of the church, the work of Wanda Allen, pictures and descriptions of the new building, information advertizing the speakers for the dedication week, and advertisements of congratulations from the leading businesses in the community. Four former pastors spoke including Jack Merritt, James Riley, Bob N. Ramsey, and M. E. McGlamery. The president of Southwestern Seminary, J. Howard Williams, spoke on Sunday morning. Clearly Allen had provided most of the information for the paper as only

---

[25] Allen interview no. 3 with Daniel B. McGee, 95.
[26] Allen interview no. 3 with Daniel B. McGee, 96.

one small column mentioned him as the last speaker in the dedication series.[27]

A tradition can also be observed emerging here in his ministry in the form of an anniversary celebration of the pastor's call, a practice that was evident in his later leadership of First Baptist Church, San Antonio. This was a celebration of accomplishments that offered an opportunity for the church to reflect on its ministry.

By the end of his second year at Wills Point, average Sunday school attendance grew to 330 with $76,570 given over the two years for the church budget and an additional $30,138.39 in building-fund contributions. Ninety-three people were baptized the first two years and an additional fifty-three in the third year for a total of 196 baptisms or an average of forty-eight each year. Sunday school attendance grew to an average of 364 by the end of the third year with goals of 400 established.[28]

While at this rural congregation, he became a member of the Texas CLC as an elected representative. He fit the profile needed by the Convention as a pastor of a small church, and as a graduate student in Ethics he could contribute to the ideas and work of the commission.

By the time his seminar work on his doctorate was completed and the dissertation was the last major agenda of his study, he was able to assume a larger pastorate and write the dissertation from the church field. So, in 1956 he moved to Cockrell Hill Baptist Church in Fort Worth. Here he found a "people's church" of "the laboring, working, hard-hat types" in a declining neighborhood with strong resistance to racial transition.[29] Again, he would give leadership to addressing ethical issues through special Christian Life weeks and church discussions. The church prospered and he became increasingly involved in the work of the BGCT.

Dissertation. A final glimpse of the rather significant change that had occurred in the thinking and approach of the youth evangelist/RA leader who was maturing into roles of pastoral leadership can be seen in the

---

[27] *Wills Point Chronicle*, 78/11, 18 March 1955, 1-16.

[28] The figures are cited from pastor-anniversary programs for years two and three of his tenure. They vary from those reported in the annuals of the BGCT. The convention statistics report for the four years of 1952–1955 a total of 162 baptisms, an increase of seventy-two members, growth in average Sunday school attendance to 361, and a total of $150,504 in receipts.

[29] Allen, Interview no. 3, 97.

dissertation he wrote for the Doctor of Theology degree. He needed a dissertation that could be written from the church field, would be largely a literary analysis of published materials, and would be significant for the field of Christian Ethics. With Maston's encouragement, he chose to compare the concept of the kingdom of God in the writings of Walter Rauschenbusch and Reinhold Niebuhr.

The culmination of the influence of the seminary in the remainder of his ministry can be seen in the intellectual framework that emerged in his dissertation. Added to his extroverted personality and his exuberant, evangelistic preaching style was a newfound focus on the broader mainstream Protestant tradition of the social application of the gospel. Allen's dissertation was a five-chapter analysis, with introduction and conclusions, of the differences between Rauschenbusch's[30] classically liberal, redefinition of the kingdom of God with Niebuhr's neoorthodox, dialectical interpretation of the suprahistorical nature of the kingdom.[31]

He reinforced the Maston methodology for theological ethics—a conservative, biblically based theology with a progressive, enlightened social practice of that theology. Thus, one can be liberal politically as long as one is conservative theologically. It proved to be a workable social ethic for Southern Baptists at least until the emergence of a new fundamentalism in Southern Baptist life that began at the end of Allen's second term as president of the Southern Baptist Convention.

Thomas Buford Maston. The impact of Southwestern Seminary cannot be complete without more detailed attention to the importance of T. B. Maston in shaping a cadre of students who would give major leadership in shaping the social ethic of Baptist life. Maston was a native of East Tennessee and a graduate of Carson-Newman College. There he met and married Essie Mae MacDonald, and in 1920 both entered Southwestern Seminary to study Religious Education. Beginning in 1922, both also taught

---

[30]One can hardly overestimate Rauschenbusch's influence in American Protestantism and among Baptists in the early decades of the twentieth century. For a brief summary of his life and work and pointers to a more comprehensive bibliography see Paul Lewis, "Walter Rauschenbusch (1861–1918): Pioneer of Baptist Social Ethics," *Twentieth Century Shapers of Baptist Social Ethics*, ed. Larry L. McSwain, 3-22, 335-36 (Macon GA: Mercer University Press, 2008).

[31]Jimmy R. Allen, "A Comparative Study of the Concept of the Kingdom of God in the Writings of Walter Rauschenbusch and Reinhold Niebuhr" (Th.D. diss., Southwestern Baptist Theological Seminary, 1958).

in the area, though Mrs. Maston concluded that role when their first son was born with cerebral palsy; she stayed at home to care for him the remainder of her life. Maston completed his study in Religious Education with J. M. Price in 1925. This ethics giant continued to teach until his retirement at age sixty-five in 1963. His doctoral study was in the area of church recreation, and his early teaching was in Religious Education where courses in applied Christianity were taught. Maston never felt called to pastor and served his entire life in teaching as a layperson, ordained to serve as a deacon at the Gambrell Street Baptist Church adjoining the seminary campus, where he and his family were members.

In addition to the courses in applied Christianity and Christian Ethics he took, Maston was influenced by the noted theologian at Southwestern, W. T. Conner.[32] Conner had studied with Walter Rauschenbusch at Rochester Theological Seminary in 1908–1910 and brought a social gospel emphasis to Southwestern.[33] This led Maston to enlarge the circle of his own education, earning a Master of Arts in Sociology from Texas Christian University and spending summers in study at the University of Chicago and University of North Carolina. He enrolled in 1932 at Yale Divinity School where he studied with H. Richard Niebuhr, earning the Ph.D. in 1939.[34] He immersed himself in study of the contemporary neoorthodox scholars Reinhold Niebuhr, Karl Barth, and Emil Brunner. This influence shows clearly in Jimmy Allen's choice of a doctoral dissertation.

As important as were his teaching and writings, Maston's influence among Baptists was also the result of his active role in the development of the Texas CLC and his cultivation of a cadre of graduates who provided its leadership for more than forty years. In 1937, President L. R. Scarborough encouraged him to shift his teaching from the School of Religious Education to the School of Theology; Christian Ethics became a department in the school. He began offering doctoral study in Christian Ethics in the 1940s and his third Doctor of Theology graduate was Foy Valentine, the

---

[32]The writing on Maston is extensive. Most of this material is drawn from John W. Storey, *Texas Baptist Leadership and Social Christianity, 1900–1980* (College Station: Texas A&M University Press, 1986), 122-43, and William M. Tillman, Jr., "T. B. Maston (1897–1988): Mentor to Southern Baptist Prophets," *Twentieth Century Shapers of Baptist Social Ethics*, ed. Larry L. McSwain, 61-80 and 334-35 (Macon GA: Mercer University Press, 2008).

[33]Storey, *Texas Baptist Leadership*, 127-28.

[34]Storey, *Texas Baptist Leadership*, 128-29.

second executive director of both the Texas CLC and the SBC CLC. Maston supervised forty-nine doctoral students, taught thousands of students in the Bachelor of Divinity program, and served on the graduate committees of a number of others who became leaders in the application of the gospel among Baptists.[35] Of equal significance to his teaching was the networking he created among these graduates. In interviews with Allen, James Dunn, and William Pinson conducted as a part of the research for this book, each identified the pattern of Maston as significant in their own career development. He kept a notebook with the names of all of his students with him and prayed for each of them by name each day. He kept up with them, and he and Mrs. Maston hosted an annual dinner in their home for all current graduate students and as many graduates as could attend. This created a network of communication that facilitated support for ethics causes. After his death, a T. B. Maston Foundation was formed with funds from his estate and gifts from friends.[36] Allen serves on the foundation board and has been its chair. The foundation sponsors an annual meeting in Texas to gather ethics graduates and students for discussions on current issues and Maston's legacy.

Conclusion

By the end of the decade of the 1950s, Jimmy Allen had completed the triad of influences that became the bedrock of his character and method of ministry for the remainder of his life. The first, as has been mentioned, was an emotional and spiritual component, rooted in the model of his father, of mystical dependence on God for a kind of intuitive leadership in whatever environment he found himself. Second was the preaching and pastoral leadership style of key pastors in Texas Baptist life, notably George W. Truett, who modeled for him the "how" of church ministry. From that came an abiding interest and commitment to the local church as the primary agenda for his leadership. And the third was the intellectual content of his

---

[35]Storey, *Texas Baptist Leadership*, 122, cites Maston as reporting forty-nine doctoral graduates and William M. Pinson, Jr. *An Approach to Christian Ethics: The Life, Contribution, and Thought of T. B. Maston* (Nashville: Broadman Press, 1979) 94-96 lists them alphabetically.

[36]Jimmy Allen, "Thomas Buford Maston: Baptist Apostle of Biblical Ethics," *Christian Ethics Today*, 9/5 (December 2003): 6-10, an address given on the occasion of the establishment of the T. B. Maston/Jimmy R. Allen Scholarship at Wake Forest University Divinity School.

study at Southwestern. The passion for evangelism was as hot as ever, but balanced with a newfound concern for the social application of the gospel in the fabric of the public life of the church in all its settings—local, statewide, national, and international. Jimmy Allen was ready to move into the next phase of his life and ministry.

Chapter 5

The Mandate for Applied Christianity

> Jimmy Allen, Foy Valentine, Bill Pinson, and James Dunn were in a den of lions in a dream I had one night. Jimmy was organizing the lions. Foy was lecturing the lions, Bill was praying for the lions, and Dunn was going around kicking every lion in the nose
> —William M. Pinson, Jr., quoting an unknown CLC supporter

Jimmy Allen was thrust into the spotlight of ethical leadership for Texas Baptists at the age of thirty-two. He gave dynamic leadership to the Convention's Christian Life Commission (CLC) when it was a rather fledgling organization facing the civil rights movement as the major moral issue of the decade. It was an agenda he pursued with as much vigor as the conservative ethos of Texas Baptists would allow.

His decision to accept the invitation to become director of a small and relatively new effort to address the moral and ethical concerns of Texas Baptists was his most agonizing vocational struggle. It put him on a course that thrust him into the spotlight of controversy, growing connections and involvements in national social policy, and effective change in the moral landscape of Texas.

Allen's leadership broadened his identity from that of a young pastor of smaller Texas Baptist churches to participation in White House conferences, board membership on national organizations such as Americans United for the Separation of Church and State and the Baptist Joint Committee on Public Affairs, and sermons printed in the *New York Times*. The CLC gave him a base for drawing on all of the skills of his personality, talent, and education.

Texas Baptists have a rather distinctive historical role in relation to the larger Southern Baptist Convention. The Baptist General Convention of Texas (BGCT) is the largest state convention in the nation's largest Protestant denomination and exerts considerable influence by virtue of the amount of money it contributes, the number of Baptists and churches in the state, the size of particular congregations, and the role of pastors who have been models for others to emulate.

Geographically, the state is a challenge. The drive from Texarkana to El Paso and from Brownsville to the Oklahoma border of the Panhandle exceeds eight hundred miles each. Population growth has been phenomenal. By 1980 the population of Texas surpassed that of New York, making it the second most populous state in the nation, next to California.

Thus, Texas has enormous influence on the body politic of the nation. Since World War II, three U.S. presidents were Texans—Lyndon Johnson, George Herbert Walker Bush, and George W. Bush. As goes Texas, so goes much of the nation.

Christian Life Commission

The Christian Life Commission in Texas was not yet a decade old when Allen assumed its leadership.[1] The commission was formally approved by the BGCT at its convention in 1950. Its first leader was Acker C. Miller who had been serving the convention as leader of the Department of Ministry with Minorities since 1944, giving attention to issues of race and ethnicity.

A. C. Miller was one of the remarkable early leaders of applied Christianity in Southern Baptist life who is often overlooked for his contributions. Raised in Texas and a graduate of Hardin-Simmons University, he migrated to Louisville, Kentucky, for his seminary study in 1917. He was introduced to Rauschenbusch and became a strong advocate for applied Christianity. After serving several small churches in Oklahoma and Texas, he joined his long-time friend from Southern Seminary days, J. Howard Williams, in work at the BGCT.[2]

T. B. Maston was integral to the formation and development of the commission. He was a member of the study committee that recommended it and served on the CLC board for eighteen years. He helped Miller shape the focus of its work which addressed from a scriptural basis the issues of family, race relations, public morals, economic life, and world order.[3]

Miller also led the commission to adopt its primary strategies on how to accomplish its work. These included conferences in churches and associations, pamphlets published by the thousands and distributed free to churches and individuals, and articles for publication in denominational

---

[1] Billy David Stricklin, "An Interpretive History of the Christian Life Commission of the Baptist General Convention of Texas, 1950–1977" (Ph.D. Diss., Baylor University, 1981); John W. Storey, *Texas Baptist Leadership and Social Christianity, 1900–1980* (College Station TX: Texas A&M University Press, 1986) 122-71; and Harry Leon McBeth, *Texas Baptists: A Sesquicentennial History* (Dallas: Baptistway Press, 1998) 244-46.

[2] Storey, *Texas Baptist Leadership*, 148-50.

[3] McBeth, *Texas Baptists*, 245.

publications. Maston was one of the most prolific writers of these materials through the years.

Miller's tenure at the fledgling Texas organization was brief. Texas had set the example for the larger SBC. It soon adopted the Texas model by moving and expanding the work of its previous Social Service Committee to the SBC Christian Life Commission. A. C. Miller was tapped to be the first executive director of the newly organized SBC CLC Commission. He accepted this new role in June 1952, moving to Nashville, Tennessee to give leadership to a national effort.

Miller's successor in Texas was Foy D. Valentine.[4] A product of East Texas, Valentine accepted a call to preach as a teenager; graduated from Baylor University; spent the summer of 1944 with Clarence Jordan at Koinonia Farms near Americus, Georgia; and finished a Doctor of Theology degree at Southwestern Seminary with Maston. He served in campus ministry in Houston and was pastor of the First Baptist Church in Gonzalez, Texas when invited to lead the commission.

Valentine continued the Miller approach of publishing pamphlets and numerous articles. He also began in 1957 an annual Christian Life Conference on the campus of SWBTS to explore a variety of social and moral issues confronting the churches. This annual conference became a source of bringing together like-minded Baptists and generating strong opposition from those who were not. He recruited William Pinson, Jr. to join the staff as associate director while Pinson was a student at Southwestern Seminary, and expanded significantly its work.

Pinson's assignment was to tape all of Maston's lectures and write research drafts on various ethical issues. Valentine proved to be a diligent editor of these materials. Pinson recorded in an interview, "I learned writing basically through Foy. He was a superb writer and a very gifted editor. . . . He would take something I had labored over and thought was just wonder-

---

[4]Valentine is something of a legend in his own right and deserves a full-length biography of his life and contributions. Storey, *Texas Baptist Leadership*, 151-55, summarized key events of his life. For a more recent summary of his work and bibliography of his published books, see David Sapp, "Foy Dan Valentine (1923–2006): Helping Changed People Change the World," *Twentieth Century Shapers of Baptist Social Ethics*, ed. by Larry L. McSwain, 296-310, 342-43 (Macon GA: Mercer University Press, 2008).

ful and would just cut it to pieces. But it was always in a way to make it better. He was a very, very good mentor and supervisor."[5]

Allen was also a part of that young talent identified by Valentine. While he was pastor of First Baptist Church in Wills Point, Allen was elected to serve on the BGCT Christian Life Commission. This put him a position of working with other commissioners and the staff in crafting materials and conferences to address social issues confronting the churches of the state. It also provided the connections for a lifelong friendship between Valentine and Allen, one that lasted until Valentine's death in 2006.

A New Vocation

Foy Valentine followed in the footsteps of A. C. Miller in 1960 when Miller retired from the role of executive director of the Southern Baptist Convention CLC. Valentine was pursued by the national group to succeed Miller and he quickly accepted their invitation. The issue now for the Texas group was who to choose as his successor.

By this time, Allen had completed his three-year term on the Christian Life Commission and was serving as pastor of the Cockrell Hill Baptist Church in Fort Worth. He had been elected to a seat on the Education Commission of the BGCT where he focused on student ministries.

It was of little surprise that Jimmy Allen would become the choice of the CLC to succeed Valentine. Harold Basden, long-time friend of Allen's and pastor of the Gaston Avenue Baptist Church in Dallas, was chair of the commission. T. B. Maston was chair of the search committee to find a successor; after consulting with the search committee he called Jimmy with a request he consider the position. Allen faced a major crisis in his life as a result of that call.

Jimmy's entire ministerial life had focused on preparation for a major pastoral leadership opportunity. He had the doctorate. He had been at Cockrell Hill Baptist Church long enough for a logical move to a larger church. What would he do? Only he could describe adequately the intensity of the decision:

> I knew churches don't call controversial pastors. So I went into a real soul searching. I asked, "Is my role to be as pastor of a major church?" I thought I would not be able to do that if I were to become involved in those controversial

---

[5]William M. Pinson, Jr., Interview with Jim Newton, Dallas, 1 July 2005, 8.

issues which were burning in my mind. So I went out to Mt. Lebanon encampment . . . on a spiritual retreat for three or four days engaging in self-examination, prayer, and seeking to know what was right. I was trying to figure out what I was supposed to do with my life. It was really a critical moment for me because I knew if I accepted this task it would probably mean I would never have the opportunity to pastor one of these major churches which is what had been instilled in me as what I should do. . . . So it was a real surrender, almost a dying to self experience. . . . But there come times when the chips are down and you are looking at the very essence of who you are. And that was one of them. I came away from that experience with the conviction that I was never going to be pastor of a big church and I was not going to worry about it. I was going to take this task because this [racial discrimination] was the most critical, devastating, powerful, destruction that was happening to the mission cause I believed in. That racism was crippling us around the world. It was not what the Bible taught, but it was also what would not work in our world.[6]

When Allen drove to East Texas to share the news with his parents, they "were aghast. You know, they had envisioned me pastoring some big church sometime, and they knew that the people who go to the CLC do not pastor big churches."[7] In what is clearly historical irony, Allen reported this during an interview in the pastor's office of the 7,000-member First Baptist Church of San Antonio.

Allen began his new role with the staff inherited from Valentine—Pinson as the part-time associate secretary of the commission and Barbara Humphries as the full-time staff secretary.[8] Two years later the total budget of the commission was less than $60,000.[9] No sooner did he arrive at the new role in June 1960 than the question of its very survival was at stake.

Allen soon learned the value of denominational coordination and even denominational politics. The new executive of the BGCT was Thomas Armour Patterson, previously pastor of the First Baptist Church in Beaumont.[10] He was elected in September 1960, allowing him a few months

---

[6]Jimmy Allen, "The Christian Life Commission and Texas Baptist Life," interview no. 3 with Jim Newton and Larry McSwain, Big Canoe GA, 14 November 2004, 44-46.

[7]Jimmy Allen, interview no. 3 with Daniel B. McGee, Baylor University Program for Oral History, San Antonio TX, June 1973, 105.

[8]Allen, "Christian Life Commission," 46.

[9]McBeth, *Texas Baptists*, 309.

[10]McBeth, *Texas Baptists*, 285.

to adjust to the new role before Forest Feezor's retirement on 31 December of that year. Feezor had paid little attention to organizational matters and delegated many leadership decisions to J. Woodrow Fuller as associate executive secretary. Fuller was a strong, effective administrator who could also threaten persons in power with his abilities. Patterson neither wanted the associate role on the staff nor Fuller's strong power base within the staff. Allen understood the tensions and moved to become a balance in the power between them. He suggested openly in interviews:

> So, in that process we were trying to figure out how to keep the CLC from being vulnerable and I was going up and down the halls meeting with committees to make sure we had an identity. We were small, we had a small budget, and a big job. I went to Dr. Patterson and asked him what my role was in his administrative staff. He was in a bind in that he had a heavyweight in the room he was trying to deal with [Fuller] and he needed some votes in the administrative staff. I told him we were not as big as the other commissions and were more like the Public Affairs staff. So he said that I should sit in the administrative staff meetings. In later days I told people we survived because I have a large bladder. I never went to the restroom. I stayed in every meeting all the way through because a voice is better than a vote. If you're in the meeting you are alive. . . . Because we were not a threat to anybody, we could work with all the various groups trying to get ethics into their programs. That is what we tried to do.[11]

In addition to a large bladder, Jimmy had a knack for careful timing of his travel schedule. He never missed a meeting of the convention staff in his first five years at the CLC, often arriving after flying in from elsewhere in the state, only minutes ahead of schedule.[12] He felt it was important to be at the table for the exchange of information and ideas.

In addition to Patterson, he sought to connect to each of the other commissions of the convention by assuring them, "we were not trying to program, not trying to threaten them, not trying to be what they were, but

---

[11] Allen, "Christian Life Commission," 47. Story, *Texas Baptist Leadership*, 160-66, is even more explicit about the reorganization process. He also reports more fully on the role of Fuller who left the convention staff in 1964 to become associate pastor to W. A. Criswell at First Baptist Church (F.N. 85). Fuller later became the executive of the Florida Baptist Convention.

[12] Allen, interview no. 3 with McGee, 111.

that we were going to be available to them on these specific areas."[13] In a folksy philosophical summary he concluded:

> You can be hurt by your friends as well as by your enemies if your friend is an elephant and you are an ant, you know, and so they could easily step on you without ever realizing they were doing it. And we had enough enemies who really wanted to do us in that it just became a major challenge.[14]

Allen worked as positively as he could with Patterson throughout his tenure at the agency. They shared a mutual commitment to missions and evangelism and he and "Dr. Pat"—his common nickname—were both cut from the cloth of a conservative, Landmark theology in background. Allen remembers:

> I did my best to help him be the best executive secretary I could help him be. . . . That is what I interpreted my role with him to be. I did not try to get him fired or try to oppose him. I did advise him and tried to help him not get his foot in the bucket too often. He knew me as a person who was not trying to undercut him. . . . That bond kept us going. He never opposed me in any kind of dramatic way.[15]

Developing allies was another of the strategies Allen followed in his tenure at the CLC. Among the most significant was E. S. James, editor of the *Baptist Standard*. The editor of this largest of the state news publications was in many ways the most powerful religious voice in the state, a fact that often irritated the state executive secretaries, and none more than Patterson.[16] Allen clearly understood the power of this position and acted proactively to develop a close friendship with James. He says:

> He [Patterson] was upset that I was close to E. S. James. I had lunch with E. S. James every week I was at the CLC. We talked about everything. I listened to every editorial he wrote before he printed it. [Laughter.] It was an interesting thing. We argued on everything. He grew out of segregation into integration during that time. It was a beautiful thing. We had that kind of relationship. He was not a seminary graduate so he was willing to learn. We even discussed the grammar of his work. He taught me honesty and how to look at the truth and say it like it is. In fact, it was through E. S. James, Abner

---

[13] Allen, interview no. 3 with McGee, 111.
[14] Allen, interview no. 3 with McGee, 111.
[15] Allen , "Christian Life Commission," 70-71.
[16] McBeth, *Texas Baptists*, 287-88.

McCall says, Kennedy won Texas [in the 1960 U.S. presidential election]. Nixon was dilly-dallying on the church/state issues. E. S. James's cousin was Jack Porter, a member of the Republican National Committee. He [James] called him [Porter] and told him that his candidate had to come out on what he was really going to do about tax money and the churches. Nixon came out on it. James said it [Nixon's stance] is not right and that Kennedy had the right position on it. Actually I helped set up the meeting in Houston with churches where they asked him [Kennedy] the questions. That was a part of Bill Moyer's influence. In the process, E. S. James was my friend and T. A. Patterson knew it. He knew I was going to have lunch with him every week. He wanted to control the *Baptist Standard* and couldn't. So I think it was a combination of common interests, some tentative trust, and a realization there was power over you that you had to deal with. So we got along fine.[17]

Continuity and Change in the Christian Life Commission

The approach of the CLC for the next several years was basically one of continuity with the earlier patterns established by A. C. Miller and Foy Valentine. It was more a difference of style than of substance. The commission and staff continued to produce brochures and pamphlets by the thousands,[18] channel articles on practical social issues through the *Baptist Standard* and other press resources, lead in local conferences on applied Christianity, and work behind the scenes with various community groups and convention agencies.

A major emphasis of Allen's work was the annual CLC conference held on the campus of Southwestern Seminary. In 1960 and 1965 the topics addressed were "Christianity and Political Action" with Governor John Connally a featured speaker in 1965.[19]

In 1962, Allen decided it was time to deal directly with the issue of race as the focus of the annual conference. He consulted with Charles Myers, chair of the commission and pastor of First Baptist Church in McKinney, who agreed to support a conference on the Bible and race. Participants included Marvin Griffin, the first African-American graduate of SWBTS; journalist and lecturer Charles A. Wells; and Kyle Haselden, editor of the

---

[17]Allen, "Christian Life Commission," 71-72.
[18]Story, *Texas Baptist Leadership*, 154, reported the first year of Valentine's leadership the number of pieces of such materials was 25,000; his last year it was 1,235,000 pieces.
[19]Story, *Texas Baptist Leadership*, 155.

Christian Century. Haselden, according to Allen, called the meeting "the largest gathering of evangelical Protestants he had been to that was talking about race."[20]

But the meeting also generated controversy, a usual experience for all of those who led in the emphasis on a social application of the gospel. One of the group leaders at the meeting was Guy Moore, pastor of the Broadway Baptist Church in Fort Worth, who led a discussion group on integration of public schools. When the *Fort Worth Star-Telegram* published a news account with the headline, "Baptists Criticize Tarrant County School Board," a group of Fort Worth pastors was upset.[21] Fred Swank, the popular, fundamentalist pastor of Sagamore Hills Baptist Church and critic of most things progressive, tried to get the meeting cancelled in midstream which Allen refused to do.[22] Swank was successful in organizing a group meeting of his supporters with Allen and Patterson in Arlington a week later. He demanded an apology from Allen for the conference to which Allen responded, "I can't apologize for something I am not ashamed of."[23] Patterson was neutral in the meeting but refused to fire Allen as the group was demanding.

One of the byproducts of these kinds of encounters was a kind of clarity of style for Allen. He assumed a less-anxious response to his critics, at least in public, and often reacted to them with calm or humor. In repeated interviews with him about a number of aspects of his ministry through the years, he was often reluctant to describe, much less name, opponents or critics. He developed a kind of thick-skinned unwillingness to react in kind to his harshest critics while maintaining a firm stance on whatever position he was advocating.

Such was not always the case, however. Pinson, his colleague for Allen's first three years at the commission, recalls a tendency for Allen to

---

[20] Allen, "Christian Life Commission," 53. Storey, *Texas Baptist Leadership*, 189-90, also describes the program.

[21] Allen asserts the article, written by a former RA camp acquaintance, Jim Jones, was an accurate depiction of the discussion, and the meeting included the superintendent of the Tarrant County school system. However, since Baptists had opposed the location of a brewery in Fort Worth, Allen believed the publisher of the paper was seeking to embarrass the group with the headline. Allen, interview no. 3 with McGee, 117-18.

[22] Allen, interview no. 3 with McGee, 119.

[23] Allen, "Christian Life Commission," 54.

burn with anger within, while not expressing it externally, when organizational or issue conflicts emerged. His ears turned red when he was angry. This anger was not expressed personally at persons, but it was present.[24]

Phil Strickland evaluated him, "There is a character consistency in Jimmy that has always led him to live out what he believed. He has always had the courage to do that. He would take positions and take the consequences."[25]

The young prophet also used wisdom in the midst of controversies. Skip Allen recalls as a child living in Dallas:

> One of the other things I'm proudest of about my father is that he was so hated when I was very, very young because he felt so strongly about integration. At the time in the 1960s when there was so much racial tension here in Dallas, Texas he was a civil rights worker. It is interesting, looking back, that we [kids] were not even allowed to answer the phone at our house until I was ten or twelve years old. We weren't allowed to answer the phone because there were so many hateful calls that came to the house. If Mom and Dad wanted to talk to us, they would call the house, let it ring once, hang up and then call back. Then we knew it was safe to pick up the phone. There were periods of time when the tensions were incredibly high. People hated him. Fortunately he had allies, like James Dunn, Foy Valentine, and James Cooper, who were part of that same movement. He was not alone; but he felt so passionately about it and was so verbal about it, that he stirred up a lot of trouble.[26]

With experience and maturity, Jimmy seemed to manage the kind of control that allowed others such expressions while he maintained his own demeanor. In response to a question about threats against his life, he opined, "Yeah, you know, there were anonymous threats, but we didn't take them seriously. Even at San Antonio we had to empty the building a time or two because of bomb threats. If you live your life listening to that, that is what you will hear."[27]

Alliances in Austin. One area of innovation for Allen at the CLC was his greater involvement in the political arena in Austin. Pinson suggested it was a departure for the CLC that continues to the present:

---

[24]Pinson, interview with Jim Newton, 7-8.
[25]Phil Strickland, interview with Jim Newton, Dallas, 4 July 2005, 4.
[26]Skip Allen, interview with Jim Newton, Dallas, 1 July 2007, 16.
[27]Allen, "Christian Life Commission," 56.

> One of the main differences between Jimmy and Foy at the CLC was Jimmy was politically inclined. . . . So as Foy majored on getting the commission on a sound footing and positioning itself within the convention producing pamphlets and materials . . . and establishing an annual conference, Jimmy became active in lobbying in Austin and set a tone there that James Dunn and Phil Strickland followed.[28]

It is an assessment with which Allen agreed as early as 1973 when he stated:

> So I began doing the citizenship information type things that now have evolved into, I think, a very effective program under the current leadership of James Dunn and Phil Strickland. . . . Foy had gone down to Austin a time or two to testify, but had never really seen the CLC as an action-oriented group. It was sort of idea-oriented, sow the seed, be the salt type thing under his leadership. . . . That was all that the Baptists could take at that time and it was a strategy, partly because of his disposition, also. Though he has a lot of concern for political things, when it came down to actually walking the halls of the legislature and dealing with that sort of thing, I found that my interests were far stronger than his were.[29]

It was a pattern Jimmy seemed to relish. In fact, he considered at one point in his career a race for governor of the state, but concluded his service in ministry was a higher calling. It does offer some understanding of his later involvement in national issues during the presidency of Jimmy Carter and his own election as president of the BGCT and then the SBC.

Allen worked to maintain a strong presence whenever the state legislature was in session in Austin. One of the Maston/Valentine philosophies was that activity on behalf of moral issues that were popular with Baptists, like opposition to alcohol and gambling, gave legitimacy in dealing with less popular ones. Allen embraced that philosophy with aggressive activity on those issues. His strategy was clear for him:

> The hottest issue at that time was the race issue. One of the philosophies we had was you help people out of the consensus of what they already believed and help them believe what they ought to believe. So we did a lot of work on the issues of alcohol and gambling because there was a great consensus about that. The gambling issue gave us great access to the legislature and the *Baptist*

---

[28]Pinson, interview with Newton, 12.
[29]Allen, interview no. 3 with McGee, 109-10.

> *Standard* was strong with us on that. My philosophy was you get the maximum amount of social control, legal control, according the consensus that your public will allow on the issues that you are trying to hold in check. You are protecting the young and the weak. There is no justification for social legislation that doesn't protect the young and the weak.... What we tried to do is to hold a limit on the erosion of morality that would legally be the base for that kind of thing. The real task is education and commitment so we tried to do all we could to understand the issues and the biblical responsibilities for responding to that and to act in ways that would make that happen.... So I dealt a good deal with the gambling issue. We kept racetrack gambling out of Texas the whole time I was there.[30]

It was an approach that was continued by his successors, James Dunn, Phil Strickland, and now Suzii Paynter. Changes in the context of such work in the 1970s led to the CLC becoming a registered lobbyist in Austin under the leadership of Phil Strickland. Allen considered such a move unnecessary during his tenure. But much of the activity of the commission staff at that time had a lobby tone to it. He provided an example of the tradeoff that strength in one issue provided for dealing with others with the following story.

> I could also drop into the dean of the Senate and talk to him about the fact they had a racist realtor law that the realtors were trying to get through, to give realtors the ability to sell according to race and that would tear up the state. At seven o'clock one morning Weston [Ware, his associate after Pinson] and I got with Senator Aiken and I said "This [pending legislation on allowing discrimination in housing markets] is going to tear up things, this is going to tear up the community and you don't want that to happen." And he called the guy who was sponsoring it, the senator, and he said "Grady, ain't you done all for those realtors that you can do from this law, 'cause we got a man named Jimmy Allen here, and he wouldn't lie about it and he insists its going to tear up the whole state if we pass this thing.... Why don't we just kill it?" And he hung up the phone and said, 'You don't have to worry about that."[31]

Over time, the nature and number of issues addressed at the political level have been significant. What Allen initiated as an approach became a standard method of operation for the next several decades. The issues addressed would require more space than is possible in this book, but they

---

[30] Allen, "Christian Life Commission," 51-52.
[31] Allen, "Christian Life Commission," 52-53.

include the full range of social and economic issues. Dunn identified racial integration, support for workman's compensation, support for bilingual education for Hispanics, and juvenile justice reform as major issues.[32] Strickland identified opposition to legalized gambling; a strict separation of church and state stance on involuntary school prayer and school vouchers; and the formation of Texans Care for Children, a child advocacy group he founded, as notable issues for commission action.[33] Storey traces the CLC story to the departure of Dunn from the CLC and identifies in addition to these issues lobbying for increases in welfare support, allowance of therapeutic abortions in some circumstances, consumer protection measures, upgraded conditions for farmworkers in the Rio Grande valley, and prison reform.[34]

Racial Crises. Allen led the commission at the height of the civil rights movement of the 1960s. His activism was real, but less obvious and public than that of many in the larger civil rights struggle. He never marched with the several activists in Dallas who supported a more aggressive stance with Martin Luther King, Jr. and others. It was neither a part of his disposition, heritage, nor the influence of his mentors to do such. Pinson summarized it for the Maston tradition of ethical activism:

> None of us really was involved in that way. It may have been Dr. Maston's influence that we just never did that. I never did. Foy never did. I don't think Jimmy did. It was not that there was not a deep desire for racial justice—you know Dr. Maston had his famous illustration with the rubber band. I think he felt like for Baptists at that time and in that setting it would have broken the band if the CLC and others were involved in that. So he was probably more a grand strategist than some of us would have given him credit.[35]

Allen did engage publicly on the issue. Civic leaders in Dallas were working to avoid the kind of explosive resistance to racial change many cities in the Deep South experienced. Among these efforts was a group called the "(Dallas) Citizens Council"—not to be confused with the white-supremacist "*White* Citizens Councils" in other areas—that included people

---

[32]James Dunn, interview with Jim Newton, Dallas, 1 July 2005, 9.
[33]Strickland, interview with Newton, 7-8.
[34]Storey, *Texas Baptist Leadership*, 169. His last chapter, 172-224, summarizes responses to issues over thirty years of convention work.
[35]Pinson, interview with Newton, 13.

like the mayor, Robert Thornton, and business leaders like Stanley Marcus and Carr Collins. Collins was a wealthy Baptist leader who had worked to attract Bishop College to Dallas and had been involved in convention activities. He was also a member of the Park Cities Baptist Church. This group met weekly with other citizens at the YMCA building for more than a year working on practical steps for integrating the city. Allen attended and was involved behind the scenes.

Jimmy's "white-hot" preaching style also endeared him to African-American pastors. He was invited by M. K. Currie to participate in a major preaching conference at Bishop College in the mid–1960s where he began what became deep relationships with key leaders of black Baptist life. These included William Shaw, who had just become pastor of the White Rock Baptist Church in Philadelphia. Shaw is still pastor there and is also president of the National Baptist Convention, USA, Inc. and a major leader in the New Baptist Covenant. Henry Mitchell, the noted professor of preaching was on the program as was J. Alfred Smith, still the pastor of the Allen Temple Baptist Church in Oakland, California, and a major leader in the Progressive National Baptist Convention. Tim Chambers, pastor of the Good Street Baptist Church in Dallas, and later a pastor in the Watts neighborhood of Los Angeles, was a participant. Jimmy was invited to lead a revival in Shaw's church and arrived the week after the Philadelphia riots. It was such a memorable week, he was invited to return on the fortieth anniversary of Shaw's service as pastor as it was the most important event in the church in the decade of the 1960s.

Among his most unusual experiences was preaching at the church of Rev. Tim Chambers in Watts during the week of the first of the major racial riots to tear at the fabric of the nation. Jimmy took his son Skip with him to Glorieta where he spoke in August 1965. Then he planned to travel to Los Angeles to speak at a Brotherhood meeting in Los Angeles and take Skip to Disneyland. While in Glorieta, the riots in Watts began, but Jimmy went anyway. His host communicated to Chambers he would be there and his African-American friend invited him to preach at his church. No one could get into Watts until Thursday of that week, so Jimmy went to the location of the devastation of the neighborhood. Skip tells the story of their Sunday experience:

> Dad promised me a trip to Disney Land, but I got a trip to Watts instead. Actually we did go to Disney Land after the riots calmed down that Saturday, and he told me he would be preaching the next day at the First Missionary

Baptist Church of Los Angeles. I wasn't excited about that one, because I never did like going to churches that I wasn't familiar with. Later on, he told me that the church was a black church that happened to be in the middle of Watts. I had watched the riots live on television, and I was scared to death. They came and picked us up, with body guards, in a big limo, and I was thrilled to be in a limo, but that was all I was thrilled about. They made me sit in the choir loft, with body guards on both sides of me, because there was a true threat of danger physically. We were the only two white faces in this sea of black faces in the church. . . . I mean, it was frightening. There were still buildings smoldering, and cars overturned in the streets that we had to drive around to get to the church. But I remember Dad standing up, and walking up to the pulpit, and I was looking down from the choir loft at all of the activity in the room. Then everything got real quiet. And this is one of the purest memories I have of him. He stood up there and gripped the pulpit and, waiting with a pregnant pause, he said: "I'm here today to talk to you about healing." And you could have heard a pin drop. He went on from there. I've been to enough black churches to know that everyone gets up, walks around, and talks. But not that day. . . . I remember very clearly getting back to the hotel and the emotional and mental exhaustion that we both experienced. He said something to me that I also haven't forgotten. He said "You will never forget this day." And I haven't.[36]

Among Jimmy's strategies was an invitation to his African-American pastor friends to join him for lunch to desegregate public facilities in both Dallas and San Antonio. When Allen heard that Carr Collins was desegregating a cafeteria he owned across the street from the Baptist building, he called his friend Rhett James who was pastor of one of the African-American churches. He tells the story: "I said, 'Rhett, let's go to lunch together.' He said 'Where?' I said, 'We will go over to Carr Collins's cafeteria. I got word today they are going to let blacks and whites eat over there.' 'That couldn't be true,' he responded. 'Let's go find out,' I said. So, we went over and went through the line. I heard someone behind us say, 'That damn Baptist foundation is trying to run this world.' [Laughter.] So I went back to the foundation people and told them I was sure glad they were getting paid for what I do!"[37]

He would act similarly when he heard about the desegregation of Joske's Department Store dining room in San Antonio. He called his pastor

---

[36]Skip Allen, interview with Newton, 2-3.
[37]Allen, "Christian Life Commission," 58.

friend Claude Black, flew to San Antonio, and the two were the first to eat there as a racially inclusive restaurant.[38]

This kind of commitment and connections, along with his relationship with Bill Moyers as Sargent Shriver's deputy for the Peace Corps and later press secretary for President Lyndon Johnson, resulted in an invitation to participate increasingly in Washington events and conferences. Among these was the White House Conference on Civil Rights in 1966.[39]

The Kennedy Assassination

Major events of crisis are remembered with amazing detail by persons experiencing them. Most people can tell you where they were and what they were doing if they were living on Pearl Harbor day, the day of John F. Kennedy's assassination, the day of the assassination of Martin Luther King, Jr., the events of the first successful manned space flight to the moon, or 11 September 2001.

Certainly, the day of the assassination of John F. Kennedy and the shooting of Governor John Connelly in Dallas, Texas on 23 November 1963 was engrained in the memory of Jimmy Allen. Under ordinary circumstances Allen would likely have been present somewhere in the festivities of that event. He had, by this time in his work, been closely connected to the civil rights efforts of the national administration through Bill Moyers. Allen had become friends with Moyers when he attended Southwestern Seminary with Bill Pinson. Moyers joined the staff of the vice president when Johnson was a senator. Pinson and Allen stayed in contact with Moyers as he rose into much higher roles in the nation's political structure.

About three months before the Kennedy visit to Texas, Allen attended a clergy meeting with E. S. James and another Texas pastor summoned to the White House by the president to discuss racial integration across the country. Allen recalls:

> They presented the challenge of trying to go ahead and integrate racially. In the process Bobby Kennedy asked what we could do in Texas to help. He reported

---

[38]Allen, "Christian Life Commission," 61-62.

[39]Allen, "Christian Life Commission," 61. The commission was called by President Lyndon Johnson 1-2 June 1966 to develop strategies for improving racial tensions in the nation.

the trouble spot for us right now is Tyler, Texas and help is needed for school integration. I said, "I will take that on. I will do that." I came back and set it up, actually with Bill Shamburger [pastor of FBC, Tyler] and some other folks in Tyler with the black preachers and the white preachers and Dr. Patterson. I asked them to be my guests in Dallas for lunch.[40]

Allen also reported that he discouraged President Kennedy's visit to Texas in telephone conversations with Bill Moyers, given the toxic political tension within Texas at that time. But Moyers responded the decision had been made and was not to be changed. He also asked Jimmy if he planned to attend the luncheon for the president and his party at the [Dallas Trade] Market, but Allen responded he had set up the meeting with Tyler clergy that same day. He reported:

So I told him [Moyers] I would fly down to Austin and be there for the dinner that night. Going up the elevator with Dr. Patterson and a couple of the African-American pastors, the man in the elevator said, "The president's been shot. And the governor too." I could not believe it. I got to the floor and called KIXL for Marvin Hillis, who was my friend from high school and was the newsman. I asked him, "Is it true?" "Yes, he has been shot and so has the Governor," he said. So we went in and had a prayer meeting with the folks and tried to talk about the subject. But it was impossible. So I was there in Dallas a few blocks away . . . trying to do something I had promised the Kennedys I would do about something that was my task as I saw it.[41]

Allen describes as "providential" his own ministry in the larger community and nation in the aftermath of the assassination. He says:

I happened to be preaching at the one service in Dallas on Thanksgiving Day they annually have. It was at Tyler Street Methodist Church. They asked me four years in a row to do that and I turned them down for three years because [usually] I went down to the lake house during Thanksgiving with my children. For some reason, I guess providentially, I told them I would do that. So on Thursday after Kennedy was shot and after [Jack] Ruby shot [Lee Harvey] Oswald, I was the speaker for the only religious service happening in Dallas on Thanksgiving Day. I preached a sermon called, "The Fifth Freedom: The Freedom from Hate." Dr. James printed it *in toto* in the *Baptist Standard* and the *New York Times* printed it on the front page that day. We had so many

---

[40] Allen, "Christian Life Commission," 63.
[41] Allen, "Christian Life Commission," 63.

hate experiences in Dallas it needed a word. Adlai Stevenson had been spit on at the city auditorium. Vice President Lyndon Johnson had been almost mobbed when he and Lady Bird came to meet President Kennedy. There were a bunch of women screaming at them. It was a city marked by hate. So I preached on [hate] that day. It was one of the saddest times. Wanda was teaching at a racially integrated school, W. W. Bushman. Even there some of the children cheered when they heard the president had been shot. It was just devastating. We lived through the trauma of the assassination trying to speak for peace. It was a tough time but it was our privilege and challenge.[42]

CLC Staff

In 1963, William Pinson completed his Th.D. work at SWBTS and was invited to join the faculty there to teach Christian Ethics. Pinson later served as pastor of the First Baptist Church, Wichita Falls; as president of Golden Gate Baptist Theological Seminary in Mill Valley, California; and, beginning in 1982, as executive director of the BGCT.[43] Allen turned to another of Maston's graduate students, James Dunn, to replace him. Dunn was deeply involved in campus ministry as the Baptist Student Union director and Bible teacher at West Texas State College in Canyon, Texas, and declined his invitation. Jimmy then employed Weston Ware, a long-time acquaintance, who worked at the commission two years before departing for Hawaii to become involved in Baptist Student Union work there. Several years later, Ware returned to the work of the commission under the leadership of Phil Strickland and became a nationally recognized expert in opposition to legalized gambling. When Ware left, Allen renewed the invitation to Dunn, who accepted, but told Allen he would only stay for two years like Ware had done. So, James Dunn became the associate director of the CLC in 1966.

James Dunn was born in Fort Worth in 1932 and was raised in the Evans Avenue Baptist Church. By his own admission, he was an ardent racial segregationist in his younger years and brought the same intensity to support that view as he later brought to the arena of racial justice. After meeting and debating with Ralph Phelps, the same SWBTS ethics professor who helped convince Allen to major in Christian Ethics, Dunn began to

---

[42]Allen, "Christian Life Commission," 63-64.
[43]McBeth, *Texas Baptists*, 360-62, provides more extensive biographical material.

soften and responded to the call to ministry as a college student.[44] Dunn graduated from Texas Wesleyan College in Fort Worth and entered Southwestern Seminary. He jokingly recalls he was able to cram his six years of seminary study into thirteen. He majored in Ethics with Maston and had completed his on-campus study when he moved to the campus ministry work in Canyon. He credits Allen for advising him to write his dissertation on the influence and contributions of J. M. Dawson, one of Southern Baptists' greatest advocates of religious liberty and separation of church and state. The dissertation on Dawson would provide more than the avenue for the degree; in 1981 Dunn became the executive director of the Baptist Joint Committee on Public Affairs in Washington, D.C., more than twenty-five years after Dawson retired from that same post.[45]

Dunn's major passion at the CLC was juvenile justice. He and his wife Marilyn never had children of their own but invested deeply in the children of others. Dunn became involved in the issue while a student pastor in Weatherford, Texas, became an outspoken critic of the Texas system of juvenile care, and attended the White House Conference on Children and Youth in 1960 as a Texas delegate.[46] His experience in addressing this issue proved helpful in furthering the cause of public morality emphasized by Allen. Dunn would stay a good bit longer than two years, actually succeeding Allen as the executive director when Jimmy left in 1967 to become pastor of the First Baptist Church in San Antonio. In 1966, the BGCT went through another of its several reorganization studies but this time, the committee conducting the study made recommendations that strengthened the commission. It was enlarged to fifteen members and the budget was expanded.[47] It no longer had to question its survival as a significant part of the work of the BGCT. With that growth, additional staff resources could now be added.

---

[44]Storey, *Texas Baptist Leadership*, 167-68.

[45]A summary of the contributions of both Dawson and Dunn can be found in J. Brent Walker, "Religious Libertarians: J. M. Dawson (1879–1973) and James M. Dunn (1932–)," *Twentieth Century Shapers of Baptist Social Ethics*, ed. Larry L. McSwain, 277-95, 323-26 (Macon GA: Mercer University Press, 2008). Walker has also collected a book of essays on Dunn's work in *James Dunn: Champion for Religious Liberty*, ed. J. Brent Walker (Macon GA: Smyth & Helwys, 1999).

[46]Dunn, interview with Newton, 11.

[47]Storey, *Texas Baptist Leadership*, 166-67.

Texas was in one of its perennial conflicts over the issue of legalized gambling in 1967. Needing help in Austin with the state legislature, Allen turned in the direction of Phil Strickland, a young attorney who was working with a law firm in Fort Worth. Strickland had attended classes at Southwestern for a year and had met Allen through an ethics retreat that was standard fare for the seminary ethics group. Strickland had worked for one and one-half years as an attorney when Allen called in 1967 and asked him to take a leave of absence from the law firm to assist temporarily on a gambling referendum before the state voters.

Strickland agreed without a stated time frame. Within days of accepting the assignment, Strickland learned from Allen he was leaving the CLC for the pastorate.[48] With Jimmy's leaving of the CLC, the future leadership and direction were not entirely clear. Dunn had not wavered in his commitment to work there for two years. Strickland was just beginning. According to Dunn's recollection, a search committee was formed. He reported:

> They came to me and said, "Are you going to consider being a successor to Jimmy?" And I said, "No, I came to be associate and do this for a couple of years and then I am out of here and I am not going to do it." So about two or three months passed and a Baptist rumor mill got going.... And when I found out who they were looking at I said, "Just a minute. I don't think you understand what is needed for this job or you would not be looking at this guy. ... If you are serious about him, put my name back in the hopper. I would consider it rather than letting the CLC go that direction."..... So they did and they elected me in March of 1968. And I had recommended to them after a lot of arm twisting and talking to Carolyn [Strickland's wife] they made Phil Strickland the associate and he agreed and they did.[49]

Strickland recalls with considerable humor the first act of the new duo: "When we got elected and the board meeting was over we walked back to the Baptist building and threw away all the pamphlets we had on dancing in public."[50] They were probably in storage from the A.C. Miller or Foy Valentine days, but this clearly was not a burning issue for the CLC. Their ardor was not diminished, however, for the many issues they would confront in the coming years. Both Dunn and Strickland continued the public activism stressed by Jimmy Allen. When Dunn left the commission

---

[48]Strickland, interview with Newton, 2.
[49]Dunn, interview with Newton, 7.
[50]Strickland, interview with Newton, 2.

to assume leadership of the BJCPA, Strickland succeeded him as executive director where he continued to serve until his death from a long struggle with cancer in 2006. At the time of his death, Strickland had more years of service than any other person in the history of Christian Life Commission work in Baptist life, thirty-nine years. True to its innovative leadership, the commission elected Suzii Paynter to succeed Strickland. She is the first female in Southern Baptist life to give leadership to a major social ethics agenda.

Conclusion

Jimmy Allen worked at the CLC for seven years. Rather than diminishing his opportunities for preaching and pastoral leadership of significant churches the visibility of this role and his temperament enhanced them. During his tenure there, he preached in a Texas church almost every Sunday and served as the interim pastor at Royal Lane Baptist Church in Dallas and FBC, San Antonio. It was to the latter church he was called at the end of 1967 to become its pastor. He would serve a major church after all.

Allen maintained one of the early philosophical stances embedded in the work of the CLC by Miller and Valentine, and continued by all his successors. The commission was able to deal with so many issues that some found offensive and others organized to oppose because of a fine line of communication each of its leaders maintained. The CLC was always clear in its reports to the BGCT, its many publications, its conferences, lobby activities, and public pronouncements that it spoke "to" Texas Baptists and never "for" Texas Baptists. It was a distinction the convention was able to accept.

Chapter 6

San Antonio Beckons: Visionary Pastoral Leadership

> There is something about the mystique that God creates between a shepherd and the people if he will be open to it that will teach him more about God than any other laboratory I know of.[1]
>
> —Jimmy Allen

Jimmy Allen's dream of serving as pastor of a significant congregation in Texas came to fruition in the late 1960s as he assumed the pastorate of the large and influential congregation of the First Baptist Church in San Antonio, Texas. Some dreams are fantasy; the dreamer is so out of touch with reality they are more hallucination than vision. Others are too small; the dreamer cannot let go of deeply held experiences and traditions long enough for a new possibility to break through. A few dreams are nightmares; in the dark night of the soul fear reigns, and the powers of evil and sin reign to conspire against the holy and good.

Then there are the divine dreams. All of the human aspirations and inclinations of the dreamer are infused with the divine inspiration of a thing we call providence. God moves in the life of the dreamer and blesses the dream. When that happens life becomes different, new history is written, and we look back on the stories of those events with awe and wonder. It happened to Moses when he encountered a bush "burning with fire, yet the bush was not consumed" (Exodus 3:1). It happened to some women at an empty tomb when they heard, "He is not here, but He is risen" (Luke 24:6). It happened on the day of Pentecost when Peter proclaimed a new vision and the church was born (Acts 2). And it happened in the First Baptist Church, San Antonio during the leadership of Jimmy Allen.

The story of a pastor is triangular. It is the story of the pastor's personality, skills, motivations, and piety. It is the story of a congregation with a history, a personality, a set of theological commitments, and its openness to the leadership of God in its midst. And it is the story of the movement of God's Spirit, an unexplainable, mysterious, yet essential part of a vital congregation's story. When Jimmy Allen went to San Antonio the triangle intersected. There a man was energized for kingdom work in new and exciting ways, a church was renewed, and hundreds of lives experi-

---

[1] Jimmy Allen, interview no. 4 with Daniel McGee, Baylor University Program for Oral History, San Antonio TX, 28 August 1973, 102.

enced an encounter with God that transformed their lives. Most of the following words you will read describe mostly the perspiration that went into the work of this ministry. But without an equal infusion of inspiration of the Holy Spirit, all of the work would have been fruitless.

San Antonio was one of the faster growing cities in the nation in the decades between 1950 and 1970. It was ranked the twenty-fifth largest urban area in 1950 with a population of 408,442, and grew to 587,718 by 1960 with a rank of seventeenth largest urban area. By 1970, it had grown to 654,153 with a ranking of fifteenth. When Allen left the church in 1980, the city population was 785,880 with a national ranking of eleventh.[2] While complete figures are not available for the decade of the 1950s, the city of San Antonio was a majority Hispanic city during the entire three decades from 1960 to 1990. By 2000, the city had a population of nearly 1.3 million with a sixty-one percent Hispanic majority.

Of equal significance was the explosive growth of military personnel in San Antonio. The nation was at the height of the Vietnam War in 1968 when Allen assumed the pastoral leadership of the church. Lackland Air Force Base was a dominant part of the incredible change of new faces and families that flowed through the community during those years.

An Unofficial Interim

First Baptist Church was led from 1937 until 1961 by Perry F. Webb, Sr., a pastor of distinguished service in the church and with Texas Baptists. His tenure was a period of "great growth in programs, physical properties, and membership."[3] In the latter years of his tenure, as is often typical, the church experienced some loss of energy and growth. The Trinity Baptist Church was formed during this time by a group of FBC members who wanted a more vibrant expression of church. First Baptist was a traditional Southern Baptist Church with a typical revivalist approach to evangelism, ministry, and worship. Webb was followed by Chester Bowles who came

---

[2]Campbell Gibson, "Population of the 100 Largest Cities and Other Urban Places in the United State: 1790 to 1990," Population Division Working Paper No. 27 (Washington DC, June 1998) <http://www.census.gov/population/www/documentation/twps0027.html> (accessed 22 August 2007).

[3]"Biography of Perry Flynt Webb," *In the Shadow of His Hand, First Baptist Church of San Antonio, Texas Supplement I—1961–1981* (Austin TX: Hart Graphics, 1981) 9.

to the pastorate from the Hunter Street Baptist Church in Birmingham, Alabama. Unfortunately, Bowles suffered a heart attack the first week of his ministry in San Antonio, an event from which he never fully recovered his former energy and health. Additionally, his wife died of a malignancy during this time, adding to the personal pain of his tenure. Bowles was a revivalist pastor and is remembered for unique revivals featuring nationally known evangelists during his five-year tenure.[4]

Allen had never preached at this historic church until 1967, even though he was often in San Antonio. His relationship with one of the leading African-American pastors in the city, Claude Black, was recounted in the previous chapter as they integrated Joske's department-store dining room. He preached often at Trinity Baptist Church where Buckner Fanning was pastor as well as Baptist Temple and Manor Baptist Church where Don Anderson was pastor. But these were more progressive congregations in relation to the CLC agenda. Yet, one of those providential events in Allen's life occurred on a Saturday evening in 1967 when E. S. James called him at his home in Dallas. James was scheduled to preach at First Baptist the next day, but had become ill and was unable to go. He asked Allen if he could go in his place. In response, Allen said, "You don't know what you are asking. I have never preached there. Those folks think I am too controversial to preach there!"[5] But the *Baptist Standard* editor called Luke Williams, minister of education at the church, and he readily called Allen to issue the invitation directly. Williams and Allen had known each other since college days and Williams had joined Bowles on the staff from the church in Birmingham where they had served together.

So Allen preached that Sunday in San Antonio. Not long after that event Charles Bowles succumbed to another heart attack. The church requested Jimmy to come again to preach, on which occasion the Interim Search Committee asked him to consider service as their interim. The BGCT discouraged convention staff from accepting interim assignments to ensure broader exposure to the churches in the state. The policy prevented preaching in the same church for more than three Sundays in a row. Allen

---

[4]"Biography of Charles Cornelius Bowles," *In the Shadow of His Hand, First Baptist Church of San Antonio, Texas Supplement I—1961–1981* (Austin TX: Hart Graphics, 1981) 11.
[5]Jimmy Allen, "Service as Pastor of First Baptist Church, San Antonio," interview no. 5 with Larry L. McSwain, Big Canoe GA, 7 March 2005, 76.

went to T. A. Patterson to seek his counsel before responding. Allen's recollection of the conversation was that he suggested to "Dr. Pat," something like, "You know, First Baptist Church in San Antonio has asked me if I can come and preach for them. I don't know how you feel about that but it's a strategic place and maybe I can do some good there." The BGCT executive responded, somewhat humorously, "Well, why don't you not call it an interim. Make sure you don't preach more than three Sundays in a row."[6] Thus, the "soft" interpretation of bureaucratic rules was given, which often occurs in organizational life.

The next several months Allen traveled from Dallas to San Antonio to serve as the interim pastor of the church without being the interim officially. He decided since this was his one opportunity to influence the church he would be as challenging and stimulating as he could be. He suggested, "I decided I would never have the experience of preaching there again so I decided that I was going to preach the gospel the way I believed it while I was there. So I did everything I could possibly do to communicate the ethical responsibility and the evangelistic intertwining I could."[7]

Allen used the pulpit on Sunday mornings to challenge the congregation toward a new future with his passionate evangelistic preaching. On Sunday nights he planned a series of sessions designed to educate the congregation to the new challenges of a church in the 1960s. Tom Skinner, a popular African-American evangelist and author of books on race,[8] was brought in to lead discussions during the Church Training hour. Sessions were organized dealing with the war in Vietnam, race, and a host of social agendas confronting the larger society.

The church responded positively. After the years of decline during Charles Bowles difficulties, Allen's enthusiasm energized the church. He said, "I tried to get everything exposed to them I could possibly do during that time. Well, God had his hand on it. And there was a real response. The

---

[6]Allen, "Service as Pastor of First Baptist Church, San Antonio," 77.
[7]Allen, "Service as Pastor of First Baptist Church, San Antonio," 77.
[8]See Tom Skinner, *How Black Is the Gospel*? (Philadelphia: Lippincott, 1970); *Black and Free* (Grand Rapids MI: Zondervan, 1971); *Words of Revolution* (Grand Rapids MI: Zondervan, 1971); and *If Christ is the Answer, What are the Questions?* (Grand Rapids MI: Zondervan, 1974). His papers are housed at Wheaton College and a brief biography can be found at <http://www.wheaton.edu/bgc/archives/GUIDES/430.htm> (accessed 27 August 2007).

church was growing in the middle of its interim."[9] The church and the city were growing on Allen as well. Here was a city and a congregation that would test to the fullest his vision of what God could do in the lives of people.

Soon the Pastor Search Committee, under the leadership of the chairman Cleo Crouch, approached Allen about becoming the pastor of the church. He was presented to the congregation, and Jimmy received the invitation from Crouch to accept their call via telephone while attending a meeting in Nashville in the fall 1967. The chairman reported, "Dr. Allen, we have recommended you to the church this Sunday morning and there was a standing ovation." I said, "Now Cleo, as many things as I have said and done, I just can't believe that." "Yes sir," retorted Crouch, "there was a standing ovation."[10] Allen accepted the call of the church and found out later more details of the "standing ovation." It seems when Chairman Couch presented his name to the congregation a woman in the choir screamed loudly, "Oh my God, NO!" But the youth in the church heard the remark, stood up and began cheering, and the whole congregation stood in support. Allen reports about eight people left the church over his coming, though six of them later returned. "That particular woman," he recalls, "became a member of a Bible church and never did believe I was not a communist."[11]

Allen resigned his role at the CLC and began his official responsibilities in January 1968. He served for the next twelve years providing energetic, creative, and aggressive leadership that established the church at the forefront among Southern Baptists as a successful model of an "old first church" in the center of a major city, integrating evangelism and social ministry. His purpose in going was clear. He desired to lead the church to become a pacesetting congregation in the values that had shaped his own personality and theology of ministry—a coherence of evangelism, community ministry, and ethical relevance. He mused to himself:

> Here is a laboratory that God could use to set a pace to help people understand that a dynamic, Bible-believing bunch of people can do this kind of work where we are if we have the energy of God to do it.[12]

---

[9] Allen, "FBC, San Antonio," 77-78.
[10] Allen, "FBC, San Antonio," 78.
[11] Allen, "FBC, San Antonio," 78.
[12] Allen, "FBC, San Antonio," 79.

It was his personal Camelot.

First Steps in a New Pastorate

Jimmy Allen moved into this pastorate of his dreams like a dynamo. It was the most innovative, creative, and productive period of his long ministry. He began with a series of challenging messages to the congregation around three specific themes. First, he addressed in his preaching, teaching, conversations with staff, and activities the question, "Who in the World Are We?" Second, he sought to work on the question, "Why in the World Are We Here?" and third, "How in the World Can We Do the Task?"

In addition to challenging the church, Jimmy immersed himself in seeking to understand the city. Allen knew San Antonio had been the subject of numerous governmental studies and analyses. He called his long-time friend William Crook who was working with the Office of Economic Opportunity (OEO) in Washington, D.C. The OEO had been established by President Lyndon Johnson to declare war on poverty in the United States. Crook responded by channeling reams of government studies on the social context of the city.

Soon he tapped into the resources of the social ministries programs of the BGCT and enlisted James Bailey, a Master of Social Work student in Dallas, to engage in a survey of the ministry potential in the city. Bailey spent a month in San Antonio interviewing fifty-five staff members of community agencies about ways in which churches could be helpful in their work. From his study came a catalog of ideas and information of what the church could do in the city. It provided information to guide the church for several years.[13]

The city leadership began responding to his presence. He was invited to join in a reevaluation of the social services of the city being conducted by the Community Welfare Council. The rabbi of the local Temple, David Jacobsen, and his wife Helen, were friends of Jimmy.

> Helen decided I ought to be on that committee. They said they had never had a Baptist preacher who wanted to know about that sort of thing. So they put me on the committee to survey the social ministries that were going on in the city. So I got involved early on in visiting and knowing what the city was

---

[13] Jimmy Allen, interview no. 5 with Daniel McGee, Baylor University Program for Oral History, San Antonio TX, 28 August 1973, 175-76.

doing for its poor, its bilingual population, and for its neighborhoods. So in serving in that capacity, I began looking for what we as a congregation could do. So the first innovation was I began a study of what the church could do for outreach ministries. And the way we did that was we got groups of people to go visit and find out what was happening.[14]

Allen was elected to the board of directors of the Community Welfare Council. The board chair at that time was Patricia Ayres, who became a lifelong friend and financial supporter of many of Allen's causes through the years. She quickly became impressed with Allen's interest in the social welfare of the city, was baptized by Allen and joined FBC in 1976. Patricia served in many roles within Baptist life after that including terms of service on the CLC of both the BGCT and the SBC. She also was formative in the foundation of the Cooperative Baptist Fellowship and served as the second moderator of this emerging mission organization in Baptist life. Ayres found Jimmy's leadership of the church impressive. She evaluated his ministry at First Baptist in a personal interview:

> Probably the most significant was the vision he had for developing the church's ministry in the downtown area—ministry with refugees, street people, all of that complex of ministries. He just had great vision for and tremendous energy to pull all that off. And it is still functioning, although not in the way it was. The energy of that vision sustained it a long time. In the midst of all that he was an excellent preacher and found time to be also very engaged in the pastoral ministry of the church, calling on prospective members and so on. He seemed to be able to do that with all the other things he was doing. He was president of the Texas Convention at that time, the SBC president, did a radio program, wrote columns for the paper. You name it. I think energy and vision are the two words that I think of.[15]

The revivalist heritage of the church was also changed early in his tenure. First Baptist had a tradition of having four revivals each year and Allen began canceling them as he could. At first there was some resistance to the change, but his leadership in instituting lay training in evangelism and mission outreach resulted in better evangelistic response than the revivals had generated. He says, "We emphasized enlistment and nurture and fellowship and taking care of doing our thing for God with an

---

[14]Allen, "FBC, San Antonio," 81.
[15]Patricia Ayers, interview with Larry L. McSwain, Atlanta, 11 November 2004, 2-3.

evangelistic thrust while we were looking at calling out the talents of the people to the task."[16]

Distinctive Programs

Jimmy Allen was never a programmatic leader. That is, his philosophy was not built around establishing programs or building buildings as the magnets for attracting people. His leadership style was to be the charismatic visionary who cast a dream of what the church could be and do, to motivate people to respond to the vision as a matter of heart religion, and to lead staff to organize avenues for lay involvement in making the vision happen. He was largely the catalyst for ideas and depended on others to take the ideas and "run with them" in action.

The Woman's Missionary Union of the SBC was heavily involved at that time in a programmatic emphasis on mission action for local churches. A series of workbooks on various approaches to mission action were published by the organization and these became standard fair in the training processes at FBC.

Much of Allen's success in San Antonio can be attributed to the staff which he inherited and developed. Luke Williams was the administrator of the church whose role was to take the pastor's ideas and translate them into workable programs that could be supported by the people. Luke's administrative skill and his personal friendship with Jimmy cannot be overestimated. Jimmy considered Luke the brother he never had. He said of him, "The chemistry was right between us. Luke was quiet and detailed. I was noisy and full of ideas. He was the implementer, and I was the innovator. Together we energized a giant downtown church, launched an international missions program through the Southern Baptist Convention, and founded the ACTS satellite television network."[17] According to Allen, "He [Williams] used to say he came on Wednesday night with a notebook in hand to find out what his job description was for the next week. I came to talk about the dreams of what we were supposed to be doing."[18] Williams would then work with the staff to develop a workable means to implement Allen's dreams.

---

[16] Allen, "FBC, San Antonio," 80.
[17] Jimmy Allen, *Burden of a Secret* (Nashville: Moorings, 1995) 23.
[18] Allen, "FBC, San Antonio," 98.

Within a few months a new team of staff emerged to work toward the new vision in the church. Lanny Allen began as Minister of Music in May of that first year. Bob Oldenberg had served at First Baptist previously and returned in the role of Minister of Youth Education and pianist. R. B. Cooper, Jr. joined the staff in August 1968 and led the community ministry outreach of the church until his retirement in 2006. Cooper and Allen were long-time friends from Dallas days; he was the brother of James Cooper. He had served as a pastor in economically disadvantaged communities and served a Spanish-speaking congregation in Falfurias, Texas. His fluency in Spanish made him the ideal person to serve in San Antonio. After accepting the staff role as Minister of Community Ministries, he earned a Master of Social Work degree and became the catalyst for many of the programs to the poor, transients, and refugees flowing through the city. Ron Willis, was a well-known street activist in San Francisco prior to moving to Bangor, Maine. He moved to San Antonio and served in outreach to the city for a period of years. Other staff additions during these early years of Allen's service were Al Ringle, Minister of Recreation; Jimmie Winter, Elementary Director; Royce Calhoun, Minister to Families; and William Mahoney, Minister of Pastoral Care.

This energetic staff was willing to try almost anything to move the church forward in its outreach to the city. Some of what they attempted worked. Within the first five years of Allen's ministry a number of new efforts were begun. Allen says there were twenty-eight community ministries supported by the church by the end of his ministry there, most of which were begun during his tenure.[19] These included a mobile chapel the church purchased to take to mobile home parks in the community to begin mission churches. These are often the least-churched communities in the city and small groups of Sunday schools and worship services were begun through this effort. Under the leadership of Ron Willis, a bar ministry was begun that lasted several months. Members would secure the approval of the bar owners to sit in the bars as available listeners and pay "whiskey prices" for soft drinks until the early morning hours. The stress of this ministry proved burdensome to most, but it demonstrated the willingness of the staff and members to go anywhere to share the gospel.

---

[19]Allen, "FBC, San Antonio," 83.

The staff soon discovered the opportunities for outreach were greater than the available resources of the congregation, so First Baptist became one of the first churches in the country to develop a talent bank of member interests and skills. Profiles were developed and Williams contracted with Trinity University to use their computer resources to develop a member data bank. From this effort, at least one church database business was developed in Arlington to copy this effort. First Baptist became a pioneer in a practice that is now standard for larger churches.

Al Ringle was called to serve as a minister of recreation for both members and the community. Out of his ministry a recreation trailer was assembled that could be moved easily from neighborhood to neighborhood. It had a collection of athletic gear so that an instant game of basketball or horseshoes could be started almost anywhere. It became a way of connecting with city youth, most of whom were unchurched. The educational program of the church was also focused on the community with Jimmie Winter leading WMU groups and Sunday school classes to conduct Bible studies for youth and children in the community.

Among the most-lasting outreach efforts was the development of a center for neighborhood ministry across the street from the church. San Antonio was a major center of the migration of "hippie" cultures during the 1960s as youth disaffected with the Vietnam War and the culture trekked from California to Colorado to Florida. San Antonio was on this path, and street culture thrived there during this period. The Episcopal Church had begun a coffee house in a ministry called Metro House across the street from the church, but with limited success. After several visits there, Allen recommended First Baptist buy it and adjoining property with a forty-one-unit hotel and six apartments. Soon the Fourth Street Inn was operational providing short-term residences for refugees and transients. It began as a conversation place but then a restaurant began for business people in the area. The proceeds from the restaurant provided help to the residents, a ministry that continues to this day. In 1975 the church purchased the United States Services Organization Service Center at Third and Alamo for $71,000. It became a Community Ministry Center and housed refuges and feeding program for transients.[20]

---

[20]*In the Shadow of His Hand*, 94.

R. B. Cooper became the primary minister within this community center that developed into a full Christian Social Ministries center. To provide the volunteers necessary for staffing, a training program was begun providing fifty hours of training in cultural sensitivity, sharing one's faith, and working in teams of two to bear a witness for Christ. No one was allowed to participate in these challenging opportunities without training. Anytime a need surfaced, these teams would be sent to investigate needs for ministry and with Allen's prodding in the media, the community often responded, allowing the church to focus its efforts where most needed. A free medical clinic in the Westlawn neighborhood was one of these innovations. Allen summarizes:

> Anyway, we had medical clinics, we had dental clinics, street recreation ministries, the street ministry in the bars, and a jail ministry in a juvenile detention center. What we would do is find the ministry, talk about it, and God raised up the people for it. Then we felt that was His response to enter into it. Then we had these testimony times (on Sunday evening worship times) when people told what was happening. So it became a mark of the fellowship that this was a part of who we were. At the same time, we were doing witness training. We put together what we called the "Barnabus Program." We said, "Everybody does not have the gift of a Paul, but everybody can be an encourager. . . . One of our principles was we did not ask anybody to do anything we did not train them to do."[21]

Along with the enlargement of social ministries, the church participated in the expansion of its outreach to the diverse ethnic community of San Antonio. The strategy of multiplication of congregations through the formation of homogenous ethnic congregations was growing in popularity among Southern Baptists as the result of the leadership of the Home Mission Board. First Baptist had a long history of ministry with the Chinese population in San Antonio. General John J. Pershing imported more than 500 Chinese to the Southwest to support his military excursions into Mexico to fight Pancho Villas. The immigrants settled in San Antonio after the military ventures ended in 1917, and First Baptist supported early ministry to the group. The Chinese Baptist Church met at First Baptist. With a large indigenous Hispanic population in San Antonio, the church supported congregational efforts in a variety of locations. During Allen's

---

[21] Allen, "FBC, San Antonio," 85.

tenure a Spanish language congregation met at the church with a pastor from the Mexican Baptist Institute, now the University of the Americas. As many as 500 persons were involved at various times in the congregation. Five other smaller Spanish-language mission congregations meeting in various locations in the city were supported as well. Allen confesses to a sense of failure to achieve the vision for this ministry he once thought possible. When asked to describe his greatest disappointment in his ministry at First Baptist he responded:

> One of the major disappointments was that I thought we could create a Hispanic ministry there that would have a tuning into the Spanish culture. I was down in Brazil preaching and discovered this place where . . . they had developed a Portuguese language ministry with 25,000 people coming to it. It was a kind of Pentecostal thing. But they built it on the discovery that in the Hispanic community the little churches get to the size of the extended family, seventy to one hundred, and then they crack up. That is the clannishness of that culture. They found a way to worship together on Friday night and train the ministers for these little house churches to meet on Sunday. They would bring the offering to the rally on Friday night. I came home thinking, "Now here is the way to reach the Hispanic culture." If we could find a dynamic preacher to do the Friday night service, we have the television setup for him to be on television in the city. We have the Hispanic seminary to provide leaders for the house churches. So we could do the Friday fiesta celebration time and build a tremendously successful Spanish language ministry. So, I looked for the man who would do that. I looked at the theatre we might start in. I spent a lot of time trying to put it together and I could not do it. I still think it would work. It works in São Paulo and I think it would work in San Antonio. But it did not work. It was one of those ideas that did not jell.[22]

The Vietnam War served to enlarge the international flavor of San Antonio even more. Lackland Air Force Base had a program called the English Language Institute which brought internationals from all over the world to receive both English instruction and military training. First Baptist had an international ministry that would provide English as a second language classes and a variety of services for family members, including regular luncheons at the church for various national groups. It is ironic that one of the groups the church hosted at a lunch in 1979 was a group of some seventy-five Iranians. Allen would meet some of them again only a few

---

[22] Allen, "FBC, San Antonio," 97.

months later when he visited Iran during the hostage crisis following the deposition of Pahlavi, the Shah of Iran, an experience described more fully in a later chapter.

San Antonio also became a reception area for a significant influx of Southeast Asian immigrants, especially after the withdrawal of the United States from South Vietnam. Among the most significant catalysts for the church's ministry was

> a man whose name was Otho Griffith who was the credit manager for Joske's. He was one of the most powerful laymen I have ever met. He came to me and said he had a heart problem. The doctor told him he was going to have to retire. He came to me to tell me had wanted to do some things since he had been a Christian, but had not.... He got involved in the Juvenile Detention center and our International Ministry. Otho Griffith became one of the most powerful witness persons I ever met. He was a quiet guy and would just tell the Gospel quietly in love. In the process, once he got the Juvenile ministry going he became interested in Internationals.... The impact of the Vietnam War and the placing of the English Language Institute at Lackland brought in people from all over the world to study English before they did any kind of military training. We recognized an opportunity because we had military personnel in the church. We put together an international hosting ministry. Otho started working with that. The Sunday school class for this group had to be done in basic English and stress the fundamentals.... So he became the teacher.[23]

The church began sponsoring and ministering to Asian refugees and that generated the need for purchasing the hotel property near Fourth Street Inn.

> Otho was so effective that when Southeast Asia fell he came to me with a burden.... In the process we sponsored 235 refugees. It started to grow and developed into a Cambodian Baptist Church and a Laotian Baptist Church in San Antonio.... I went to Otho Griffith's funeral two years ago [2003] in Dallas. Laotian people drove in from all over the country for his service. After I got through with the service they asked for the privilege of telling their stories. It was the most powerful moment to see what God had done with their lives through this man and this congregation.[24]

---

[23] Allen, "FBC, San Antonio," 86-87.
[24] Allen, "FBC, San Antonio," 87-88.

Outreach to the Military

First Baptist Church emerged by the early 1970s as the most effective congregation in the SBC in the quantitative measures of evangelistic success—number of baptisms. In both 1973 and 1974, the church led the Convention in baptisms, 539 and 553 respectively. Much of the reason for that success was the aggressive outreach by the church to Lackland Air Force Base. Jimmy invited all of the Baptist military chaplains in San Antonio to a luncheon at the church to engage in dialogue about how the church could be supportive of their work. Since the active-duty personnel were allowed to leave the base only one weekend each month, most of the ministry needed was on the base. Out of that group a fellowship group of chaplains met regularly. One of those leaders, a Southern Baptist chaplain now endorsed by the Cooperative Baptist Fellowship, Charles Baldwin, later served as Chief of Air Force Chaplains at the Pentagon. They asked for assistance in follow-up for the airmen making professions of faith and the church sent a cadre of lay persons to provide training for new Christians.

In the course of ministry on the base one airman named Bob Sandole made a profession of faith in Christ and became a part of First Baptist. He was a cross-country champion from New England, a competitive athlete, and aggressive personality. Bob appeared in Allen's office shortly after his conversion to announce he had sent his testimony to the paper for publication. "Bob, they are not going to put your testimony in the newspaper," Allen responded. "Yes," he said, "they have already printed it!"[25] Soon he was discussing with his pastor concern that there was not a chapel service at the base with the enthusiasm and tenor of the worship at First Baptist. He did his research on military policy and concluded he could ask for a distinctively Baptist service on the base. With Allen's encouragement, he discussed this with his base chaplains and began such a service in spite of some resistance to the idea. Some 250 airmen attended the first service and that soon grew to 400. The church provided counseling and support for those making professions of faith. Allen reports: "It grew until they moved it to the gymnasium. They were having the largest worship service in the military in the world out of that Baptist service. I took Bill Glass out there to preach one morning and they had eighty seven professions of faith that

---

[25] Allen, "FBC, San Antonio," 95.

morning."[26] Because of the involvement of the church, a chaplain asked if they could move their baptism services to First Baptist from another area Baptist church. The response was positive and a significant portion of the increase of baptisms for the church came from this ministry of outreach.

Soon Sandole completed his term of military service and became the manager of the Fourth Street Inn. He opened the restaurant there with an Italian menu as there were no other Italian restaurants in the area. He also knew this food had the best markup in price over cost of any other kind, and his success provided resources for the other ministries of the church.[27]

Connecting through Media

No decision proved to be more innovative or more life changing for Allen than his efforts to direct his energies toward involvement in the media of the city. The airwaves were much less saturated with religious programming in those days than in the present, and there was some resistance within the media to having specific religious programming. The local ABC affiliate, KSAT on channel 12, had a weekly worship broadcast that moved from church to church during each month. So, First Baptist had some exposure through television. When Allen approached the ABC station manager, Jack Carroll, about purchasing weekly broadcast time,

> He said that the FCC was wanting more locally approved programming and . . . that is not preaching that would be on Sunday morning. That [conversation] was on Thursday and said I would be back Monday. I had never done a program, did not know anything about what that was. But I had been around a lot of talented people. So I sat down and worked out a thing with folk singing. Bob Oldenburg was on the staff. We offered Carroll a discussion format with some folk singers and talked about teenage issues. I took it to him and he said, "We will do it." He called it Good News. Every Saturday we would tape the program and it would be played on Sunday morning. No self-respecting teenager is looking at television on Sunday morning. But I knew if we did that there would be parents looking and we needed to attract younger families to the church.[28]

The Good News program lasted for about three years and from it the church began attracting more families with teenagers. Allen says, "The

---

[26] Allen, "FBC, San Antonio," 96.
[27] Allen, "FBC, San Antonio," 97.
[28] Allen, "FBC, San Antonio," 89-90.

image of the church shifted as people saw young people talk about drugs, racial issues, and other youth concerns. People began bringing their kids to our church. We had a spurt of growth from that effort."[29] But more important was the growing visibility of Allen and the church in the community. He was learning how to communicate through a new medium and establishing contacts in the industry. Soon he was approached to participate in a talk show called "Controversy" on KENS, the CBS affiliate on channel 5, a discussion featuring a rabbi, priest, and minister. Next came an opportunity to offer a commentary on a moral issue for the Saturday night news on Channel 12. Allen recalls:

> That is where "Moral Side of the News" began. On Saturday night I would have ninety seconds to talk about an issue from a Christian point of view. It got popular enough they moved it to Wednesday night. And for five years, every Wednesday night, I was on the 10 PM News as a part of the ABC station talking about moral issues. In the process of that, we ended up with a think tank of people in our church to feed that. So every Tuesday I would meet with people we had in our church—the editor of the *Chamber Magazine*, the editorial page writer for the *San Antonio Express-News*, the reporter covering the city in the *San Antonio Light*, and the treasurer of the city. So we had good representation from areas of the city. Their assignment was to think of the hottest and most pressing moral issues in our city. We would talk about those and I would pick one and that night I would write the ninety-second commentary. I would go to the station every Wednesday night and do a live presentation of that commentary as a closing part of the news story. That did several things. One was it gave me an opportunity outside the pulpit to talk about moral issues confronting the city. So I did not have to use pulpit time to call people to those thoughts. It created "hall talk" which became an educational process to my people as they discussed what I had said. It also gave us some impact in the city for action to get things done. One of the major byproducts was it put the issue on the agenda of these five people in the think tank for their participation in the city. So I would see in the newspaper editorial things we did not get to in the "Moral Side of the News." We discussed among us ethical issues and that became a school of input for these folks. I did not think of it but it worked that way.[30]

---

[29] Allen, "FBC, San Antonio," 90.
[30] Allen, "FBC, San Antonio," 90-91.

Fortunately, copies of the teleprompter texts for these commentaries are available in Allen's files from 30 January 1972 to 18 August 1974. They are a treasure for capturing his thinking on a host of topics. The texts address "hot topics" including such issues as drug abuse, President Nixon's trip to China, ethics in the Texas House of Representatives, pornography, health care for the poor, racial violence, legalized gambling, city elections, Watergate, energy crisis, emergency ambulance service, the San Antonio jail, and a host of other similar issues. He addressed local, statewide, and national issues through this medium. The tenor of these commentaries is tough—names of politicians who voted the wrong way are identified, practices of conflict of interests in both the city council and the state legislature are identified, and sides are taken in behalf of the electorate on issue after issue. These commentaries established Allen as a voice of speaking truth to power and an individual willing to become controversial.

Jimmy's activities in the public arena became an educational process within First Baptist Church. This weekly research group developed new sensitivities in their own spiritual development. One of these "think-tank" members was Roddy Stinson, at that time the communications director for the San Antonio Chamber of Commerce and now a columnist with the *San Antonio Express-News*. Stinson credits Allen with becoming for him the most important spiritual influence in his life. Stinson and Allen first met, according to his recollection, when he was a journalist for the Brotherhood Commission of the SBC. After his move to San Antonio, he joined First Baptist and began a long pilgrimage in Christ; he credits Allen with decisive influence in his growth. Stinson recalls:

> In this largely Catholic city, Jimmy became the face of the Protestant community . . . to a large extent because of one of his most creative and risky leaps of faith into television broadcasting. . . . Because he handled himself so well and was instantaneously articulate about virtually any subject, he became a favorite interview for the local media . . . newspaper and TV alike. Also, his willingness to reach out to other denominations and their pastors helped him become a major figure in the larger church community.[31]

Other media became important as well. Allen used his weekly column in the church newsletter, *Reflections . . . by the Pastor*, to address issues both within and beyond the church. He saw this as an educational process

---

[31]Roddy Stinson, e-mail interview response, 28 August 2007, 2.

for topics he often did not address from the pulpit where he preferred to teach biblical concepts and inspire for application and life. A collection of these articles (undated) assembled by church member Margille S. Stroud, is also in his files. He addressed internal issues of the church and practical suggestions for daily living of the Christian life. But he also used this column to write of local, state, and national trends, often quoting from current news reports and literature to buttress his positions. Again, he was educating the congregation in a holistic application of the gospel.

He was offered a column in the *San Antonio News-Herald* in 1971 which was named *Down to Earth*. He again addressed a variety of issues and concerns ranging from church-state separation, to government aid to parochial schools, the appointment of an ambassador to the Vatican during the Carter administration, taxation of the churches, the program of reparations for African-Americans proposed by James Forbes, and government aid to Baptist colleges and universities. These were syndicated and published in twelve other Texas newspapers. Allen's columns were also published in the *Baptist Standard* which created *Baptist Press* releases and wide circulation of his thought through the network of Baptist state papers. Allen quickly emerged as a national clergy voice. He addressed a wide-ranging variety of issues from the routine to the controversial. He never seemed to shy away from the challenging issues of the time. An illustration is a straightforward discussion of abortion. After describing the extremes of opinion on the issue he voiced his own:

> The complexities of the question of competing values, the silence of the Scriptures about the point in which a fetus becomes a person, and advances of science, with its "medical mistakes" such as the famous Thalidomide-deformed child, makes men [*sic*] of genuine Christian concern take differing positions on abortion laws.
>
> My position is that there is a time before a fetus becomes a person. In this sense aborting is not murder. However, society should place reasonable restrictions on the process to avoid an unimpeded trend toward devaluation of the innate worth of every human person.[32]

The final piece in the media strategy that was emerging was a weekly television broadcast of the worship of First Baptist. When Allen heard a rumor that the ABC affiliate was considering sale of time for worship

---

[32] Jimmy Allen, "Is Abortion Murder?" *Baptist Press*, 17 April 1971, n.p.

broadcasts as a result of ownership changes, he met with the station manager, James Chavone. He confirmed the change and Allen immediately began meeting with lay leadership and the church made the commitment to this new form of outreach, sometime in 1974. Ever the networker, Allen had preached at the Evangelism Conference for the Baptist State Convention of New York when he met William Howard, a Baptist living in New York City. Allen tells the story:

> It turned out he was a graduate of Howard Payne College. I asked him what he did and he said he was an engineer for NBC. It turned out he had brought the first color television station on line in Pittsburgh for NBC. In the process he said he always wanted to do something for the Kingdom of God but never had a chance to do it. I remembered that conversation when we had the television opportunity. So I called him and said, "Bill, I am looking for some cameras. We don't have much money but we are going to go on television." He said, "You know we just took the cameras off the *Today* show to replace with new ones. They are old, but in good shape and I think I can get them for you." I said, "How much would they cost?" He said, "They are $80,000 each, but I can probably get them for about $8,000 each." I said, "I will take four of them." He said he would like to come down and help us with that. So Bill Howard came down at his own expense to help engineer the job at First Baptist.[33]

New opportunities for the expression of talent within the church were created by the beginnings of this new ministry. One such story was the involvement of a key layperson in this new ministry. When the cameras were installed, Allen recalls,

> We had a guy in the church whose name was Chester Wilkes, who I remember vividly because he wore a Stetson hat. He was chairman of the Parking Committee. Every Deacon's time he would talk about parking. When we got the cameras he asked if we had any schematics for them. I said we had some paper work. He took them and looked at them. When Bill Howard came down he asked what he [Wilkes] did. I said, "He works for the military out here at Lackland." He said, "That man can go to work for me any day." It turns out he was a troubleshooter for the military security services. When they had problems with their satellites, he would go solve the problem. And we had him parking cars. And the fact was he loved God enough to do that and he was good at it. [Laughter.] He became the most fulfilled man you ever saw

---

[33] Allen, "FBC, San Antonio," 92.

becoming involved in that TV ministry. It was a matter of matching talent with the opportunity. God gave us both and we matched it. And praise God for what happened with them. Also, we had to affirm them when it got tough.[34]

Results

How does one evaluate the ministry of a pastor and the congregation being led during the tenure of that ministry? It is fair to say Jimmy Allen's move to First Baptist Church had the effect of a Texas "whirlwind" on the congregation and the city. If there is one word that captures every portrait that emerges of him it is "energy." He brought significant change to the church during his eleven years of ministry leadership there. He lived in a vortex of change in both the larger society and the city in which he served. At the same time he expended enormous energy caring for illness within his immediate family that will be described in a later chapter and was elected president of both the BGCT and the SBC. An examination of copies of his personal calendars during these years and interviews with persons who worked with him at this time document the workaholic lifestyle he lived. Jimmy is one of those rare persons who seems to need little sleep, usually four hours each night. With his innate energy, daily infusions of coffee, and a divine sense of call, he made a difference in the lives of people, a church, and indeed a denomination.

Buildings, Budgets, and Baptisms. The three Bs of Baptist success are usually the concrete, statistical measures one can apply to determine the effectiveness of a leader. Jimmy Allen certainly excelled in these areas.

First Baptist engaged in a number of building expansion efforts during his tenure. Interestingly, the majority were external to the church facilities themselves. With his move to the city, the church sold its parsonage and purchased a new one for the Allen household.[35] The educational building was remodeled in 1970 and included a prayer chapel named in honor of Charles Bowles.[36] In 1975 the church purchased the United States Services Organization Service Center at Third and Alamo for $71,000. It was used for a Community Ministry Center and housed refuges and a feeding program for transients.[37] Metro House, a forty-one-unit apartment building,

---

[34]Allen, "FBC, San Antonio," 92.
[35]*In the Shadow of His Hands*, 92.
[36]*In the Shadow of His Hands*, 93-94.
[37]*In the Shadow of His Hands*, 94.

and six apartments in the rear of the Metro House were purchased at the same time for the expanded community ministry. From 1979 to 1981, extensive renovation occurred to the educational and worship spaces of the church buildings.

The budget was $499,699 in the first year of Allen's pastorate. The 1979 budget, his last year in leadership there, was $1,170,927.[38] I remember his presentation in a seminary class while he served as president of the SBC in which he described his common practice of challenging the church to add a special project requiring "over and above" the budget giving each year as a way of stretching the congregation toward its potential. Obviously it worked in this case. The total receipts for the church in the last year of his ministry there were $1,476,685.[39]

The number of baptisms was probably the most successful numerical measure of his leadership. During the twelve years of his tenure, the church baptized a total of 3,576 people. When one adds the number in his preceding churches, Jimmy Allen baptized more than 4,000 people in his years of Texas pastoral ministry.

Another measure of numerical strength can be seen in Sunday school attendance. Certainly the level of enthusiasm and growth for the church was most evident in the worship services and external ministries of the church. On some Sundays of special emphasis the attendance would reach as many as 2,000 people. In reality, the average attendance over the period of Allen's ministry did not change appreciably. The peak year was 1,637 in 1971. By the end of his ministry the average attendance was slightly below that of his first year of service, 1,462. In the area of total membership the growth was dramatic—from 7,799 in 1968 to 9,720 in 1979.[40] There is a reasonable explanation for this size factor. Allen steadfastly resisted the suggestions by layleaders and staff to "winnow" the membership files to reduce to the level of active participation. Allen defends his practice with a story:

> The church roll was big because we had a lot of people who came through and we did not know where they were. When some of the leaders wanted to

---

[38]*In the Shadow of His Hands*, 85.

[39]Compiled by Clay Price from BGCT annuals and recorded in e-mail to the author, 24 August 2007.

[40]Compiled by Clay Price from BGCT annuals and recorded in e-mail to the author, 24 August 2007.

clean it up I asked, "Have you ever seen a church that got greater and deeper because they were able to count better and have few folks on the roll to send their money in." I said we were going to keep doing what we were doing. I started to cut everybody down to size at the time we did the television thing. Then I got a check for $68,000 from a guy in Corpus Christi who had not been in our church for twenty years who just heard about our going on television. Because we stayed in touch and called him a member that check convinced me we should not eliminate people from the roll wherever they were. We had more than 7,000 members when I went and nearly 10,000 when I left.[41]

Qualitative Measures. The more difficult measurement of effectiveness is in terms of the significance of lives changed, spiritual experience deepened, and commitments to the mission of God in the world enlarged. There is no accurate means of such measurements. Yet when one talks with the people who have known him, worked with him, and have been recipients of his ministry, the reports are glowing. A subjective appraisal would indicate several strengths of his work at San Antonio.

First, Jimmy Allen's style is of one of effecting change without stiffening resistance. He evidently learned well the famous lecture of his mentor T. B. Maston using a rubber band—the challenge of change is to stretch the people to a new shape without breaking the rubber band. Allen's positive approach was to encourage people to respond out of their discipleship to Jesus and obedience to God as Father when faced with difficult actions. Roddy Stinson reported Jimmy's willingness to declare himself as a part of this change ministry. "About two years into Jimmy's ministry, a deacon told him:

> "If (Hispanics) continue to join our church, a lot of members will leave." To which Jimmy responded, "And if we *don't* continue to reach out to them, I know of at least one family that will leave—mine." Today, FBC has many Hispanic members, several in leadership positions . . . all a legacy of Jimmy Allen's courage and belief in doing the right thing regardless of the consequences to him personally.[42]

His leadership had an impact in the area of staff relations as well. He was able to recruit and maintain a stable, creative, and loyal group of

---

[41] Allen, "FBC, San Antonio," 94-95.
[42] Stinson, e-mail interview, 2.

persons who adjusted to his personality. He reported terminating only one staff person in his years of service there.

One of the persons who knows him as well as any other outside his family was his secretary for almost fifteen years, Janice Brake, whom he baptized as a young woman. She served with him from 1974 until his resignation from the Radio and Television Commission. Her appraisal:

> Dr. Allen is a driven, competitive (try to play scrabble with him!) and immensely confident person—who has a vision for the grand plans of God. He expects the best of others and he was candid about what those expectations were. I remember once just after I had started working with him that he called me into his office. He said, "Why is all this on my desk?" And he started stacking into my arms every file on his desk. After that I knew that he wanted me to take care of all those files! One of the things I most valued in the working relationship was that I could count on his candor about what was expected and where things stood. I would say he largely delegated to staff, but at the same time if he felt it was important he was not reluctant to be involved in how a detail was handled. He has the quality of being able to listen and to hear what is being said, so I would say he was reasonable in his responses to staff if they felt differently than he did about something.[43]

Allen wears well in congregational life and seemed to avoid many of the explosive conflicts that characterize much of congregational life today.

Second, Jimmy was willing to take the risks of failure in order to accomplish the possibilities of success. Stinson considered his leadership style a

> whirlwind. Something new and different in the areas of evangelism and/or ministry were being discussed, organized and implemented constantly. Some were successful, some weren't. But the process of trial and error was exceedingly exciting . . . even fun for this young adult. I chaired the committee that formed Fourth Street Inn in 1974. Thirty-three years later, it is still in operation. I ate there last week.[44]

This quality may be the most important in understanding the contributions of Jimmy Allen. Brake's appraisal seems appropriate:

---

[43] Janice Brake, e-mail interview with Larry L. McSwain, 9 September 2007, 2.

[44] Stinson, e-mail interview, 2.

> I think Dr. Allen accomplished many different things at one time because he lives in the present. For example, when he had a speaking commitment or other meeting, we started a folder. Everything related to the commitment went in the folder as the information came in or was generated. I made reservations, prepared an itinerary, and he held out his hand as he walked out the door. I was always rather amazed by this level of trust! But I think he could not have been involved in as much or focused on big issues if he had not been able to trust the moment and not dwell on details. He had basic ways of dealing with logistics—he ALWAYS received a pocket-size calendar of appointments and reminders for the next day before he left each day. He trusted Luke Williams to know what to do to manage the operations of the church. He had friends he called on to discuss issues and ideas. He has an immense intellectual ability to plan and to see things as whole or completed. He has a great deal of energy. Setbacks do not get him down. He has amazing perception. He has great faith—he often mentioned the faith of his parents in his childhood for the provision of each day's needs—and he seemed to live that as well.[45]

Allen is self-aware of his failures as well as successes. He described some of those failures. "We did some magnificent failures in the process. I tried to have a program in the San Antonio auditorium with Pat Boone after his conversion. We managed to fill the place by about eight percent. I tried a week of preaching at the theatre on Easter the way W. A. Criswell had done. I talked to him about it and it was a failure. We did a bunch of things. We learned to fail without being a failure. You know, everything does not work. You try and see where it goes."[46]

The third critical assessment of his leadership is his ability to communicate clearly, energetically, and creatively. Allen is gifted with speech. There is universal recognition of his enthusiasm as among the attractive features of his communication style. Brake recalls:

> Dr. Allen was a dynamic preacher who built the ministry of the church around the strength of his preaching. His sermons were based on scripture first. They were unfailingly interesting often with an unexpected twist or surprise around an idea. He was able to paint a visual picture using various illustrations from a movie, a play, a piece of literature, a poem, or a quote to communicate an idea. Because his sermons were biblically based with a traditional faith

---

[45] Brake, e-mail interview, 2.

[46] Allen, "FBC, San Antonio," 89.

while at the same time often tying in current events or literature, I think they had a wide appeal to many different people for the many different levels of his approach to a subject. He did not seem to plan sermon titles and subjects far ahead—but preached out of his impressions in a more fluid way.[47]

Sometimes that creativity was not appreciated, especially when, as Stinson reported, was the experience of his wife; he revealed the end of a movie plot before parishioners had seen it. His preaching and addresses are marked by literary allusions, contemporary events, and popular culture illustrations from movies and television programs.

Jim Newton has known and worked with Jimmy Allen for more than forty years, interviewing him on numerous occasions. His appraisal of Allen's ministry in San Antonio is perceptive:

> I have never known a pastor who portrayed the model of a prophet and priest as well as Jimmy Allen. He was a priest, that is a pastor, to the people of the church as he sought to minister to their spiritual needs. He was also a prophet, challenging the people to become involved in the life of the community, the city of San Antonio. . . . It was a very unique time in the life of that church and the life of that city.[48]

Finally, Jimmy made ministry to people the focus of his service at the church. Yes, buildings were expanded and renovated in two of his pastorates. But most of the building emphasis in San Antonio was one of outreach to the community. He reflected many years after leaving San Antonio:

> But I lament that, like many families, the family of faith is not functioning as it was intended by its Founder.
>
> I have watched a creeping paralysis develop in many groups of believers who began with the best of intentions. Most Christian churches begin with the goal of meeting the needs of people with the spiritual message and ministry they communicate. Because such a church will inevitably become a place where battered, broken, bruised people congregate, the church soon begins to grow. With size and success come the need for bigger buildings, larger budgets, and specialized institutions, all ostensibly for the purpose of more-effective ministry to hurting people. Gradually, leadership roles are redefined

---

[47]Brake, e-mail Interview, 3.
[48]Jim Newton, telephone interview with Larry L. McSwain, Atlanta, 2 July 2008, 2-3.

and pastors and spiritual leaders find themselves becoming managers rather than ministers.[49]

By 1979, the ebb and flow of providence were moving in new directions for Allen. After twelve years he concluded his ministry in San Antonio with a trip to Iran with a group of clergy seeking to facilitate the release of hostages taken in the capture of the American embassy in Tehran. Church leaders would not be surprised to see stories of their departing pastor on the pages of the *New York Times*. His arena had shifted to a global stage with an even-bigger dream than any he could imagine in San Antonio. It was now the world as the stage for a bold initiative of mission action. He would attempt to do that from the platform of the presidency of the Radio and Television Commission of the SBC, a role he assumed in January 1980.

---

[49] Allen, *Burden of a Secret*, 211-12.

Chapter 7

Denominational Leadership: Enlarging the Vision

> Our president is not omniscient. He doesn't know everything. He is not all-powerful. He is not omnipotent, but he may be omnipresent.
> —William M. Pinson, Jr.
> introducing Jimmy Allen at a denominational meeting

The most natural evolution in leadership for Jimmy Allen was the concentric circle of influence that enlarged from his involvements in San Antonio. He was already a well-known voice in Texas Baptist venues from his extensive network of connections from his RA and CLC work. As pastor of the First Baptist Church, his successes in leadership enlarged his profile as a potential elected denominational spokesperson. Communicating his views via media, especially his articles that extended statewide by 1971, made Allen an easily recognizable denominational leader. That has always been a prerequisite to election in Baptist circles.

President of the Baptist General Convention of Texas

Allen's in-depth knowledge of the BGCT added to his effectiveness when he was elected to leadership roles as he was never interested much in being a figurehead leader of any entity. Always the activist, Jimmy was determined to make a mark when he could. It was a part of his political instincts and his innate compulsion to change things. Allen's first foray into elective denominational leadership occurred at the annual session of the BGCT meeting in Fort Worth in November 1968. There he was nominated by Russell Dilday and elected vice president of the Convention, less than one year into his service as pastor at First Baptist, San Antonio.

The next year the convention met in San Antonio. It was an unwritten tradition in the BGCT for pastors of churches in the "home town" of the Convention meeting place *not* be nominated for president. It was viewed by some as "home field advantage" for such a practice to be followed. Allen assumed the same in 1969.

Several currents were swirling within the BGCT at that time. The perennial issue of government loans for Texas Baptist colleges and universities continued through most of the 1960s. Convention reorganization was on the agenda with a "Committee of 100" studying again the structure of the BGCT staff. The tenure of T. A. Patterson as executive director was drawing to a close as the result of Patterson's own efforts to mandate a fixed retirement age of sixty-seven prior to his election to the post. Patterson wished to continue his service, but was boxed in to his own leadership on that point. He had also generated some controversy with a major effort to involve Texas Baptists in a crusade evangelism approach to overseas partnership evangelism, especially in Japan and South America. The move had been expensive and strained relationships with the Foreign Mission Board of the SBC. Not all Texas Baptists or FMB missionaries shared his enthusiasm for this approach. The level of his commitment to this strategy was obvious. The day after his retirement with the BGCT, 1 January 1974, he began working as executive vice president of Dub Jackson's World Evangelism Foundation, the primary advocate for crusade evangelism.[1]

The most visible candidate for president of the BGCT in San Antonio was William M. Shamburger, pastor of First Baptist Church of Tyler. He was viewed as a strong Patterson supporter and possible successor to him, representing the more conservative East Texas constituency of churches. The political customs of that time were against any overt campaign effort for elective denominational offices. Rumors would circulate in advance of the convention as to potential nominees. The nominator was usually a widely recognized leader with a following who would often be the deciding factor in an election. Clearly a "telephone" campaign among networks of key leaders might take place prior to the convention. But announcements of potential candidate or the appearance of a campaign was often anathema for victory.

Allen avers he refused to respond favorably to encouragement from friends to be nominated prior to the convention meeting.[2] But on the morning nominations were to be made, shortly after midnight, he received a telephone call from a group meeting at a local hotel,

> who had been in a prayer meeting and a discussion time and felt that they needed the option of my nomination in order to give the people a chance at that point. I yielded to that reasoning and to that request and the next day was nominated. I had no idea that I would be elected and so I didn't even tell my wife at breakfast that was going to happen. I didn't even go to the Convention that morning because I didn't want to be around when that sort of thing was in the air. I went into my office and worked that morning. I went down to the

---

[1] Harry Leon McBeth, *Texas Baptists: A Sesquicentennial History* (Dallas: Baptistway Press, 1998) 283-324.
[2] Jimmy Allen, interview no. 5 with Daniel McGee, Baylor University Program for Oral History, San Antonio TX, 28 August 1973, 189.

convention to see the lieutenant governor [Ben Barnes] who was a friend of mine and was there to bring a speech that day. . . . He told me that I'd been elected . . . when I met him and he said, "Congratulations, you've been elected without a runoff." . . . So I felt thrust into leadership at this point.[3]

His first act as the newly elected convention president was to inform Wanda. "I said, 'My soul, I've got to call Wanda.' I had not told my wife I was being nominated. So I called her and said, 'Honey, there is something I forgot to tell you at breakfast. I did not think it would happen.' She said, 'Yes, I know. It's on the radio.' [Laughter.] I was in the doghouse. I never quite recovered from that."[4]

Knowing well the machinery of the Convention, Allen began meeting as an ex-officio member of the most significant committees of the Convention, making suggestions and moving key ideas forward. The most significant power of the state convention president is the power of nomination to key boards and committees. Allen immediately worked to broaden the range of persons in his nominations for these roles. Included were ethnic leaders and women at a new level of involvement.

The major innovation of his two years of leadership as Convention president in 1970–1971 was the formation of the Urban Strategy Committee. Allen raised the importance of the demographic shifts from rural to urban realities and a growing urban mindset in the state in his addresses and committee meetings. The cities became the theme of the annual meeting in Austin in 1970 with William Pinson a keynote speaker and convention approval of the appointment of the Urban Strategy Committee. The committee was charged with studying the population changes in Texas and developing convention strategies for future work. Out of it came an Urban Strategy Council.

The council moved to develop a formal relationship between the convention and Southwestern Seminary. Soon urban conferences and classes were added at the seminary and a person was employed as a liaison

---

[3] Allen interview no. 5 with Daniel McGee, 190. Allen reported in "The Christian Life Commission and Texas Baptist Life," interview no. 3 with Jim Newton and Larry L. McSwain, Big Canoe GA, 14 November 2004, 49; the people in the room included "Abner McCall, James Landis, Ray Worley, and five or six others."

[4] Interview no. 3 with Jim Newton and Larry L. McSwain, 50.

between the two entities to provide communication and awareness of mutual resources.

In an interview during the year following his service in this role, Allen reflected:

> I would say that, of the two years of my presidency, that may be the most significant thing that happened. . . . I hope history will show that it was a pivotal time to turn our attention to the cities and that we will out of that . . . come to a gearing of the mind set of Baptists to the facing of the challenges of the cities. You see, the Southwest as you know is always some years behind the urban processes and the secular man processes of the Northeast. We still have enough spiritual energy, enough churchmanship, if we can be alert and learn the lessons of our brethren up in the North, to affect the city. We can actually affect some of the very changes that are happening if we've got both the vision and the nerve to do it. And I am hopeful that we are at the beginning of that process. We are late in the game now, but we may be able to do something about that. And I would like very much to see that done not only here in San Antonio where I have a direct role, but also in each of the urban centers of our state. And so I would say that as I look back on the two years, if there's any one thing I take great delight in, it is that we got the Convention's attention about the urban scene.[5]

The Urban Strategy Council changed both the philosophical mindset and then the core leadership of the convention staff. But the event Allen talks about most and shaped his public persona for the next thirty years occurred in the second year of his presidency. It was traditional for the convention president to meet annually with the presidents of the various Black conventions in Texas. Most of the African-American convention presidents held lifetime roles while the BGCT role changes at least every two years. So, there was not a sustained ability to work together on common projects. Allen had worked at the CLC on numerous statewide issues with the African-American leadership group; he had a deep personal connection with the members of the group. When he met with them there was trust already established.

> We decided that it was time for us to do something together as a people. And out of that came a decision that we would move our conventions together, for the first time in the history of Texas Baptists. . . . we spent a year putting

---

[5]Allen, interview no. 5 with McGee, 194.

together a forum in which we changed all the Convention plans for meeting for six different conventions. [They moved] from wherever they were going to meet to Houston and had the second session that I was president [of the BGCT] simultaneously with the other Black conventions. The centerpiece of that meeting was an evangelistic rally which we had at the Astrodome. I spent the last year of my presidency, the last six months of it I spent a fantastic amount of my energy helping to promote that Convention because I felt it was a center of the stage to show that Baptists were reaching across ethnic lines in fellowship. That we were joined together in a purpose of witnessing and winning people to Christ and that out of it the exposure would have a great deal to do with what happened in the future.[6]

The planning for the event proved to be a monumental challenge. Arranging the logistics for securing and managing the Astrodome was a major challenge. But probably a bigger one was the resistance Allen experienced from the convention staff. Since the emphasis was on evangelism for the event, the Evangelism Division of the convention would need to be involved. C. Wade Freeman, the long-time and powerful leader of the division, was opposed to the plan. Allen moved aggressively and sometimes with force to push the convention to provide the resources and personnel needed to make the event happen. As it turned out, the meeting proved to be a major success. Allen concluded that

> there was more at stake than a meeting. That it was a symbol and an opportunity to say something that I had felt God wanted to have Baptists saying a good while. Which is that we are one in the spirit and that there is a oneness of brotherliness and of concern for a lost world and city. So this was put together without any great outstanding personalities. Billy Graham was not there. . . . We had 41,777 people by Astrodome count at the meeting that night [with 970 professions of faith and 445 reaffirming their faith]. It turned out to be the largest Baptist meeting thus far in the history of the founding of the United States. . . . The fact is that we had a phenomenal happening that night, which affected the attitudes of program planners tremendously. Since that time our evangelism conference, for instance, is now cosponsored by the Black convention(s) and ours. . . . I felt that the other thing I took a great deal of delight and thank God for, was the fact of that meeting and the significance of it in the aftermath in the lives of so many people and program planning among Baptists. So the two things that I thought were most important—the cities on the one hand, the ethnic and the racial problems on the other, both were

---

[6]Allen, interview no. 5 with McGee, 195-96.

addressed by the Convention during that time in a way that I was very grateful to respond to.[7]

The event became a model for Allen's future leadership. He would replicate a similar effort as SBC president in 1979 and later as the program chair of the Celebration of a New Baptist Covenant in 2008.

Allen continued to have significant influence on a key decision after his term of service as president concluded. As the time for T. A. Patterson's retirement approached, the process for election of the executive director of the convention changed. Until that time, each executive was chosen in a "round robin" process of voting by the executive committee from all persons nominated from across the Convention. Now a nominating committee for the new executive was selected and Allen was chosen to serve on it. When the committee met, it elected Allen as the past Convention president its chair. So he gave leadership to the selection of the critical person for the future of the BGCT.

The committee had a rather long period of time to seek a new executive and was encouraged by Patterson to delay its work until near the time of his retirement. So, three months before his retirement the committee nominated long-time pastor James Landis to succeed Patterson. Landis, pastor of the First Baptist Church in Richardson, Texas, had served as chair of the Urban Strategy Council, and brought a new emphasis on the urban context in his role. He was also favorable toward the CLC emphases within the convention.

President of the Southern Baptist Convention

The next logical step in Allen's denominational leadership emerged in his election as president of the SBC at the 1977 Convention meeting in Kansas City, Missouri. He had led the SBC in baptisms during 1975 and 1976. Traditionally that achievement brought invitations to speak at the state convention meetings across the country. For the two years preceding his election Allen preached in most, if not all, of the state conventions of the SBC, usually at the annual evangelism conference or the state convention itself. This put him at the forefront of visibility in national denominational life.

---

[7]Allen, interview no. 5 with McGee, 196-97.

The catalyst for Allen's decision to allow himself to be nominated for the post was a specific decision. James Sullivan, the long-time president of the Baptist Sunday School Board prior to his retirement, was elected to his first term of SBC president at the 1976 convention. In the course of his term, he let it be known he would not allow himself to be nominated for a second term. John Hurt, editor of the *Baptist Standard*, called Allen in San Antonio with that news. Many friends across the country had encouraged him to consider nomination for the role at some time in his ministry, so that call raised the specter of an opportunity to serve in Allen's mind. He called a dozen or so personal friends to communicate the news and seek their reaction. They included Foy Valentine, James Dunn, Clifton Tennison in Louisiana, Doug Watterson in Tennessee, and others. He was encouraged by them to allow himself to be nominated.

Southern Baptists became a new kind of denomination in the 1970s. For much of their history, they were a rather insulated Southern phenomenon trapped in the sectarianism of small churches, rural poverty, regional influence, and the burdens of racial segregation. Following World War II, Baptist people in the South enjoyed economic prosperity as the Sunbelt exploded with industry and population growth. The SBC engaged in a mission expansion across the United States and around the world. They planted new congregations in every state of the United States. The SBC became the largest Protestant overseas mission-sending agency in the U.S. The convention was focused on missions as its central unifying element and though there were skirmishes of conflict over theological issues, a traditional focus on missions and education kept the convention on track. The convention was now a national denomination in every sense of the word.

Bold Mission Thrust

The dominant symbol of that traditional synthesis was Bold Mission Thrust (BMT). Owen Cooper served as president of the SBC 1975–1976, the last layperson to do so until the time of this writing. The mission agencies of the convention were concerned with a declining growth of mission resources and personnel. Beginning in 1973, Gerald Palmer, vice president of the Missions Division, led an effort to set twenty-five-year goals for the HMB.[8]

---

[8]David T. Bunch, "Mission Service Corps History," An unpublished paper, n.d., 2-3.

So the agencies began organizing a renewed focus on mission with Cooper's blessings. Prior to the 1975 convention meeting in Miami, the Foreign Mission Board held an interagency consultation to discuss renewed emphasis on missions in the denomination. Out of that grew a study committee headed by Warren Hultgren, pastor of the FBC in Tulsa, Oklahoma. The group recommended to the 1976 SBC meeting in Virginia Beach, Virginia a set of mission goals they called Bold Mission Thrust which set the agenda of delivering the message of the gospel to every person in the world by the end of the century.

One of those goals was to double the number of persons engaged in mission service. Denominational leaders became convinced such would happen only if a significant force of volunteers was enlisted. Two weeks prior to the convention meeting in June 1977, President Jimmy Carter invited the primary leaders of the denominational agencies to the White House for a strategy meeting on creating such a voluntary force of missionaries. Jimmy Allen was involved in the planning of the meeting, but did not attend. No doubt the meeting was largely arranged by Carter's long-time friend, Glendon McCullough, executive director of the Brotherhood Commission, and Owen Cooper. Carter suggested to the gathered leaders establishing a force of volunteers who would serve with support for expenses, but no salary, for two years. His idea was modeled on the approach of the Church of Jesus Christ of Latter Day Saints which requires such service of all young males. It was agreed a goal of recruiting 5,000 volunteers would be added to the BMT goals at the convention and Carter would address the messengers via videotape encouraging the program. He became the first president of the U.S. to address the SBC and promised to support personally a volunteer for two years.

It seemed an idea whose time had come. In 1975, the four primary mission agencies of the convention had organized Volunteers in Missions, an effort to create interagency coordination of efforts in enlisting volunteers and develop a database of volunteers with a goal of documenting up to 100,000 volunteers.[9] When the convention met in 1977, it approved a new set of goals for BMT that included doubling the number of appointed missionaries to 5,000, enlisting 5,000 volunteers for missions, and doubling Cooperative Program receipts to $300 million dollars, all by 1982.

---

[9]Bunch, "Mission Service Corps History," 2.

The effects of BMT were electric at the Kansas City convention for many of the messengers in the room. Daniel Vestal was one such person. He describes the effect of this dramatic mission emphasis on him:

> That was the pivotal convention for me. I was a young pastor, thirty-two years old. I had gone to First Baptist, Midland, Texas in May 1976. So, in 1977, I went to the SBC. Jimmy Carter spoke about BMT and MSC. The convention acted, and I stood on the floor of the Convention and wept. And I said, "I can give my life to this." Now, I look back and realize that BMT had a lot of naïveté about it, maybe even some triumphalism. But . . . that captured my imagination and my heart. I went back to First Baptist and led the church to continue to increase it's giving to the Cooperative Program. We led the SBC in cooperative giving for ten years.
>
> We initially moved thirty percent of our giving to the Cooperative Program. Soon we were giving $1 million or more each year. We didn't do that to be number one. We didn't do that to be noticed. We did that out of a belief that we could do more together in missions than we could by ourselves. And, when I left First Baptist Midland, we were giving forty-four percent of our budget to missions, thirty percent through the Cooperative Program, and fourteen more percent to direct involvement.[10]

Allen was nominated at the convention by Edwin Young, then pastor of the First Baptist Church in Columbia, S.C. Jimmy had Ed preach a revival in San Antonio, and Young was a "rising star" on the preaching circuit at the time. Interestingly, Ed Young moved to Second Baptist Church in Houston, became involved in the "conservative resurgence" movement after 1979, and served two terms as SBC president. Also nominated were Richard Jackson, pastor of the North Phoenix Baptist Church and close friend of Allen. Jackson had committed his support to Allen prior to the convention, but then was nominated himself, along with Dotson M. Nelson of Birmingham, Warren C. Hultgren of Tulsa, Oklahoma, and Clifton W. Brannon of Longview, Texas. The "conservative" standard bearer was Jerry Vines, then pastor of the Dauphin Way Baptist Church in Mobile, Alabama. After the first ballot Vines and Allen were in a runoff and Allen won by a vote of 5,100 to 2,300. Allen credits the providence of God with his election. He recalled:

---

[10]Daniel Vestal, interview with Larry L. McSwain, Atlanta, 16 July 2008, 1.

The thing that sealed it for me was when I sat there and they had the opening of the service before the nomination, they had the opening worship time. And they flashed on the board the scripture of the day which was John 15:16 "Ye have not chosen me, but I have chosen you and ordained you that you go and bring forth fruit. And that fruit abide, and whatsoever you shall ask in my name, I will give you."

You will find it on the wall in my office. It is has been the theme of my life. It was given to me as a theme back when I was in seminary and pastoring at Will's Point in a time of crisis that came to me and became the scripture that I write into the Bibles as I sign Bibles for children.

And when it flashed on the wall I was sitting there with Wanda and I had this sense of "Ahha" you know? . . . And I told Wanda, that we need to go to the room, we have a job to do. So, we went over to the room we had a prayer time together as the votes were being counted. And we were over there in the room. They called to say it is a run-off "between you and Jerry Vines." I didn't go over to the second session to even vote. I just stayed there and waited and sure enough, I won. And so, that was how I became president of the Southern Baptist Convention.[11]

Year One

Allen thrust himself with his usual intensity into the planning for the SBC meeting in Atlanta, Georgia in 1978 where he would preside. In a press conference at Kansas City following his election, Allen identified himself clearly as a "conservative theologically and a progressive on social issues" with a traditional SBC position (at that time) of opposition to abortion on demand with support for therapeutic abortions, opposition to homosexual behavior, but "concern and compassion" toward them, and "increased opportunities" for women. He also defended Jimmy Carter's brief televised message to the messengers of the 1977 convention in support of BMT as the voice of a churchman declaring his Christian commitment rather than a politician violating the separation of church and state.[12] He became increasingly visible as a spokesperson for a host of issues and the pace of his speaking to agencies and conventions increased even more.

---

[11]Jimmy Allen, "President of the SBC," interview no. 6 with Larry L. McSwain, Cumming GA, 20 September 2005, 124.
[12]Bill Kenyon, "New President Feels Baptist Faith Maturing," *Dallas Morning News*, 16 June 1977, 12A.

Allen embraced the goals of BMT enthusiastically as the newly elected president. Ever aggressive, his first task was to meet with Porter Routh, the executive secretary of the Executive Committee of the SBC.

> Early on I had a visit, right after my election, with Porter Ruth, who did, I think, to every president the same thing. . . . I went to Nashville and he came in and we visited and he says, "You know, the constitution of the Southern Baptist Convention says that the task of the president is simply to preside over the annual meeting and to appoint the members of the committees."
>
> And I said, "Well, Porter, I am sure that is what the constitution says. I haven't read it, but I am sure that is what it says. And at one time in Southern Baptist life that was probably a very good description, but you know, the president of the Convention is the only man in the country who is elected by the total constituency. We have an annual meeting and there is only one person elected to be leader at that time in the total constituency. Therefore, he has to listen to the folks that elected him. And the mandate of this convention is BMT. And therefore, I plan to do what the mandate says. I am going to go help the Convention do what they voted to do."
>
> And so he just kind of stuttered and that was basically the meeting. He gave me the stuff he had. Anyway, it was an interesting kind of reaction, and it was the pattern of our relationship the whole two years. I felt freedom to be the president and he felt freedom not to like it. . . . I became an ex-officio member of all the boards because of the way things worked. So I went to the meetings. I was, as Bill Pinson once introduced me to say, "Our president is not omniscient. He doesn't know everything. He is not all-powerful. He is not omnipotent, but he may be omnipresent."[13]

Allen's travel schedule became legendary among the press during his two-year leadership. One frequently repeated joke among them was. "Do you know the definition of frustration?" The answer: "It is Jimmy Allen looking up at an airplane in the sky and bemoaning the fact he is not on it."

Mission Service Corps. During that summer he called together two staff members from each of the key denominational agencies—Brotherhood Commission, Women's Missionary Union, Sunday School Board, Foreign Mission Board, and the Home Mission Board—to work on implementation of Volunteers in Mission goals. The group set forth a support budget of $7,800 per year for each volunteer. Any congregation could authorize the volunteer and a background check would be done by the agencies with the

---

[13] Allen, "President of the SBC," 130.

HMB certifying volunteers in the U.S. and the FMB doing so for overseas volunteers. That brainstorming meeting also came up with the idea of the name of the program as Mission Service Corps modeled after the language of the Peace Corps.

Soon the publicity mechanisms of the denomination were at work advertising the new program and providing information in as many publications as possible. Allen's former BGCT colleague and friend, Jim Newton, published a special foldout on the program as editor of *World Mission Journal*. Thousands of copies were printed and circulated in the December 1977 issue as well as many other denominational publications.

David T. Bunch was employed 1 January 1978 by the HMB to establish a denominational system matching volunteers with mission opportunities, tracking money given to support the effort, and publishing resources for supervision volunteers. A film, "The Gift of Love" was produced for distribution as well a pamphlets and news articles.[14]

Allen pushed the agencies with more pressure than they appreciated at times. There are in his presidential files at the Southern Baptist History Library and Archives multiple letters communicating gifts received, individuals interested in the program, needs for volunteers, and cajoling of agencies to act quickly on specific persons. There are also some mildly reactive letters from agency personnel. In one particular letter from William Tanner, president of the HMB, dated 7 November 1977, he wrote, "I have one word of advise for you, my dear brother president, take time to let your soul catch up with your body and your mind and spirit to join each other. In other words, pace yourself well. You have much to offer, and hopefully many good years to contribute, so take care of yourself." Ironically, Allen has now outlived Tanner by several years.

The MSC group was aware of the difficulty of funding the program through the normal channels of denominational funding, so the idea emerged of a special fund-raising effort to support it. Allen and Owen Cooper accepted responsibility for putting together a fund-raising event that would involve President Carter to raise one million dollars for the effort. After meeting with Carter and securing his willingness to help with the effort, Allen sent monthly reports to the president detailing progress in the program. His reports included rather critical comments about the resistance

---

[14]Bunch, "MSC History," 7-9.

to the concept from some state convention executives as well as Porter Routh and his associate, Albert McClellen, at the SBC Executive Committee. But the plans continued to grow.

A meeting was scheduled at the Mayflower Hotel in Washington, D.C. on 2 May 1978. One hundred and six invitees attended the dinner. President Carter invited the attendees to a reception at the White House preceding the event and then spoke at the dinner. Russell Newport was enlisted to sing. Allen turned to his friend and church member, Patricia Ayers, to support the effort and she made the largest gift to it in the amount of $185,000. She gave a testimony at the event as to why she did that. A total of more than $750,000 was committed at the event and more followed to achieve the goal. It is not clear that the total amount was finally collect from the several multiyear pledges made. Among the gifts committed was a check in December 1978 from Rosalynn Carter in the amount of $3,500 to support one of the first appointees to Brazil.

Some controversy did follow the meeting. Jack Harwell, editor of the *Christian Index*, criticized it for its blurring the lines of church/state separation and functioning outside the financial plan of the SBC.[15] Allen was given space on the editorial page of the *Christian Index* the following month to defend the dinner.[16] What was likely not made public was the fact the White House reception cost $6,686.53, all of which was reimbursed with $3,000 gifts each from the FMB and the HMB. Allen and Cooper paid the additional $686.53 personally.

Allen was the recipient of generous support from a variety of friends for his many ventures beyond FBC, especially Patricia Ayers. Another helpful support couple were David and Gloria Smith, members of Trinity Baptist Church in San Antonio. Smith had sold his business inherited from his father and enjoyed flying his two-engine Piper aircraft. So Smith offered his services to fly Allen to many of his speaking engagements and denominational meetings at a personal cost of $50,000 annually.[17] On one of the flights with Smith and his wife, Allen suggested they become MSC volunteers. They accepted and were the first couple in the San Antonio area appointed in the program, with appointment by Trinity Baptist Church. A

---

[15]Jack Harwell, editorial, *Christian Index*, 25 May 1978, 2.
[16]Jimmy Allen, editorial, *Christian Index*, 15 June 1978, 2.
[17]John Rutledge, "Layman Acts as Pilot, Inspiration to Allen," *Baptist Standard*, 27 July 1977, 6.

host of persons across the country were appointed and a formal commissioning service was held for them at both the SBC in Atlanta in 1978 and in Houston in 1979. Twelve hundred people were appointed at the Houston convention and another 1,000 volunteered during a session preached by Billy Graham. Bunch reported in the first twenty-five years of the program, 7,862 adult volunteers were assigned through the HMB.[18]

The Atlanta Convention, 13-15 June 1978.[19] The Atlanta meeting of the SBC in 1978 was Allen's first opportunity to exert his influence in the shape of the convention. It was a convention that lived out his promises of greater inclusivity in appointments and programming. The most visible change in the nature of the convention was in the number of women who were involved in it. Jimmy appointed Marian Grant, the wife of the editor of the *Biblical Recorder*, Marse Grant, as chair of the Program Committee, the first (and last) women to serve in such a visible role. Fifteen women were appointed to the committees of the convention that year. Five more women had roles on the program, most significantly an address by Coretta Scott King and testimony by Ruth Bell Graham. Ethnic leaders were included as well, though not in large numbers given the newness of their participation in denominational life.

Jimmy's sermon to the Convention, "Where There Is Vision, The People Flourish" was an inspirational challenge for embracing BMT. He spoke of the source of the vision, its shape, steps toward accomplishment, and strength for fulfilling it. He challenged the messengers to capture the current moment as one in which God was stirring people to respond amid a confused, seeking, hurting, and hungry world. Allen also challenged the convention not to respond to the currents swirling within SBC that would become a vortex of change the next year. He encountered head-on the growing accusations of theological liberalism within the convention. Though he does not mention them by name, critics of seminaries and SBC

---

[18]Bunch, "MSC History,", 17.
[19]The information for this section is from *Annual of the Southern Baptist Convention*, Atlanta, Georgia, 13-15 June 1978.

agencies were publishing evidences of alleged liberalism within them.[20] He suggested:

> We don't have time or need to debate the authority and accuracy of the Bible. Our confused world does not need to be treated to the scene of Christians tearing at each others vitals over whether their beliefs are being described in just the right jargon. The urgency is for us to announce his word, explain his word, live his word, share his word. The Bible is true truth. While we are debating the various ways of describing our ammunition, the enemy is taking our world.
>
> ... But the basic problem about the Bible is not whether we agree on how to describe its authority, it is whether we trust its promise. Depend on its power enough to obey its command and to share its message. A confused world needs no theoretical explanations. It needs the one who is God's answer to man's need ... Jesus.[21]

Allen made a strong appeal for Southern Baptists to give generously to the efforts of the FMB to fund hunger relief. He suggested that if every Southern Baptist would give one dollar per week the board would have $676 million in a year for this effort. He announced an offering for World Hunger at the conclusion of the convention, and a little more than $14,000 was given.

On the surface it appeared Allen's approach was one reflective of a new progressivism in the largest denomination of the U.S. The 1978 SBC was a seminal moment in the history of the convention. It was the largest gathering in Convention history to that time, with 22,903 messengers registered. One major flurry of controversy broke out during the week when 2,000 gay activists marched through the streets of Atlanta to the Georgia World Congress Center to protest the appearance of Anita Bryant before the SBC Pastor's Conference, chaired by Bailey Smith. The 20,000 in attendance at the Pastor's Conference cheered loudly as she sang "The Battle Hymn of the Republic." Bryant was a former Miss America who led

---

[20]The SBC controversy has been addressed adequately in other sources. Within months of the convention meeting, Harold Lindsell, *The Battle for the Bible* (Grand Rapids MI: Zondervan Publishing Co., 1978) was published, and quotations from multiple writings of seminary and agency personnel were being circulated by Judge Paul Pressler.

[21]Jimmy Allen, "Where There Is a Vision, the People Flourish," sermon to the Southern Baptist Convention, Atlanta, 13 June 1978.

a grassroots campaign for a special election in Miami, Florida to repeal a municipal law prohibiting discrimination in employment and housing against homosexuals. Her efforts had brought national media attention to her and she came to Atlanta to be nominated for first vice-president of the convention. But the enthusiasm was not translated into votes. She was defeated overwhelmingly by Doug Watterson, pastor of First Baptist Church in Knoxville, Tennessee and a close friend of Jimmy. Later in the convention a resolution commending her stance on the issue of homosexuality was passed. Another Allen friend, William L. Self, pastor of Wieuca Road Baptist Church in Atlanta, was elected second vice-president.

The postwar mission synthesis within the SBC reigned supreme. That synthesis was shaped by traditional pastoral leadership with a conservative theology, passionate emphasis on unity through missions rather than theology, and growing participation in an emphasis on the relevance of the gospel to the social agendas of the larger economic and political landscape. The machinery of the convention was revised with a major modification of the bylaws and procedures with little discussion. Dramatic BMT Goals for 1979–1982 were adopted. Agencies reported their activities with little opposition or questioning. Leaders of the traditional synthesis were elected to leadership roles as officers with ease. Allen was reelected to a second term as president by acclamation. Mission programs were well attended and focused on BMT. Personal testimonies featured diverse voices with a more profound feminine touch. Coretta Scott King, the widow of Martin Luther King, Jr., spoke in place of his father who had to withdraw from a previously confirmed commitment to speak. Elton Trueblood, the noted Quaker philosopher-theologian, and Ruth Bell Graham, wife of Billy Graham, participated in a panel of speakers on the family. Jesse Fletcher, president of Hardin-Simmons University in Abilene, Texas, and well-known mission leader, preached the convention sermon.

The 1978 convention marked a significant high point in the influence of the Christian Life Commission of the SBC as well. Harry Hollis, a member of the CLC staff, presented a major report on "Morality in Television— A Plan for Action." The CLC presented as a part of its agency report a "Declaration of Human Rights." It was a thoughtful, biblically based statement affirming global political action within the framework of the United Nations' Universal Declaration of Human Rights. In all, twenty-two resolutions were passed by the convention and most of those with substance were introduced or guided by the staff of the CLC. They included positive statements on racism; opposition to pornography; a reaffirmation of previous resolutions on abortion recognizing its appropriateness in cases of rape, incest, or threat to the life of the mother; concern about global terrorism; the need for economic responsibility in the form of responsible government spending; opposition to tuition tax credits; support for religious liberty in Israel; and previous Convention resolutions on the use of alcohol. The tenor of the Convention seemed to convey ease in the Southern Baptist Zion!

An intended highlight of the Convention was an address by President Jimmy Carter to a postconvention meeting of the Brotherhood Commission. Glendon McCullough reserved space for 16,000 people at a breakfast where Carter would speak. When the sale of expensive tickets for $12.50 lagged, event planners scrambled to fill the room with an effort to recruit members from Atlanta area churches to attend. McCullough attributed the low sales to the predominance of pastors and denominational leaders with only seventeen percent of the messengers at the convention being laity. Others suggested Carter's negotiation of a controversial treaty ceding the Panama Canal to Panama diminished his popularity with his own Baptist family. Carter was enroute to Panama to sign the treaty when he stopped in Atlanta for the speech. A more practical explanation was likely the fatigue of the messengers after three days of meeting and the limits of expense accounts to pay for another day of activities.[22]

Carter seemed unconcerned about the crowd of 6,000 when he spoke to the assembled group, joking,

> "I understand Glendon McCullough was trying to finance a cooperative program [referring to the breakfast ticket prices]. This may have worked with Episcopalians and other wealthy people but Baptists have a limit on what they can contribute toward breakfast. Perhaps, if he had asked Anita Bryant this morning there may have [been] some more success." Carter proceeded to link his service as president of the U.S. to his faith and BMT. "Politics is not unsavory. It's not degrading. It's not something of which we need to be ashamed. In my acceptance speech at the Democratic convention almost two years ago, I said that I wanted an opportunity to translate, aggressively translate, love into simple justice. Well, that's my chance as one individual, no better than you, to adopt a bold mission. All of us in this room, in our own special way are influential and, we know that Christ said that unto whosoever

---

[22]Louis Moore, "Baptists Trying to Find Crowd for Carter Speech," *Houston Chronicle*, 14 June 1978, 2, 1.

much is given, much will be required, and to whom men commit much, they will demand more."[23]

He commended the Convention on its "Declaration on Human Rights" and urged action on it as well as defended the approval of the Panama Canal treaty in the U.S. Senate as members of the Revolutionary Communist Youth Brigade displayed an anti-U.S. banner during the speech.

But there were signs of impending change, a change that would assert its full force the following year at the annual meeting in Houston, Texas. When the obligatory reaffirmation of the Baptist Faith and Message (1963) statement on the Bible was offered as a resolution, messenger Broadus Moody (S.C.) moved to amend it:

> Be it further *Resolved*, that the Southern Baptist Convention, meeting in Atlanta, Georgia, June 15, 1978, go on record as clarifying our belief that the Bible is infallible, inerrant, verbally inspired Word of God as recorded in its original manuscripts.

The amendment failed. But Jimmy Allen's presidential sermon had fallen on deaf ears for some in the room. Within a year fissures in the traditional synthesis of Convention leadership would appear. Those fissures would lead to a major crack that would break open the unity of the SBC and inaugurate a transformation of the denomination into a new entity.

Year Two

The first action of the reelected president of the SBC following the intensity of the Atlanta convention was to take a month-long vacation. One of the affects of his lifestyle was extended absences from his family, a reality he spoke of with regret through much of his later life. He did, however, attempt to make up for those periods with extended family vacations and periodic trips which included occasional cruises to the Middle East and other venues. After returning to San Antonia, it was full-speed ahead.

Jimmy Allen was now, more than ever, a national figure. Invitations flowed into his office to speak, to comment on issues both denominational and those affecting national social and political issues, and to participate in more meetings than one human could manage. The local media in San Antonio praised his election and leadership. The *New York Times*, the

---

[23]"Carter's Text: 'I Want Our Country to Be Strong,' " *Atlanta Journal Constitution*, 17 June 1978, A5.

Washington Post and other national media quoted his responses to critical issues. He travelled internationally to mission settings where he preached and met an increasing array of Baptist leaders around the world. He was a man upon whom the tug of involvement was monumental. Never one to shirk either travel or involvement, life for him became more hectic than ever before. Allen was absent from his church more frequently, but managed to be in San Antonio on most Wednesdays and Sundays. He met with the staff on Wednesday, visited people in the hospital, and spoke to the congregation on Wednesday night. Telephone contact with the staff members was regular, even from distant places of the world. The staff carried increasing responsibilities for the work of the church and the church seemed to manage well his external involvements. He made every effort to be in his home pulpit on Sundays and often put the final touches on his sermons in the early morning hours of Sunday after reading and thinking about them on his latest airplane trip.

Allen and the Carter White House. Jimmy Allen first met Jimmy Carter as he campaigned for the U.S. presidency in San Antonio in 1976. He became more personally involved with him as SBC president. Ironically, Jimmy's first act as the newly elected SBC president in 1977 was to oppose publicly Carter's appointment of an envoy to the Vatican. In spite of his criticism, it never seemed to strain their relationship, one that has developed into an endearing and lifelong friendship.

Jimmy became a strong defender of the president and his policies. By Allen's second term as SBC president, the White House was gearing up for a second term campaign and he was contacted for support and assistance more frequently. He was enlisted to raise funds for the campaign and invited to attend several events at the White House. He was now on the national platform of religious leaders who were involved in both private conversations and public events in Washington, D.C.

His most visible support for Carter was for his efforts to negotiate peace in the Middle East. If there is a highlight of the Carter presidency, it was the successful negotiations between Israeli Prime Minister Menachem Begin and Egyptian President Anwar Sadat to conclude a treaty of peace between their nations. The framework for that treaty was the now-famous Camp David Accords, developed by the three leaders between 5 to 17 September 1978. Allen joined other national religious leaders in calling the nation to prayer for the success of the accords. When the treaty was signed formally, Jimmy Allen was among the invited guests on the south lawn of the White

House on 26 March 1979. He met with Carter in the oval office on that occasion as well as attended a formal state dinner that same evening celebrating the event.

Another of Carter's significant accomplishments was the negotiation with the Soviet Union for the release of five dissidents in exchange for commuting the convictions of two Russians agents of espionage. Among the five was Georgi Vins, a Baptist pastor from Kiev who was a part of the underground church movement in Russia. Vins had served eight years in prison and was under sentence for five more years of internal exile when Carter announced his release 27 April 1979. Vins was allowed to emigrate with his family to Canada or the U.S. The SBC had called for his release in a resolution passed at the 1976 convention.

Within two days of his release, Vins was worshipping with President Carter at the First Baptist Church in Washington, D.C. Pastor Charles Trentham and Olin Robison, president of Middlebury College in Vermont and a graduate of Baylor and Southwestern Seminary, had worked for his release and had met with members of his family in Kiev in the summer of 1978. With White House encouragement, Allen immediately joined Trentham and Robison to raise support and assist Vins in his adjustment to a new environment. Allen travelled to Vermont, met Vins, and invited him to address the SBC meeting in Houston.

Other events took Jimmy Allen to the White House. He participated in efforts to enlarge the funding for international aid and was invited to join the elite leadership of the nation at Camp David 6-11 July 1979 as Carter sought to develop responses to the energy crisis and malaise of feeling that swept the nation toward the end of his first term. Allen was among ten of the nation's religious leaders included in the list of 130 governmental, academic, and business leader attending the consultation. The ten religious leaders met with him the afternoon of 10 July. Carter addressed the nation with new promises of energy independence, new vision for the nation, and reorganization of his staff after the consultations.[24]

---

[24]"To Lift a Nation's Spirit," *Newsweek*, 23 July 1979, 20-30 and "Clerical Group Urges Americans to Support Carter 'Call to Action,' " *New York Times*, 17 July 1979, n.p.

The Houston Convention, 12-14 June 1979.[25] The 1979 SBC meeting was scheduled in the Summit in Houston, Texas. Allen continued his strong support for a visible presence from women in the convention. Five women either read Scripture or voiced prayers on the Convention platform. He appointed fourteen women to the three committees for which he had responsibility. None served as chair, however, as had been the case in Atlanta. James Pleitz, pastor at Park Cities Baptist Church in Dallas, was chair of the Committee on Order of Business and his dependable associate Luke Williams chaired the Committee on Committees. Allen's former mentor T. B. Maston opened the meeting in prayer.

But the mood of this convention was decidedly different from Atlanta. The Pastor's Conference had been ceded by the traditionalist leaders of the past to an emerging fundamentalist leadership of the largest Convention churches. The Pastor's Conference preceding the Houston Convention was a programmatic attack on the institutions of the Convention, most notably the seminaries. By the conclusion of the conference meeting, a full-blown plan for affecting the outcome of the Convention was revealed publicly. In an article on the polarization evident in the meeting, Paige Patterson, then president of the W. A. Criswell Institute for Biblical Study College in Dallas, documented an eighteen-month effort to organize messengers to attend the meeting to vote for a "conservative" president and approve a statement on the inerrancy of the Bible. Judge Paul Pressler, Civil Appeals Judge and long-time Houston resident, was his partner in the effort. Patterson admitted to organizing "captains" in thirty-three state conventions who in turn enlisted two to ninety assistants in each convention to recruit messengers to attend the meeting. Pressler secured access to four large skyboxes above the Summit from local friends and set up "caucus rooms" to guide the strategy of taking over the Convention.[26] The established leaders of the traditional SBC synthesis were blindsided. Allen reports his own mother was offered free hotel accommodations by the hotel clerk when she checked in, "'Judge Pressler will pay your hotel bill.' And she drew herself up to her 4 feet 11 inches and said, 'Do you know who I am?' She

---

[25]The details of this section, except where noted otherwise, are taken from *Annual of the Southern Baptist Convention*, Houston, Texas, 12-14 June 1979.

[26]Louis Moore and Tommy Miller, "Polarized Political Views Evident as Baptists Meet," *Houston Chronicle*, 12 June 1979, 1, 8.

said, 'No.' And she said, 'I am Jimmy Allen's mother and Judge Pressler will not pay my hotel bill tonight.'"[27]

The convention was constituted on Tuesday morning with 12,514 registered messengers. At the time for miscellaneous business, the intensity of the mood was immediately evident. Wayne Dehoney moved a reaffirmation of the Baptist Faith and Message statement on the Bible, which was challenged later in the meeting. Gene Anglin of Texas moved to amend the SBC Constitution requiring the rejection of the ordination of women by missionary appointees. By ballot vote, the motion carried by a 58.5 percent margin, but did not have the two-thirds majority required to amend the Constitution. Jimmy preached his presidential sermon on "Bold Mission Thrust: While It Is Yet Day. . . ." True to form, it was an inspirational challenge to embrace BMT. Allen drew from the text of the blind man in John 9:1-9 to describe the challenge of the darkness faced in the world, the choice of allowing God to transform through human agency, and an appeal to commitment "While it is yet day." His call to commitment was to both evangelism and to feeding the hungry and affirming human rights and religious liberty around the world. He appealed to the commitment to BMT as a priority above any other warning:

> As I perceive it, we are being pressed by good and sincere people right now to alter our agenda from Bold Mission Thrust. In this very crucial time of gathering momentum toward increased mission lives, increased mission giving, increased mission praying, some want to change our agenda from missions to orthodoxy. We must resist that temptation. We must remain a Bible-believing, Bible-sharing, Bible-obeying people committed to the lordship of Christ. The Bible says, "Go ye into all the world and preach the gospel to every creature." When Simon Peter suggested an alternative agenda to Jesus, he said, that the voice is the voice of a friend but the message is the message of the enemy.[28]

That stance earned Jimmy the title for many as the last moderate Baptist president of the SBC.

The major agenda of the Patterson-Pressler skybox caucus meetings was the election of Adrian Rogers as president. When the nominations were made that afternoon, six candidates were on the ballot: Ed Price (PA), A.

---

[27] Allen, "President of the SBC," 142.
[28] Jimmy Allen, "Bold Mission Thrust: While It Is Yet Day . . .," A sermon to the Southern Baptist Convention, Houston TX, 12 June 1979, 10.

Douglas Watterson (TN), Adrian Rogers (TN), Robert Naylor (TX), William Self (GA), and Abner V. McCall (TX). A total of 11,938 votes were cast with Adrian Rogers winning on the first ballot with 51.36 percent of the vote. The Patterson-Pressler caucus effort had won.

But the voting pattern changed after that seminal event. Hundreds of messengers who showed up for that vote disappeared! Most of the rest of the Convention's votes rejected the Patterson-Pressler influence. Abner McCall, retired president of Baylor University, was elected first vice president in a runoff with T. A. Patterson, father of Paige Patterson. Only 7,746 ballots were cast for that election. More than 4,000 messengers had left the room. By the time of the announcement of the runoff Tuesday evening and a second ballot, 5,336 ballots were cast. The ballot for second vice president brought a runoff between Harold Lindsay, Sr,, the nominator of Adrian Rogers and Don Touchton. Touchton won on the second ballot Wednesday morning with a 56.89 percent majority, with 2,879 votes.

The exodus of the caucus machine meant the remainder of the Convention was more similar in outcome to the Atlanta convention. Resolutions recommended by the Resolutions Committee were approved on domestic violence, support for the preservation of family farms, support for public education while recognizing the validity of church-related private schools, abstinence in use of alcohol, encouragement of reform of television media, support for alleviation of hunger, opposition to nuclear power plants, the vital work of peacemaking, efforts to alleviate inflation in the economy, and ministry outreach to migrant farmworkers.

There were continuing fireworks, however, on several issues. When the resolution on abortion was presented, supporting the "right of expectant mothers to the full range of medical services and personal counseling for the preservation of life and health," an obvious reference to therapeutic abortions, an amendment of the whole resolution was offered by Gary Tebbets (MO). When he moved for a "Constitutional amendment which would protect the personhood of all human life at all stages of development, whether born or unborn, and ensure every conceivable human being of his inalienable right of life and liberty." It failed, and the original resolution was approved. On Thursday, a resolution "On Gratitude for our Seminaries" was debated at length, but passed. When a resolution on the IRS investigation of tax-exempt schools that were not racially integrated was presented, a lengthy debate ensued. It was passed after amendment. The controversy created by the Patterson-Pressler caucus was also addressed in a resolution

"On Disavowing Political Activity in Selecting Officers" which passed. A motion was also approved directing the registration secretary to report any voting irregularities to the Executive Committee and needed action to the next SBC.

In spite of the controversies of the meeting, Allen's agenda of highlighting BMT was a major feature of the meeting. Goals extending BMT and incorporating MSC in the BMT process were approved. The Convention sermon was peached by William Hinson, pastor of First Baptist Church, New Orleans, Louisiana on "God's Great, Glad Day."

But the most significant event of the meeting was a missions rally in the Astrodome on Wednesday evening. Allen had spent months organizing the rally, reminiscent of his similar effort when president of the BGCT. The Home Mission Board and Foreign Mission Board made their reports to the estimated crowd of 50,000 people. New mission appointees were introduced including some 1,000 Mission Service Corps volunteers. The event was concluded with a message by Billy Graham, long-time friend of Allen. Allen had attended Graham's sixtieth birthday party in Charlotte, North Carolina the preceding month and was one of the many who praised the noted evangelist. When the invitation was given by Graham "to go where he wants you to go, and be what he wants you to be," more than 1,200 persons responded. Allen considers this rally the major achievement of his many years of leadership.

The final program of the week on Thursday evening proved to be a disappointment, however. The events of the preceding two days had exhausted both messengers and local church members alike. An embarrassingly small crowed showed up to hear an address from Georgi Vins, the Soviet dissident released from confinement only weeks before. Manuel Scott, famed African-American pastor from Los Angeles, preached to a handful of the faithful.

Allen's elected leadership came to an exhausting end. He and his family took a much-needed vacation in the mountains of the West for a month. He returned to a warm reception at First Baptist Church on 15 July and announced renewed efforts in leadership of the church, pledging a goal of doubling the membership of the church during his remaining tenure.

In reflection many years after the events of his dramatic leadership of a convention in change he commented on his legacy in that role:

> I think the opportunity that comes to you as president of the Southern Baptist Convention to deal outside of Southern Baptist life to represent what

you believe to be the best of the Baptist tradition is a tremendously exciting opportunity. I found myself in all kinds of places doing that thing, including speaking at Harvard and other places for Harvey Cox and trying to explain to secular-minded people who we are at our best.

I think it presents a tremendous opportunity that enriched my life and I am very glad about it. I sorrow when I see people missing that by becoming the captives to the people in power. It seems to be one of the things that I was glad I was able to do was to be with people in power without being either fooled about that, knowing the limitations that we have. I really felt gratified that God gave me enough self-awareness and God-awareness to be a conscience voice where I could be without being captured by the folks I was dealing with and I think that was the greatest challenge that I had to face.

People operate off the illusions of power. Nobody has power. They just think they have it. Or somebody else thinks they have it, and they operate. And I was able to do a lot of things with a lot of people without losing my compass and I think that is my greatest satisfaction.[29]

---

[29] Allen, "SBC President," 148-49.

Chapter 8
Ventures in International Relations

> Ethical acceptance of the world contains within itself an optimistic willing and hoping which can never be lost. It is, therefore, never afraid to face the dismal reality, and to see it as it really is.
> —Albert Schweitzer[1]

Service as the president of the Southern Baptist Convention brings with it automatic requests from many areas of the world for assistance and involvement. When one has the access of a Jimmy Allen to the president of the United States, the nature of those requests is even more significant. Appeals include requests for intervention with government agencies for individuals, assistance for individuals desiring immigration to the U.S., financial support for Christian organizations and individuals, and involvement in issues of moral and political importance. Jimmy became involved in two most-significant agendas of international concern during his active denominational leadership.

Religious Liberty in Israel

The issue of religious liberty in Israel arose during the first year of Allen's SBC presidency as the result of concerns about new legislation passed by the Knesset, Israel's parliament, in 1977. The law was introduced by Rabbi Yehudah Meir Abromowitz of the ultra-Orthodox Agudat Israel Party, passed on 27 December 1977, and scheduled to take effect 1 April 1978. The law "Penal Law Amendment (Enticement to Change Religion) Law, 5738," stated:

> 1. Whosoever gives or promises to a person money, money's worth or some other material benefit in order to induce him to change his religion or in order that he may induce another person to change his religion is liable to imprisonment for five years or a fine of 50,000 pounds.

> 2. Whosoever receives or agrees to receive money, money's worth or some other material benefit in return for a promise to change his religion or to cause another person to change his religion is liable to imprisonment for a term of three years or a fine of 30,000 pounds.

---

[1] Albert Schweitzer, *Out of My Life and Thought: An Autobiography*, trans. C. T. Campion (Repr.: New York: Holt, Rinehart & Winston, 1961 [1933]) 241.

The language of the law, especially the punishments to be levied under it, created an immediate outcry within the Christian community in Israel and among Christian missionaries in particular. Their concern was twofold: that certain benevolent mission activities such as social services and health care ministries could be interpreted by the government as inducements to conversion, and the law would give encouragement to radical Orthodox Jews to engage in acts of violence against Christians and their property. Reaction from the United Christian Council in Israel (UCCI), a group of Protestant leaders, including long-time SBC career missionary, Robert Lindsey, was immediate. In an emergency meeting of a committee of the council in January 1978, a telegram was drafted to Prime Minister Menachem Begin protesting the hasty passage of the law during the Christmas season and ignoring UCCI concerns about it.

Soon the anxiety of the missionary community in Israel spread to denominational offices in the U.S. They began immediate lobbying efforts with U.S. Jewish organizations. Within weeks, the pressure from the U.S. was bringing clarification from Israeli officials including a commitment from Shmuel Tamir, minister of justice, that "instructions have been given by the attorney general that no action or even inquiry be instituted by virtue of this law without the prior direct authorization of the attorney general in person or the state attorney in person."[2]

By the time the law took effect on 1 April 1978, the Baptist Joint Committee on Public Affairs (BJC), of which Allen was a board member, was organizing to address it. The board expressed concern about the law at its March 1978 meeting and began documenting public reaction and communicating with Jewish groups who were already announcing opposition to it. The UCCI continued to press its case with Israeli officials and documented instances of local police actions of harassment against a minister, Baruch Maoz, with no apparent knowledge by the police of the promised interpretations of the law. By 1 September 1978 the BJC had arranged for a meeting by a delegation with the Israeli ambassador in Washington, D.C., Simcha Dinitz. The meeting was attended by seven representatives of Baptist groups on the BJC board, including Allen and J. D. Hughey representing the FMB. Hughey reported in letters to SBC

---

[2]Transcript of a telephone transmittal from Shmuel Tamir to Richard Maass, president of the American Jewish Committee, 8 March 1978.

missionaries in Israel a most productive meeting, including commitments to clarify the law.

A week following this meeting, President Carter, President Anwar Sadat of Egypt, and Prime Minister Begin met for the historic exchange of diplomatic agreements known as the Camp David Accords. Allen was included in national religious leaders invited to call the nation to prayer for the success of this historic effort and to attend a formal ceremony of celebration at the White House on 18 September when Carter addressed the Congress to announce the results of the accords.

Meetings in Israel 1978–1979. Through the fall, 1978, the accounts of continuing concern for some formal change in the Israeli law on "anti-Missionary activities," as Christians characterized the law, continued. Allen planned a trip to Israel after Christmas. Wanda and their son Michael and Robert and Patricia Ayers and their children joined in the trip as well. Allen decided to take informal initiatives to meet with Israeli leaders on the religious liberty issues that had arisen. He made contact with his friend Congressman Jack Hightower, whose staff provided to him up-to-date names and backgrounds of the members of the Knesset and Israeli cabinet. Jimmy communicated with Robert Lindsey in Israel and made arrangements to meet with attorneys who could help him identify the legal issues. Rather than create the media attention of an announced visit as SBC president, he made informal contacts through friends in Jewish circles to meet with persons in Jerusalem while members of his tour group were visiting historic sites. Jimmy's visit occurred exactly one year after the passage of the offending Israeli law.

Allen's schedule of contacts included a mix of official meetings as a part of the tour of which he was a part and private meetings set up by the Ministry of Foreign Affairs. On 28 December 1978, his tour group attended a reception hosted by the president of Israel, Yitzhak Navon, for the heads of the Christian communities in Israel. Navon's published remarks affirmed the commitment of Israel to "freedom of religion, freedom of worship and free access to the holy places." The mayor of Jerusalem, Teddy Kollach, and Baptist missionary Robert Lindsey were also present.

Allen's most important visit was with the minister of justice, Shmuel Tamir, at his home some thirty miles from Jerusalem on 1 January 1979. Tamir had offered an interpretation of the law reported in the U.S. in March 1978 that limited an aggressive application of it in Israel. In conversation with Allen, he offered to engage in a process that would ensure a public record of that interpretation by setting up an official questioning in the Knesset by a member of another party of how it would be interpreted. He committed to mailing to Allen a copy of the Knesset process which he would initiate within two weeks. Israel has no constitution, and there was open discussion of the importance of one that would include a commitment to the United Nations Declaration on Human Rights. The meeting concluded with a cordial commitment to continuing correspondence.

Allen convinced his hosts in the Ministry of Justice that any process that did not include concurrence with this strategy from the originator of the original legislation would likely be met with resistance. Thus, he met in Tel Aviv on 3 January 1979 with David Glass, chair of the Knesset committee recommending the law to forbid enticements to change religion.

Glass was an orthodox Jew and somewhat antagonistic toward Allen at the beginning of their meeting. Allen recalls the tone of the conversation:

> And when I went into meet him, the first thing David said to me was, "Dr. Allen, I don't think there ought to be any Christian missionaries in Israel." And I said, "Well, David, we know now what we don't agree about. Let's see if there's anything we do agree about." [Laughter.] I said, "I can tell that you take God very seriously in your life." He said, "I do." I said, "We agree about that. I take God very seriously in my life. And I take it that you want everything that is done to be done in a way that God will be honored, and his reign will be forwarded." He said, "I do." I said, "We're together on that. I want that also. Now, our perception is different because I think there ought to be freedom for my faith and your faith to communicate its beliefs without the interference of law, and I know we don't agree on that. But I want to tell you how much I appreciate the fact that, in this political situation, you have agreed to allow this to happen." And so he said, "Well, I didn't do it because I wanted to, but I felt the situation would make that acceptable."[3]

Jimmy learned of Glass's plans to visit the U.S. in the spring of that year. He extended an invitation for him to visit in San Antonio, which Glass did; that visit is described later in this chapter.

A meeting was scheduled with Prime Minister Menachem Begin on the same day. Allen had arranged for a photographer to take pictures of the event and their discussion was cordial. It did not focus on the law issues at hand, but more generally on the Camp David process and the encourage-

---

[3]Jimmy Allen, "Israel and Iran", interview no. 7 with Larry L. McSwain, Big Canoe GA, 2 March 2006, 165-66.

ment of Southern Baptist support for Israel as a nation that valued freedom. It had been made clear to Allen that Begin had been briefed on the agreements from Tamir, but he did not want to discuss the law in question.

The remainder of his time in Israel was spent with more social visits with several hosts from the Ministry of Religious Affairs and participation in the activities of his tour group. He followed up with several who had assisted him with letters of appreciation for their help.

Fortunately, Jimmy dictated summaries of his conversations at the time. The most productive for his purposes were with David Glass and Shmuel Tamir. The minister of justice was true to his word to Allen. In a letter dated 24 January 1979, Allen received a five-page summary from Michael Pragai documenting Tamir's official response to Knesset questioning on 16 January 1979. He provided for the public record the statements circulated in the U.S. in March 1978, including the commitment,

> I can assure you that there is no intention whatsoever on the part of the Israeli Government to restrict in any way religious freedom of the Christian community or any other community in Israel or to impede them from the pursuit of normal educational or philanthropic activities.

Pragai provided further a copy of the Hebrew record translated into English noting,

> On January 1st, 1979 I met with Dr. Jimmy R. Allen, president of the Southern Baptist Convention in the United States. In response to his inquiry on that occasion, I likewise informed him of this stand of the Government of Israel.[4]

Allen was asked by the Israelis to disseminate broadly in the press the results of his visits. *Baptist Press* reported the essence of the Pragai letter and it was published in the Baptist state convention papers. The actions that followed seemed to reassure the Christian community in Israel and there seemed not to be further repercussions from the offending law. Correspondence from both Robert Lindsey from Israel and Baker James Cauthen, executive director of the FMB, offered strongly affirming appreciation for the outcome of this venture.

Meetings in Israel 1980. The successes of Allen's building personal relationships with Israeli leaders did not end with his first trip as SBC

---

[4]Letter from Michael Pragai, office of the Consulate General of Israel in New York, 24 January 1979, 5.

president. He followed his visit with letters of appreciation to every governmental official he met. Jimmy also extended an invitation to David Glass to visit San Antonio when he learned of his plans to visit the U.S. Allen remembers his comments to Glass, "What happens with so many people in Israel—they go and see the East Coast—you haven't seen the United States until you come to the heart of the United States, and I want to invite you to come be my guest. And I want to show you our version of Masada." I said, "I live and preach eight blocks from the Alamo. And I want you to come, and I want to show you the place where we drew a line in the dirt. People volunteered themselves to stay and die for what they believed." And he said, "I've heard of the Alamo." And I said, "Would you come?" And he said, "I will." So he came to San Antonio to be my guest.[5]

Glass did visit San Antonio. Allen discovered he would have to import a unique form of kosher food from New York to meet the dietary needs of the devout Orthodox man. During that visit Allen arranged for a visit to the ranch of his friend, Tom Martin, next to the famed King Ranch. He recalls:

> So I took him to the ranch, and Wanda went with us. . . . We went down in Dave Smith's airplane and landed there and toured the ranch. In the process of that particular flight, Glass asked, "Dr. Allen, would you come and testify to my committee on your belief that we ought to adopt the United Nations' statement on human rights?" And I said, "Well, David, I'd be glad to. If you want me to, I'll do that." He said, "I would like for you to. I'll write you a letter when I get home." And so, out of that visit to the ranch and the visit to San Antonio, he did indeed write and ask me if I would come and testify to his committee about why religious liberties are important and why they ought to protect it.[6]

Glass returned to Israel and issued an official invitation to Allen to testify before the Constitution, Law, and Justice Committee of the Knesset.

Allen went back to Israel in May 1980 to testify before the committee with funds provided from the FMB for his travel. A careful draft of his testimony was developed in consultation with Robert Lindsey and local attorneys. Both Lindsey and Herbert Kerrigan, a Scottish expert on international law, participated in the committee hearing as representatives

---

[5] Allen, "Israel and Iran," 181.
[6] Allen, "Israel and Iran," 182.

of the UCCI, as did Zwi Werblowsky, a Hebrew University professor and representative of the Israel Interfaith Committee.[7]

Jimmy provided printed copies of his testimony for the committee and shared them with others during his visit, including a second visit with Prime Minister Begin. It was a carefully presented summary of the identity of Baptists and their commitment to religious liberty, It included a clearly stated word of appreciation for the actions of the committee in the previous year in providing limits on the administration of the antibribery law. He encouraged the committee to embrace the concept of freedom of conscience in matters of religion, building specific safeguards into the law to ensure them, and offered language from international human rights declarations for their consideration. He provided texts of the United Nations Declaration on Universal Human Rights (1948) in articles 18 and 19 and the International Covenant on Civil and Political Rights (1966) in articles 18 and 19 on freedom of thought and religion. Allen concluded his testimony with a strong word of caution about specific language before the committee that would deny free expression, "to prevent harming the values of morality or sacrilege against a religion." Though he did not say it overtly, he knew this language would allow a distinctive Jewish limitation on any religion deemed critical to that faith and would limit the freedom of Christian groups in Israel.[8]

It is difficult to assess the impact of Allen's ventures into Israeli politics. His visits actually raised the anxiety of some SBC missionaries in Israel that his visibility could bring reactions in the Knesset, resulting in more negative outcomes than the status quo. Some in the U.S. Jewish committee were encouraging a less accommodating reaction to the antibribery laws with insistence they be repealed entirely. Jimmy was convinced such was not a political possibility. So, true to his experience and realism, he was willing to settle for clarifications rather than repeal. The reality was that no attacks on Christians were reported nor were any arrests made in the aftermath of compromise on the law.

---

[7] Elizabeth F. Smith, "Religious Freedom Essential Allen Tells Israeli Committee," *Foreign Mission News*, 20 May 1980, 2.

[8] "Testimony of Dr. Jimmy R. Allen, President of Radio and Television Commission of the Southern Baptist Convention, United Stated of America to Committee on Constitutional Law and Justice, Knessett [*sic*] of Israel, in Hearing on Proposed 'Basic Law: Rights of Man,' 19 May 1980."

The state of Israel has yet to approve a formal constitution. Though such was promised within months of the founding of the state in 1948, the inability of the religious leadership of the country to agree on language related to religion that will satisfy both secular and Orthodox Jews has stymied action. The Knesset has passed nine Basic Laws that provide the legal framework for the courts of the country; however, there is still no clear statement of religious liberty embodied in any of the Basic Laws, including the Basic Law: Rights of Man.

The Iranian Hostage Crisis

The seizure of the American Embassy in Tehran, Iran on 4 November 1979 by militant student advocates of the Iranian Islamic Revolution led by the Ayatollah Khomeini created the most serious crisis of the presidency of Jimmy Carter. It established a rift that continues between the governments of Iran and the United States to this day. Mark Bowden calls this event, in pejorative style, "the first battle in America's war against militant Islam."[9] It was a dangerous time as advocates for the use of force to free the hostages within the U.S. raised their voices with charges of weakness against Carter. When the president attempted a rescue effort that failed in catastrophe in the Iranian desert in April 1980,[10] the fate of his 1980 presidential reelection bid was sealed and the election of Ronald Reagan was assured. After that attempt, any diplomacy that would result in the freedom of the hostages during Carter's tenure was essentially doomed. More critically, tension between the two nations has not abated to a significant degree to this day.

While the focus of this chapter is on Jimmy Allen's personal involvement in the crisis, some attention to the background of the events preceding the crisis are in order. In reality, the hostage crisis was one of those mass movements of impetuous crowds for which governments have little control or easy response. Iran was engaged in a revolution in 1979 and revolutions can never be controlled. In the midst of that revolution of Islamic fervor that brought the Ayatollah Khomeini from exile in Europe to Iran and thrust the Shah of Iran out of the country, competing forces were at work to control

---

[9]Mark Bowden, *Guests of the Ayatollah: The First Battle in America's War with Militant Islam* (New York: Atlantic Monthly Press, 2006) 4.
[10]Mark Bowden, "The Desert One Debacle," *Atlantic Monthly* 296 (May 2006): 62-77, documents the venture in detail.

the future of the country. But the one unifying force for the people was the collective hatred for the twenty-six-year reign of Pahlavi, the Shah of Iran, and his dreaded Iranian security forces SAVAK. Bowden says of the revolution:

> Iran's revolution wasn't just a localized power struggle; it had tapped a subterranean ocean of Islamic outrage. For half a century the tradition-bound peoples of the Middle and Near East, owning most of the world's oil resources, had been regarded as little more than valuable pawns in a worldwide competition between capitalist democracy and communist dictatorship. In the Arab states, the United States had thrown its weight behind conservative Sunni regimes, and in Iran behind Pahlavi, who stood as a bulwark against Soviet expansion in the region. . . . the Cold War would determine the shape of the world; all other perspectives, those from the so-called Third World, were irrelevant, or important only insofar as they influenced the primary struggle.[11]

Jimmy Carter's emphasis on human rights as president became the nemesis of his ability to manage negotiations during the hostage crises. The disconnect between his stated policy and the Carter administration's support of the Shah as an exile after Khomeini's return in February 1979 only incensed the revolutionaries. It gave them a cause for widening their political support among the Iranian people. When Carter allowed the Shah to enter the country temporarily on 19 October 1979 for emergency medical treatment, it created a demand from the Iranians for his extradition to Tehran, an action the U.S. could not take. Thus, Carter became the symbol for the revolutionaries of American imperialism and support for the injustices and violence of the Shah toward the Iranian people.

Revolutionary students began organizing what they considered a short-term occupation of the American Embassy in Tehran. No more than sixty students, many of whom had studied in the U.S., organized and carried out the occupation event. Once the embassy was occupied and some sixty-four people within it became hostages, the political dynamics within Iran took over and no single group could negotiate their release.[12]

Jimmy Allen was in transition during the time of these events. He had completed his service as SBC president. Jimmy was in the process of

---

[11] Bowden, *Guests of the Ayatollah*, 4-5.
[12] Mark Bowden, "Among the Hostages Takers," *Atlantic Monthly* 294/5 (December 2004): 77-96, describes the takeover based on interviews with the hostage takers.

leaving San Antonio to assume the leadership of the Radio and Television Commission when he decided to engage in the riskiest venture in his ministry. It would also be the event that brought the most criticism from letters and commentary of his long career. Allen decided to become involved in efforts to communicate directly in Iran with revolutionary leaders and seek some opening that might bring resolution to the crisis. His friend and nation were in trouble and his calling to involvement would not let him ignore an opportunity.

From Prayer to Travel. Though his term of office as SBC president was complete, Jimmy Allen continued to receive multiple invitations for involvement in national moral and political issues. His name was especially on the list of more progressive leaders of mainline Protestantism. Plus, the new fundamentalist leadership of the SBC would have little interest in such groups or issues.

The impetus for his first involvement came from the Inter-Faith Coalition of Princeton University led by Methodist-Presbyterian chaplain William Kirby and SBC campus minister John Walsh. Both were convinced the religious community might have an impact on the religiously dominated Iranian regime in ways normal political processes might not. They organized a gathering of twenty-one religious leaders at the Statue of Liberty on 13 December 1979 to make video-taped appeals to the Ayatollah Khomeini for "safe release of the hostages, affirmation of the principles of nonviolence and rejection of vengeance, and a just address of grievances."[13] Jimmy Allen was one of the twenty-one participants along with others from Episcopal, Methodist, Lutheran, Disciples of Christ, Roman Catholic, and Unitarian traditions.

As a part of the informal conversation of that meeting, the participants from Princeton University seemed to be the most knowledgeable of the resources for engaging in further dialogue. Citing the expertise of Richard Falk, one of the experts in Iranian culture and politics, Kirby and Walsh posed the possibility of a meeting with Khomeini on Christmas day. Allen recalls the conversation:

> That was an Islamic practice to have exchange visits between Christian leaders and Islamic leaders on the Feast of Ramadan and the Jesus-Mary day

---

[13]"Bishop Allin Press Faith Appeal to Iran," *Diocesan Press Service*, 20 December 1979, 2.

of Christmas. And so the idea emerged as to whether or not a group could go over to do a conversation with the Islamic leaders about the situation with the hostages . . . both to establish any kind of positive relational communication and also to discern what was happening.[14]

Allen made no commitment to such a trip but did agree to pray about it and be open to the possibility. Within days, John Walsh called him to propose the group meet with Iranian leaders in Washington, D.C. and to be prepared to travel to Tehran if the meeting were productive. With little advanced preparation, "I decided that I would be ready to go. I felt a very strong impression that it was the leadership of the Spirit, an opportunity that might be often misunderstood, but there was a conviction that God was leading in the process."[15] Allen secured a commitment from friends for private funding of the trip as well as support for three other group members. Since it was the week before Christmas, Allen arranged for James Dunn to preach at First Baptist, San Antonio in his absence; called the chair of the deacons at the church to inform him of his plans; and notified the chair of the RTVC to prepare him for the possibilities of negative reactions.

Allen had cleared the possibilities of his travel with the State Department and informed the White House of his plans without any official support from either. He was given the name of the Iranian desk specialist at the State Department, Henry Precht.

Seven people assembled at the Iranian Embassy for discussions about a possible trip with the Iranian Charge d'Affairs Ali Agah and Mansour Farhand, U.N. Representative of Iran. In addition to Allen, the group included:

The Rev. Charles A. Cesaretti, assistant to the presiding bishop of the Episcopal Church, New York.

The Rev. Charles Anthony Kimball, Ph.D., student at the Center for the Study of World Religions at Harvard University, graduate of Southern Baptist Theological Seminary, and a specialist in Islamic studies.

The Rev. Dr. William K. Kirby, Chaplain to Students, Princeton University with extensive involvement in civil rights issues.

---

[14]Jimmy Allen, interview no. 1 with Robert M. Parham, Baylor University Program for Oral History, Radio and Television Commission, Ft. Worth TX, 24 June 1983, 4.
[15]Allen, interview no. 1 with Robert M. Parham, 5.

Dr. Thomas M. Ricks, assistant professor of Middle East History, Georgetown University, with a Ph.D. in Middle East History, and a former Peace Corps volunteer in Iran. Ricks was fluent in Farsi.

The Rev. John Walsh, Protestant Minister/Chaplain at Princeton University, graduate of Harvard Divinity School, social activist, and the third Southern Baptist on the trip.

The Rev. Dr. C. Dale White, bishop of the United Methodist Church in Princeton, New Jersey with a Ph.D. from Boston University and a national leader in Methodist social causes.

The meeting with the Iranian diplomats gave them the assurance their visit would be received openly by the Minister of Foreign Affairs in Tehran Sadegh Ghotbzedeh. They were promised access without significant restrictions to gather facts about the situation in Iran, have access to key leaders of the country, and travel to visit places without restrictions. The group decided to depart for Iran the next day, 22 December 1979.

Allen had some advantages in the group in that he was a more nationally identifiable figure than the others, had a public identification with Jimmy Carter, and was experienced in relating to the press. So it was natural that he emerged as the public spokesperson within the group. He also tended to function somewhat independently at times. When he checked into his Washington hotel, he notified the State Department of his plans and Henry Precht requested he come to his office. When Allen refused in order not to become compromised as a government representative, Precht came to Allen's hotel, though angry about it. There he briefed Allen on what knowledge the government had as to the hostage situation and gave him a copy of the names of the people the department believed were in the Embassy. Jimmy never told his colleagues he had such a list but hoped to be able to confirm its accuracy. None of the group was ever given access to the hostages, so the names could not be confirmed. Interestingly, the list given Allen had every name that was a hostage at the time of their visit, with two names spelled incorrectly.[16]

Allen reported to the BJC the intentions of the group in general terms and a press release was written by Stan Hastey about the trip as a hope, "to explore in depth the implications of our mutual commitments to justice and

---

[16] A list of the hostages, those who were released early, those smuggled out of Iran through other embassies, and the eight servicemen who lost their lives in the Iranian desert is available in Bowden, *Guests of the Ayatollah*, 639-41.

to explore means of dealing with the release of the hostages." A written statement was released to the press by the group at Kennedy airport prior to their departure and again upon their arrival in Tehran on Christmas eve, where they also indicated no more press releases would be offered until their two-week visit was concluded.

Activities in Iran. The seven unofficial representatives of religious America departed from Kennedy airport in New York on 22 December 1979. They left with little expectation of meeting the hostages. Another group of clergy was afforded that opportunity. William Sloan Coffin, pastor of Riverside Church in New York; Rev. William Howard, African-American Baptist pastor and president of the National Council of Churches; and Bishop Thomas Gumbleton, an activist Roman Catholic from Detroit were granted the opportunity of leading in Christmas worship with the hostages in the American Embassy.[17]

The Princeton-inspired group had a different agenda—to meet with the Ayatollah Khomeini in hopes he would relent on religious and humanitarian grounds. They flew to Athens for a day layover to recover from jet lag and plan their strategy. A full day was spent with Tom Ricks reviewing the culture and discussing possible scenarios of strategy for arranging meetings with various officials. The group concluded they would make both group visits to a variety of venues as well as individual ones, with each person free to explore wherever each wished.

The group agreed with Ricks' suggestion that the first visit would be to the poorest neighborhoods of the city of Tehran, rather than the cosmopolitan developments of the Shah. They visited the Behesht Zahra cemetery where multiple martyrs of the Iranian revolution were buried.[18] That act was

---

[17]Mark Bowden, "Captivity Pageant," *Atlantic Monthly*, 295 (December 2005) <www.theatlantic.com/doc/200512/december-1979/3> (accessed 18 April 2008) describes the event in rather critical terms. Most of the hostages felt the group was giving propaganda advantage to their captors, especially Coffin, and none more than Bruce Laingen, the U.S. Chargé d' affaires, held at the Iranian Foreign Ministry with two of his staff. The clergy met with the three diplomats for several hours after meeting with the hostage captors.

[18]Charles A. Kimball, "Listening to the Voices of Iran," *Boston Sunday Globe*, 27 January 1980, A4; "Perspective: Mission to Iran," *Harvard Divinity Bulletin* (December-January 1980): 15-16; and "Iran's Agony—An Eyewitness Report," *Inquiry Magazine* 3/6 (3 March 1980): 6-8, provide details of the visit.

noted in the local press and opened doors to others because of the sympathy being shown.

When the group checked into the Hotel Intercontinental, they discovered it was the center of the American press, including ABC, NBC, and CBS. Wanting to avoid the press, they moved the next day to the Tehran Kings hotel. One of the unexplained aspects of the whole crisis was the seeming access of the American press to Tehran with evident confusion from the U.S. government in securing meaningful information. Bowden reported that

> dozens of American journalists moved freely in Tehran, scrambling to get access to the compound and the captives. ABC's Peter Jennings was among them, wandering the streets to solicit the opinions of random Iranians and doing feature stories about postrevolutionary life . . . yet the United States government, by all appearances, was unable even to start a dialogue with the country's rulers.[19]

The critical day in Tehran was Christmas Day. The Ayatollah had released a Christmas Day message to Christians the day of their arrival, 24 December, which angered the group, especially Allen. It was an attack against the ringing of bells in the U.S. for the hostages, an effort Allen had suggested to President Carter after calls from friends in the church of Bruce Laingen. Allen recalls:

> As I read that I realized that this was a kind of thing that we had to respond to. There we came as Christian leaders, on a Christmas season, and into this troubled country trying to understand its revolution to deal with it. And here was a bold frontal attack on us and on what Christians stood for. So I told Tom Ricks that I felt strongly that we had to answer that.[20]

Jimmy wrote a first draft which the group edited. On Christmas day they went to the offices of Foreign Minister Sadegh Ghotbzedeh to seek an appointment with Khomeini. His deputy,

> told us that just cannot be done. People wait three months for an appointment with the Ayatollah. After a great deal of conversation, a couple of hours of it, we talked about various ways of doing it and the question emerged, 'Have you asked him?' Why don't you call Qom, which was seventy miles away, and ask him if he will see us today? So he went to the phone and called Qom, and came

---

[19] Bowden, *Guests of the Ayatollah*, 245.
[20] Allen, interview with Parham, 19.

back with a great shocked look on his face and said, "I don't understand it but you have an appointment with the Ayatollah Khomeini at 5:00 p.m. this afternoon."[21]

The logistics were nearly impossible as it was nearly noon, their statement had to be translated into Farsi, and traffic was a problem. In reality, they arrived at the house where he stayed after dark and two hours late. But the Ayatollah met them, heard their statement, and offered one of his own. Allen considers the meeting and the lateness providential because their television camera crews had left for the day. Otherwise their meeting would have been broadcast on Iranian television and interpreted to suit government propaganda. It was broadcast via radio, but with less impact.

The statement these pilgrims had written was read aloud after the Ayatollah had read it in the next room. He responded with summaries offered by a translator and copies of the translation made available later. Allen reflected on the visit:

> Actually it was important that the Ayatollah and this group meet, because it opened all of the doors in Iran. You know, once you have been to the cemetery, and once you have seen the Ayatollah, then you can see everybody else. There was never another closed door that we could find. . . . And it turned out that we were the only Americans to visit with the Ayatollah during the whole hostage crisis, except for a professor from California who was a Moslem convert who travelled back and forth all during the time because he was a friend of the Ayatollah.[22]

After the most-significant visit of the trip, the group moved increasingly into individual meetings in a variety of places. Visits were made to multiple governmental leaders, some of whom maintain leadership in Iran today. Another trip was made to Qom with a lengthy meeting with Ayatollah Shaiot-Madari, a competitor with Khomeini, for discussions of Shiite understandings of the role of the Ayatollahs in political activities.

Three other particular venues were important. One was a gathering of victims of torture under the Shah at the officer's club where unbelievable atrocities were described and injuries of some 1,500 persons were displayed. Allen and Kimball went to a meeting of Friday prayers led by the Ayatollah Husayn-ali Montazari where they discussed openly the process

---

[21] Allen, interview with Parham, 20.
[22] Allen, interview with Parham, 22-23.

the Iranians would have to follow to release the hostages. They were invited to be his guests at the prayer service to pray in whatever manner they were comfortable. Pictures of Allen praying seated between a standing rabbi from Mexico and a prone Kimball circulated in major international newspapers. Jerry Falwell circulated it in his magazine with headlines that Allen was praying toward Mecca and had converted to Islam. Allen received numerous letters of criticism for praying toward Mecca with Moslems, a charge he denied as he was not aware of the direction of his prayers. It was among the more controversial of his public actions in his ministry.

The third event was a visit to the captors of the hostages at the American Embassy. After being in Tehran a week, Ricks called the students and requested a visit. Only he and Allen were allowed to attend initially. A second visit with other members of the group also occurred. The two of them spent three hours in conversation with about thirty-five students, many of whom had studied in the U.S. Allen came away from the meeting feeling the major desire of the students was to have their story of the revolution told in the American media. He had some hope that a media presentation to the American people in exchange for the hostages could be negotiated and so wrote to President Carter after the trip.

The students initially agreed to allow a return visit, but then resisted. When Allen and others went to the foreign minister's office to seek a second opportunity for access, he was surprised to be greeted by a man working there named Sedek who had been in FBC, San Antonio. Allen met at least one other person in Tehran who called him by name, having been part of the international ministry of the church. Sedek was able to work out a second meeting at the embassy on the night before the group was to leave Tehran. The entire American group was allowed to meet with about twenty students. There was more informal conversation with small groups of the individuals. Unknown to Allen, Kimball and Walsh offered to remain with the hostages and take the place of two of them if the students would allow them to do so. The students rejected the offer, but "it was a very moving moment when John and Charles said that they would stay."[23]

On 3 January 1980, the group gathered at the Tehran airport to report to the press the results of their efforts. A written release was given, including a summary of their goals and the following conclusions:

---

[23] Allen, interview with Parham, 49.

> As we leave the country to return home we report successful results on our efforts. In some of them we feel fully satisfied with progress made. On others, including the hope of forward motion in the progress for releasing Americans held at the embassy we leave with sadness that more progress could not be made....
>
> We believe we have accomplished the task of understanding more vividly the aspirations and hope of the Iranian people as they seek freedom and justice through the Islamic revolution. It is essentially a religious revolution.... We have become convinced that no military solution for the crisis should be attempted.[24]

Each of the seven returned to their respective places of service to engage the issues within their own sense of appropriateness. Kimball wrote a series of personal reflections published in a variety of venues. Bishop White was aggressive in moving within the United Methodist Church to address the issue of injustices in Iran and seek denominational statements of support for justice and peaceful resolution of the crisis. Allen wrote a long letter on 8 January 1980 to the president encouraging a media presentation of the student grievances to the American public in exchange for concessions on the hostages. He also suggested having Andrew Young or Richard Falk at Princeton University serve as intermediaries with the Iranian students.[25]

One must ask the value of this venture and others like it. When asked by Robert Parham about the historical significance of the Iranian effort by clergy, Allen's response was clearly humble:

> I think it will be a barely noticeable footnote in Baptist history. I think it was—if we had been able by some miraculous bridge-building to be pivotal in getting the hostages out, it would have made a dramatic story that would be noted. I think as it is it will be a very unimportant footnote of one group of Baptist [sic] folk who tried to do something at one time in a moment of historical crisis.... I doubt that it will be interpreted as being significant. Most of the time peacemaking efforts are not awarded with recognition unless an accident of history puts them together in such a way as to make it an actually observable success in what you've done. And so if you do this sort of thing because you expect it either to be successful and be noticed, then you have the

---

[24]Unpublished press release from the files of Bishop C. Dale White.
[25]The text of the letter is read into Allen, interview with Parham, 53-57. A copy is also in Allen's personal files.

wrong motivation and it's not going to work. My feeling was that it was what God led me to do at that time. It was important for me to do it. . . . I think it will probably not be noticed by history.[26]

Allen's appraisal is pretty accurate in the scope of the Iranian story. As evidence, one can note Bowden's negative appraisal of both groups of clergy to visit Iran that Christmas in 1979. Of the group meeting with hostages, he wrote:

> There was a natural tendency of liberals like Coffin, Howard, and Gumbleton to see dramatic change and to see any revolutionary as ideological kin, but they needed to be careful in this case about who they were cozying up to. The world was a more complicated place than they imagined. A new form of totalitarianism was taking shape, a religious variation on an ugly twentieth-century theme.[27]

His only notice of the second group of which Allen was a part was a rather disparaging comment about their support for the demands from some in the group for the return of the Shah to Iran.[28]

Clearly, Jimmy Allen is no international diplomat. What was an important success in Israel in communicating the Christian witness for religious liberty was met with limited success in Iran. The hostages were not released as a result of the visit of Christians of conviction in a hostile environment. But they tried. And they tried at some personal risk in an unusually difficult environment.

If there is one quality that can be readily observed in Jimmy Allen, it is that he is a risk-taker. His conviction of the leadership of God in going to difficult places, whether to riot-torn Watts or Philadelphia, to engage the antagonists of religious conflict in Belfast, Ireland, or to encounter the symbol of revolutionary Iran, the Ayatollah Khomeini, Jimmy mustered the courage to live out his convictions that the gospel of Jesus Christ demands involvement from Jesus followers. How many of us would do likewise?

---

[26] Allen, interview with Parham, 57-58.
[27] Bowden, *Guests of the Ayatollah*, 278-79.
[28] Bowden, *Guests of the Ayatollah*, 289-90.

Chapter 9

Kingdom Communication in a Television Age

> This is a story only history will be able to tell. Jimmy Allen had a real vision for the use of media to proclaim the gospel. Jimmy was always a big thinker. He had great plans, great visions, big ideas. Of course, his ideas also had a very high financial cost.
>
> —Jim Newton[1]

Jimmy Allen was elected on 11 December 1979 to become president of the Radio and Television Commission of the Southern Baptist Convention (RTVC) on 15 January 1980. It was a logical move for him, though he declined initially the invitation to meet with the Search Committee. He had served First Baptist Church in San Antonio for twelve years and given leadership to every important elected leadership position in the denomination, as well as dominated the religious life of San Antonio with his voice and presence. There were more mountains to climb for him in that context but to give leadership to a national, denominational effort to implement a Bold Mission Strategy via television was a bigger one.

The move seemed equally providential for the RTVC. The commission grew from the work of a committee appointed at the 1938 annual meeting of the SBC in Richmond, Virginia to "explore the field of radio broadcasting as a possible medium for projecting the Baptist message."[2] The work of the committee expanded until it became the Radio Commission in 1946. Paul Stevens became its leader in 1953, led in renaming it the Radio and Television Commission, and moved it to new facilities in Ft. Worth, Texas in 1955.[3] After more than twenty-six years of leadership of the commission, Stevens resigned in March 1979 citing disagreements with trustees who demanded more overt evangelistic programming. Stevens' management style ruffled feelings of staff members as well. The Commission was producing "thirty-two radio and television shows heard in ten languages on 3,275 stations" at the time of his resignation.[4]

---

[1] Jim Newton, telephone interview with Larry L. McSwain," Atlanta, 2 July 2008, 3.
[2] Lucien Coleman, "The Southern Baptist Convention and the Media," *Review and Expositor* 81/1 (Winter 1984): 19.
[3] Coleman, "The Southern Baptist Convention and the Media," 19-22.
[4] Pat Gordon, "Tune in to Tranquility: Baptist Broadcasters See End to Rocky Road," *Dallas Morning News*, 13 July 1980, 4.

Jimmy Allen was an obvious choice to succeed Stevens. He was a successful pastor, visionary preacher, had developed skills in the use of media in his church, and had demonstrated his leadership within the denominational bureaucracy the previous two years. He also emerged as a primary spokesperson for Bold Mission Thrust (BMT), and the denomination seemed on track to continue its focus on its aggressive mission goals. What better person to give voice to the use of media for BMT?

The new president of the RTVC inherited a technically competent staff for its programming mission. It had developed a large collection of programs that provided suitable opportunities for communicating the gospel in the media marketplace. These included "Master-Control," a contemporary radio program; "JOT,' an animated cartoon series for children; "Country Crossroads," featuring Country and Western music with well-known performers; "The Human Dimension," a television drama/documentary series; "The Athletes," with personal testimonies by Christian athletes; "Listen," a contemporary television series; "Black Beat," a radio production focusing on issues for African-American listeners; and "Invitation to Life," televising evangelistic services from selected cities.[5]

Continuity and Discontinuity at the RTVC

Allen entered a culture at the RTVC that required the balancing skills of an acrobat to administer. His personality was one to stress creativity, new initiatives, inspirational strategies, and popular support for whatever venture he engaged. Yet, he accepted the call to a highly technical enterprise that emphasized production, timelines, programming, budgeting, and delivery of content through existing radio and television media that were tested and traditional. Among his first decisions was to employ three persons from San Antonio to whom he could delegate many of the administrative tasks of the agency while he worked on the broader strategies and public-relations aspects of the role he accepted. Luke Williams became executive vice president on the RTVC staff. Ron Dixon, a San Antonio advertizing and media consultant, was added as vice president for public relations, and Janice Brake moved to continue her role as his administrative assistant. He had three persons with whom he had worked and could delegate major administrative responsibilities with a minimum of adjustment.

---

[5]Coleman, "SBC and the Media," 23.

The program reports to the various trustee committees changed little through the years of Allen's leadership. The commission staff continued to work on many of the same programs with the same strategies as before Allen's arrival. Likewise, annual reports to the SBC continued to emphasize these programming efforts.[6] What was different were the reports from the president of the commission where the focus was on overarching new initiatives and strategies, developing financial resources, and optimistic reports of progress on the development of what became the ACTS Satellite Network. When possible, he infused his own personality into the program efforts with participation in a number of the established television venues where his pastoral and charismatic concerns were voiced for viewers. He also initiated several major special programs such as the broadcasts from China described below.

Allen began his usual process of learning all he could about the new industry of which he had become a leader. He became a board member of the National Cable and Television Association and met with leading entrepreneurs in the business—Ted Turner, John Malone, Pat Robertson, and others. He connected with the National Association of Broadcasters, which put him in contact with the leadership of the national television networks and existing denominational television ministries of the National Council of Churches, the Episcopal Church, and the United Methodist Church. Alliances were explored with a host of persons including the evangelical president of the Shopping Network, Tom Paxon, who visited his offices in Fort Worth. Soon he found himself serving as informal pastor to many in the industry, offering prayers at their meetings and visiting some in the hospital when ill. He worked cooperatively with a number of denominational entities as the networks tended to provide programming assistance to those denominations working together in their television efforts.

Within months of assuming his new office, Allen became increasingly aware of the changing landscape of the media marketplace. The RTVC was connected to the traditional "big three" network delivery systems for broadcasting their productions—NBC, CBS, and ABC. The "electronic church" was in its ascendency with the rise of "televangelists" who could

---

[6]Copies of both the board minutes and program reports are on file at the SBC Historical Library and Archives in Nashville.

appeal directly for financial support. Another significant factor at the time was the emergence of religious television personalities with growing television ministries financed by their viewers. This "electronic church" moved from network to cable television with the purchase of time through networks such as Pat Robertson's Christian Broadcasting Network (CBN), the PTL Network in North Carolina begun by Jim Bakker, or the emerging Trinity Broadcasting Network. The growing visibility of these strategies brought from SBC leaders suggestions for similar strategies for the denomination.

Local network affiliates were selling their prime-time slots to these entrepreneurs. The RTVC depended on free air time, but it was increasingly made available at times such as the middle of the night when few viewers or listeners were available. Some commission members were pushing for a more overt evangelistic approach to programming in the pattern of SBC evangelist James Robison, as well as for direct appeals for funding. This latter strategy Allen knew could not be sustained for a number of reasons.

First, he seemed philosophically committed to denominational support for the efforts of the commission. He stated repeatedly in public his opposition to direct appeals for funds, saying, "Solicitations on the air are turning people away from a clear shot at Jesus."[7] He repeatedly requested, with strong trustee support, annual percentage increases in Cooperative Program (CP) support far in excess of the growth of the revenue to the SBC. There is only one year of his presidency in which the denomination came forward with such support.

Second, he believed Baptist individuals would support private fund-raising efforts to support an effective BMT strategy. As will be seen, that did not prove to be the case at the levels required for success.

Finally, it is clear he understood the bureaucratic "warfare" that would be generated from the other agencies of the SBC if the RTVC had been successful in public media appeals for funding. Such would have required the approval of the SBC Executive Committee, an action few denominational observers believed possible.

The first year of his leadership of the RTVC was one of smooth transition in which he received high marks from most observers. He moved to assemble a staff and presented Luke Williams as his choice for executive

---

[7]Kenneth Woodward, with Jerry Buckley and Eloise Salholz. "If You Can't Beat 'Em . . . ," *Newsweek*. 9 February 1981, 103.

vice president at his first executive committee meeting 11 March 1980. At that meeting, the trustees also wrote off $298,038 in outstanding campaign pledges that were considered uncollectable. The slate was clean.

National Awards. Paul Stevens had developed a tradition of awarding an Abe Lincoln Award and other similar awards to outstanding media personalities who had contributed to the industry with integrity and values. A formal dinner was held in Ft. Worth for the honorees and positive attention was given to them through the press.

There was no Abe Lincoln Award ceremony on the docket for Allen's first year, but the commission chose to present President Jimmy Carter its Christian Service Award in the White House with trustees provided expenses to attend on 12 February 1980. The Abe Lincoln Awards were soon renewed with distinguished network leaders. The March 1982 recipient was NBC News Network Correspondent John Chancellor, with comedian Grady Nutt included as a part of the program. The 1983 recipient was Gene F. Jarkowski, president of the CBS Broadcast Group. In 1984, evangelical leader Charles Colson was the recipient of the Abe Lincoln Award, and a Distinguished Communication Medal was given to Bob Mulholland, the chief operating officer of NBC. The last notation found for these kinds of awards was in 1985 when Kurt Waldheim, General Secretary of the U.N. was awarded the Abe Lincoln Award; Charles Kuralt, popular ABC commentator spoke, and Walter Cronkite, the CBS newscaster, was given the Distinguished Communication Medal. Senator Mark Hatfield was awarded the Christian Service Award. By this time in the evolution of the commission's work, it was focused increasingly on cable delivery systems and budget constraints for such costly events were becoming evident.

Change in the Air. Allen presented John Scales as vice president for development with recommendations for extensive fund-raising activities in the future at the June 1980 board meeting. The board also requested a twelve-percent increase in CP funding from the SBC. An increase of 8.162 percent was received.

The emerging and most rapidly growing market for television was in cable television at that time. So Allen called together a "think tank" of artists, technicians, and denominational leaders for a brainstorming session at the Stagecoach Inn in Salado, Texas, 26-28 August 1980. Participants included such individuals as Bob Thornton and Bob Taylor from the RTVC; communications specialist Darrell Baergen from San Marcos Academy; artists Ragan Courtney and Cynthia Clawson; and others. From that meeting came the idea of a network they called the American Christian Television Network. In a later meeting with staff of the Sunday School Board, the idea of naming it ACTS, or the American Christian Television System, emerged. It had a biblically identifiable name. It was an idea of linking the programming resources of the commission with a network of local churches, associations, and conventions in a delivery system that would reach beyond the national networks into every local community of the nation through a cable system.[8] The idea consumed Jimmy for the remainder of his time at the commission.

A critical element for the creation of a network was access to a space satellite. Many avenues were explored for creating such a possibility, including Allen's first formal recommendation on the issue to the RTVC trustees. He recalls:

> We had to get a space in the sky. At that time, they (the industry) lost a satellite and the cost for satellite space was astronomical. We are talking in terms of one, two, or three million dollars a year. One guy looked at me and said he would sell us satellite space for eleven million dollars. Well, in my typical fashion I asked, "What else will we have to pay for?" I did not tell him we did not have eleven million dollars.[9]

At the September 1980 board meeting, the trustees approved a motion to authorize $5,050,000 to purchase space on Westar V, "if and when the money is in hand."[10]

Several program initiatives were begun. Radio programming continued to be the mainstay effort of the staff with 5,186 programs aired on 3,502 stations in 1980 and 6,494 programs on 4,153 broadcast stations in 1982–1983, the peak years. A Center for Communication Studies at Southwestern Seminary, the development of Spanish-language resources with the FMB and HMB, a Videotape Network to provide broadcast resources to denominational groups, and a toll-free telephone counseling service to

---

[8]Jimmy Allen, "President of the Radio and Television Commission, SBC," interview no. 7 with Larry L. McSwain, Big Canoe GA, 12 December 2005, 151-52.

[9]Allen, "President of the Radio and Television Commission, SBC," interview no. 7 with McSwain, 152-53.

[10]Minutes of the Radio and Television Commission Board of Trustees, Ft. Worth TX, 9 September 1980, 2.

support respondents to various broadcasts were begun.[11] But most of the energy involved a major shift in philosophy to develop a new delivery system that could be utilized by churches, associations, and denominational agencies.

The ACTS Satellite Network

Jimmy Allen's first years at the RTVC coincided with a new strategy by the Federal Communication Commission to enlarge the number of low and medium power television stations across the United States. By securing a license through bidding in the open marketplace, a television station capable of broadcasts within a ten to twenty-five mile radius could be built. Costs for a 100-watt station ranged from $50,000 to $80,000 and for a 1000-watt station up to $160,000.[12] Concurrent with this development, the number of commercial communications satellites was growing. Though expensive, by leasing space on a satellite, constructing a receiving dish in a local community and building a low-power television station, the commission could beam its programming to any community in the country. The structure of ACTS was designed to provide the consulting resources to local churches, associations, and state conventions to construct low-power stations, secure downlink satellite dishes for receiving commission programs, and initiate broadcasts of their own. The idea was for these local groups to bear the costs of the local resources and the commission would receive fees for use of the satellite and programming. As the network launched, the focus shifted away from locally owned television stations to commitments on local cable systems. The costs of the television concept was too much for the fledgling effort to bear, and the complexity of securing FCC license approvals for an adequate number of local stations proved problematic.

This approach was new territory for the RTVC. Such a new direction meant the decentralization of the television ministry of the denomination from a central production operation to the full range of Baptist organizations and people. Thus, enormous energy and significant budget were expended in the years 1982 and following providing training to groups

---

[11]Summary statistics, programming information, and budget information derived from *Annual of the Southern Baptist Convention* for the years 1980–1990.

[12]Coleman, "SBC and the Media," 25.

across the country, consulting with those seeking to establish local ACTS organizations, hosting an annual National Conference on Broadcast Ministries, and expanding its offering of programming to fill the growing hours of broadcast time on new media outlets. ACTS was launched at 4:00 p.m. on 15 May 1984 with press coverage across the country in secular,[13] industry,[14] and denominational outlets. By 1985, new television programs included "Life Today," a look at timely issues from a mission's perspective; "Lifestyle," with focus on issues of interest to women; and "Cope," a call-in counseling format that anticipated many of the current talk-show formats popular in the culture.[15]

The complexities of a national network called for new management structures indirectly connected to the RTVC. The first of these efforts was the incorporation of a nonprofit Texas corporation, ACTS, Inc. This new entity was designed to provide a network for the delivery of programs beyond the current outlets available to the commission. At the same time as this effort was being made, the Baptist Sunday School Board (BSSB), under the leadership of Grady Cothen, was launching BaptistNet, another effort to beam BSSB programs through satellites to churches, associations, and conventions. Both agencies were working together on cooperative satellite leasing arrangements. ACTS Inc.'s primary function was to secure FCC permits for construction of low-power television stations and manage programming from the Commission.

The RTVC authorized a "joint venture agreement" between ACTS, Inc. and the BSSB with a line of credit of up to $10 million from the board as the basis of its financial viability with the FCC.[16] The new entity was legal 8 January 1981. A contract was signed 2 February 1981 assigning to the RTVC all of the operational responsibilities of ACTS, Inc.

---

[13]Caroline E. Mayer, "Religious Broadcasters: Beyond Pray TV," *Washington Post*, 5 February 1984, F1, 8-9; Dalene Perrigo, "Christian TV Ready to Air in Anchorage," *Anchorage Times*, 7 January 1984, C8; and Jim Jones, "Baptist Network on Air with Wing 'n' Prayer," *Fort Worth Star-Telegram*, 16 May 1984, 13-14.

[14]Victor Livingston, "Acting on Faith: The Southern Baptist Convention Plans to Launch ACTS in May with an Evangelical Bent and a Funding Twist," *CableVision*, 30 January 1984, n.p.

[15]*Annual of the Southern Baptist Convention*, 1985, 227.

[16]"Motions for Implementing Baptist TV Network," Minutes of the Radio and Television Commission, 5 January 1981.

Progress was made in the first year of the entity. The RTVC trustees approved at its SBC Convention meeting in June 1981 the purchase of interim satellite time from fall 1982–February 1984 at a cost of $1,642,000. By fall of the same year the executive committee of the RTVC authorized the expenditure of $250,000–$300,000 for a partnership with Baylor University and Southwestern Seminary to implement a low-power television station in Fort Worth to be known as Channel 31. Given the political dynamics within Fort Worth, it appears the FCC license was never approved.

It would take nearly three and one-half years before all of the details of this new enterprise could become fully operational. By the beginning of 1983, the trustees of the Commission authorized $1,303,880 in supplemental Cooperative Program funds to the ACTS network and began the approval of a series of bank loans to provide interim financing to launch it.

The implementation of ACTS, Inc. required the approval of the Executive Committee of the SBC. Within a matter of months, major legal hurdles were raised by SBC attorneys about the new entity and its potential of legal liability for the Convention. The Convention leadership insisted on greater accountability for the organization by the RTVC trustees. Related to the denominational issues was a withdrawal by the BSSB from participation in the network. Initially, Lloyd Elder, Grady Cothan's successor as president of the BSSB, was elected to ACTS, Inc. Shortly thereafter, in May 1984, Elder resigned from the board and the $10 million loan guarantee of the original partnership was withdrawn.

A second subsidiary corporation was formed, ACTS Satellite Network, Inc. (ASNI) to manage the ACTS programs. Organized in April 1983 as a nonprofit corporation, its primary role was to market the ACTS Network to cable television companies and independent stations.[17] The major difference in the structure of ASNI was that it was composed of all of the trustees of the RTVC. When the trustees met, they conducted business for both entities to assure proper accountability for the ACTS Network to the SBC.

The third essential link in a workable network was the services of a satellite for broadcasting nationally. The Commission approved a contract with GTE Spacenet Corporation for use of a satellite transponder beginning 1 October 1984 at a rate of $110,000 per month. The contract was for eighty-four months, with the option of renewal for an additional thirty-six

---

[17] *Annual of the Southern Baptist Convention*, 1989, audit note 14, 341.

months. The BSSN entered into a similar contract with the same company to launch its broadcasts of resources through Baptist Telnet.

Finally, the interflow of systems worked and ANSI launched the ACTS Satellite Network in May 1984. The launch was made in time for a network broadcast of portions of the SBC annual meeting in June of that year. The 1985 RTVC report to the Convention detailed the accomplishments of the effort:

> The initial program schedule consisted of six hours per day, and was extended to eighteen hours daily following an inaugural special televised during the Kansas City Convention on June 12, 1984. Just three months later, on September 15, 1984, the program service was extended to a full twenty-four hours per day, seven and one-half of which featured fresh new programming and the balance consisted of selective repeats to provide an adequate exposure in all four national time zones. From the beginning, ACTS has provided a new flawless service technically, logistically, and administratively as a result of proper preplanning and effective preparations by each element of the broadcast team.[18]

Though necessary to the ACTS concept, the costs of satellite transmission proved to be the "Achilles' heel" of the new cable strategy. Other competing television ministries could manage income streams to pay for such expenses through aggressive appeals for funds. The action of the RTVC not to appeal for funds via their programs meant a commitment to a high-cost technology with no clear means of paying for it short of major increases in denominational support or subscriptions/gifts from local ACTS groups. Neither occurred.

In addition to the above national entities, the ACTS staff established local groups who would be independent entities. Each local group would consist of a board of representatives from supporting churches who paid ten cents per month per resident member to the commission. Each group would be responsible for the costs of a satellite receiver and for programming for local cable systems.

---

[18] *Annual of the Southern Baptist Convention*, 1985, 227.

Money, Money, Money

Ever aggressive, the RTVC president launched new initiatives in programming, fund raising, and development of a cable network. He inherited an organization that was funded almost entirely by CP allocations from the SBC. It had a small endowment of one and one-half million dollars, including restricted investments in retirement accounts for the employees. Analysis of the audited financial reports of the agency over the years of his leadership indicate early success in enlarging designated giving, a growth from $21,632 in 1981 to nearly $600,000 in 1982 and $465,382 in 1983. By 1988, endowment had grown to more than $3,000,000, still small for an organization of the complexity of the RTVC. From 1983 until the end of his tenure, almost all fund-raising activities were focused on raising gifts for the ACTS effort.

The ability to raise development funds from individual Southern Baptists proved to be a major disappointment for the RTVC. During Jimmy's tenure, the board employed two vice presidents for development to organize national efforts at fund-raising. After 1984 that office remained vacant and Cargill and Associates, W. Tyler Associates, and Resource Development Inc. provided fund-raising consultations in repeated fund-raising efforts. The RTVC trustees approved a goal of raising $12.5 million in 1985, but the SBC executive committee approved only a $6 million campaign over three years with promises to study a five-year effort for $12.5 million.[19]

In spite of lofty goals and major efforts at creating a national campaign of support for the new network, success was elusive. The fundamentalist/moderate controversy in the SBC was at the height of its conflict from 1985 to 1990 and finding lay support for any denominational fund-raising was difficult at best. According to the audited financial reports presented to the Convention each year, a total of $3,321,000 was raised during the fiscal years 1985–1988. The costs of raising those funds were evidently more than the revenue generated. *Baptist Press* reported from unnamed sources: "At one point, Executive Committee members were told ACTS had spent $600,000 more on fund-raising efforts than had been raised."[20]

---

[19]Minutes of the Radio and Television Commission, 5 March 1985.
[20]Al Shackleford, "Radio-TV Commission Trustees Vote to Sell ACTS Network," *Baptist Press*, 15 April 1988, 2. The same assertion was made a year

Initial results from the ACTS satellite network appeared to be promising. Reporting to the 1986 SBC annual meeting, the RTVC stated that during the 1984–1985 fiscal year, "ACTS was being broadcast by 177 cable systems and six low-power stations, with a potential viewing audience of approximately 4,000,000 households."[21] The 1985–1986 report stated: "During this time ACTS has been delivering twenty-four hours of programming daily to 220 cable systems, three full-power stations, and six low-power stations making ACTS accessible to approximately 6.8 million television households."[22] An even more optimistic report was offered for the accomplishments of the Commission for the 1986–1987 year at the 1988 SBC annual meeting:

> The ACTS Satellite Network is the fastest-growing Christian television network in the nation according to the February 1, 1988, issue of *Cablevision*. This national magazine for the cable television industry reported that ACTS experienced a 28.6 percent growth in the total number of cable households in 1987. The second-place network had a growth of 16.4 percent.
> The more than 350 cable systems contracted to carry ACTS programs have 6.3 million subscribing homes. The number of households able to access ACTS programs stood at 7.9 million with the addition of low-power and full-power television stations affiliated with the network. This means that the faith and family programs produced by Southern Baptists and other mainline denominations may be seen by as many as 21.5 million individuals."[23]

It was also reported at the same meeting that four regional RTVC offices were being established to work at expanding the network and enlisting support. For all of the optimism of these reports, however, the underlying costs of the approach were proving difficult. After enlarging the staff to 261 employees in June 1984 to manage the ACTS launch, thirty-five temporary employees were terminated in September with some negative press coverage.[24] By the end of the first year of operations, the RTVC was

---

later in Al Shackleford and Dan Martin, "Network Sale Fails; RTVC to Continue ACTS," *Baptist Press*, 15 March 1989, 2.

[21]*Annual of the Southern Baptist Convention*, 1986, 234.

[22]*Annual of the Southern Baptist Convention*, 1987, 216.

[23]*Annual of the Southern Baptist Convention*, 1988, 233.

[24]Helen Parmley, "Baptist Radio-TV Commission Lays Off 35 Workers," *Dallas Morning News*, 1 September 1984, A37.

in financial crisis mode. According to a rather stark article circulated on Religious News Service by Diane Winston:

> But after eighteen months of operation, the network can be seen by only about four million people. Money has been slow coming in from all sources. . . . "It was the hardest year I ever lived," he [Jimmy Allen] said, reflecting on 1985. . . . Staff cuts have left only ninety of the approximately 170 employees who once worked at the Network.[25]

Network revenue as reported in the annual audit was growing, but inadequate for the level of expenditure being incurred. The ACTS satellite network generated $205,000 in 1986, $485,000 in 1987 and $747,000 in 1988 while total annual expenses for the RTVC were $5,277,000 more in 1988 than they had been five years earlier.

On paper, as indicated in table 1, the losses in expenditures seemed manageable. However, cash flow was bleeding from the growing costs of the ACTS network and certain accounting issues more complicated than most readers would want to know.

Table 1
RTVC Annual Budgets
1980–1989 (in $000s)

	1980	1981	1982	1983	1984	1985	1986	1987	1988	1989
REVENUE	4,004.6	5,885.4	7,659.0	7,395	9,978	10,451	11,744	11,628	8,540	8,550
CP	3,301.5	4,195.3	3,692.4	4,229	4,579	4,928	5,356	5,238	5,402	5,493
BMT			1,303.9	181						
CAPITAL			110	272						
OTHER	703.1	1,690.1	2,552.7	2,713	5,399	5,523	6,388	6,390	3,138	3.057
EXPENSE	3,935.9	5,238.8	7,471.0	6,692	9,266.0	11,718	11,504	11,977	11,357	9,923
BALANCE	68.7	646.6	188	703	712	(1,267)	240	(349)	(2,817)	(1,373)

---

[25]Diane Winston, "ACTS Network Still Struggling," *National Christian Reporter* 5/52 (28 February 1986): 1.

Table 2 provides a clearer picture of the financial situation of the Commission when one explores the debt being accumulated and the costs for servicing the debt in the annual expenses of the budget. Financially, the multiple projects of the commission during this decade proved disastrous.

Table 2
Debt Accumulation and Interest Expense
1980–1989 (in $000s)

	1980	1981	1982	1983	1984	1985	1986	1987	1988	1989
NonCurrentDebt	0	0	0	0	4,966	6,337	8,326	8,537	7,864	7,109
Interest Expense	0	0	0	0	268	949	1,120	887	955	1,067

By 1986, the financial picture of the ACTS network was sufficiently bleak that Jimmy Allen began a process of moving in a new direction. First, a ten-million-dollar loan was approved by the board in August 1986 from the Central Bank of Walnut Creek, California, pledging all of the assets of the RTVC to secure it. A new plan for development presented by Resource Development Inc. was approved the next month. Second, tension between Allen and James Edwards, the executive vice president and chief financial officer, had grown to such a point Jimmy felt it necessary to replace him with a different leader. Richard T. McCartney, editor of the Oklahoma Convention *Baptist Messenger* with whom Allen had worked at the BGCT, was employed as executive vice president, assuming that role in January 1987.

RTVC trustees were increasingly restive about finances with questions raised about the realism of future projections. They approved a motion by Mike Hamlet to request trustee Fred Roach to form a local financial advisory committee to work with staff on a monthly basis. The group was also in conversation with Dominion Video Satellite about ACTS as a channel of a new network to be called Direct Broadcast Satellite, a conversation that lasted the better part of two years without success.

The final change in approach came through 1987 and 1988 as Allen sought a potential buyer for the network that would maintain its presence, but reduce the financial liability for the denomination. The changing landscape in the industry was having an effect on the network. After the numerous scandals with Jim Bakker and Jimmy Swaggart, cable providers moved to focus on broadcasts from multidenominational efforts. Several of the nation's largest cable providers made a grant of $5.2 million to help start a new network, VISN, for "Roman Catholics, Jews, and Protestant groups."[26] The move brought pressure to the market at a time when ACTS was the fastest-growing cable system in the religious world with 28.6 percent growth in 1988.[27]

In April 1988, the trustees approved an agreement with an organization called Friends of ACTS, Inc. (FOA), led by Center (Chip) Atkins, a San Antonio businessman with national success in television marketing. The agreement provided the Friends organization ninety days to complete a proposal that would pay the RTVC eleven million dollars in cash, a promissory note of twenty-three million dollars payable at two million dollars annually at market interest rates, and three percent of the gross proceeds from the network for thirty years. The group would also broadcast five hours of RTVC programming daily for thirty years. Allen also announced if the sale were successful he would resign from the Commission and head the Friends of ACTS organization, probably weakening his continuing leadership. The motion to approve the agreement in the board included the provision that "full communication to the Southern Baptist Convention Executive Committee and all interested publics within the Southern Baptist Convention be conducted with candor and sensitivity." Thus, Allen went on record of his limited tenure at the RTVC.

Unfortunately, the FOA was never able to secure the financing necessary to complete the sale at the costs negotiated. Multiple extensions were offered until a final meeting in March 1989 when the trustees rejected Atkins' final offer and voted to continue ACTS as a RTVC operation. At its next scheduled meeting in April 1989, Richard McCartney reported the offer of employment to Jimmy Allen by the FOA. With the publicity of the repeated failure to close the purchase, three additional offers were made to the board meeting in April. John Hagee's Global Evangelism organization offered in a letter $9-million-plus based on an examination of the books; Satellite Network Services and the Veeco Group offered an amount that

---

[26]Diane Winston, "Christians Spar for Upper Hand Over Cable TV," *Dallas Times Herald*, 5 June 1988, A1, A18-19 and Susan Sawyers, "Mainline Religions Plugging Into the Power of Cable," *Greensboro News & Record*, 25 September 25, 1988, C1-C2.

[27]"Cable Stats," *Cablevision*, 1 February 1988, 64.

would clean the slate on debt after due diligence; and Ralph Tacker with FOA made an offer of $10 million at closing. The board rejected all offers and Allen resigned 11 April 1989 effective 1 May with a termination date of 30 June 1989.

The CenturyMen in China

The ACTS satellite network was Jimmy Allen's consuming effort. It was not his only effort, however. He used every opportunity to enlarge the arena of presenting the gospel in both direct and subtle messages to the world. One illustration of Jimmy's method of operation was the development of a tour that took the CenturyMen to China for the first cultural event by a Christian group after the normalization of relations with China during Jimmy Carter's presidency in 1979.

When Allen heard of a planned visit to the U.S. by Chinese Premier Deng Xiaoping, he contacted the Carter White House to seek an appointment with the Chinese leader. To his surprise, an appointment was scheduled to meet Deng in Houston. When the premier became ill, he diverted from Houston to Vancouver, and the Chinese offered a meeting with the newly appointed ambassador from China at the Chinese Embassy in Washington, D.C. the following month. Allen and other key leaders of the SBC met with the ambassador; conversations about possible cultural exchanges were begun.

In 1981, the conductor of the Shanghai Philharmonic Society Chorus and professor of music at Shanghai University, Ma Geshun, attended the National Conference on Broadcast Ministries in Fort Worth as a part of his tour of American institutions. Professor Ma had studied at SWBTS and had been a roommate with Cliff Tennison, pastor of FBC in West Monroe, Louisiana and long-time Allen friend. There he heard the CenturyMen sing and wanted them to perform in Shanghai. A formal invitation was issued by Shanghai Television 22 January 1983 for the group to perform in Shanghai, Nanjing, and Beijing.

The CenturyMen is a group of one hundred ministers of music in Baptist congregations who travel around the world, partly at their own expense, to present concerts of Christian hymns and sacred music. They were a routine part of national television broadcasts programmed by the RTVC, which provided some financial support to the group. The singing group is led by Buryl Red, New York composer and music publisher. Red is a nationally known composer, best known for his composition "Celebrate

Life," among more than 1,600 published compositions and arrangements. He has an extensive network of connections with leading musicians around the world as the executive producer of numerous music textbooks.[28]

From that meeting and others, Allen put together a delegation to visit the People's Republic of China with a goal of doing a television documentary. A Chinese travel group in New York led by Jean Cheng guided the delegation of Allen; Buryl Red; Lewis Myers with the FMB; Britt Towery, a Manderin-speaking FMB missionary; and Ralph Tacker, a Mission Service Corps volunteer with technical television skills. To Allen's surprise, Buryl Red was known by the Chinese musical leaders they met because of relationships with a Chinese music professor at Columbia University through whom he had provided music textbooks to students in China.

During that visit the group visited with Professor Ma in Shanghai to arrange for the concerts there. They made their way to Nanjing where meetings were held with Bishop K. H. Ting, principal of the reconstituted seminary there.[29] They also visited the printing work of the emerging Amity Press, formed by the Amity Foundation, a major organization of the Three-Self movement in China. Myers established a relationship with the Amity Foundation that opened new doors for the FMB with Amity Press and the China Christian Council, the government-approved organization of the Chinese church. The outcome was the establishment of Cooperative Services International, an FMB-supported program providing English-language personnel to work in China. Multiple connections were made that allowed for development now of more than twenty-five years of growing relationships between Baptists in America and Chinese Christian leaders. Visits with a variety of officials in the Ministry of Culture in Beijing completed the journey.

The full details of planning the trip are more complex than can be covered in this book, but the connections that emerged are clearly providential. One detail must be covered to communicate Allen's networking skills.

---

[28]More information is available at <thecenturymen.com> (accessed 12 August 2008).

[29]Britt Towery, *Churches of China: Taking Root Downward, Bearing Fruit Upward*, 3rd ed. (Waco TX: Baylor University Press, 1990) 58, reports the Nanjing Theological Seminary had graduated no students for twenty years and reopened in 1981 as the Jinling Union Theological Seminary, becoming the strongest theological school in China.

After meeting David Wong, former BWA president from Hong Kong, he discovered Wong's niece, Dorothy Cai, was visiting Oklahoma Baptist University in the states. Allen contacted her, invited her to visit the RTVC offices, and discovered she was the staff person in the Bureau of Music of the Ministry of Culture in Beijing who would have to clear the music to be sung by the CenturyMen! With her approval, a variety of music was sung, including Christian hymns.

An added feature of the event was the inclusion of a camera crew from the RTVC and a producer from NBC to assist in producing a television program recording the events. The program, "China: Other Voices," was broadcast on 26 February 1984 on the NBC network.

After much negotiation, planning, and rehearsals at the RTVC studios, fifty-two members of the one-hundred-member group travelled to China for a series of concerts October 24–November 9, 1983.[30] The trip was an adventure for the group as this time frame was only a few years after the Cultural Revolution that devastated so much of China's art, architecture, and institutions. Shanghai Conservatory of Music was rather small and drab with some 500 students at that time. Yet, next to Beijing Central Conservatory, it was the second most prestigious music school in the country, with some one hundred faculty, including twenty voice faculty. The "cultural exchange" event involved joint performances by the CenturyMen and the Shanghai Philharmonic Choral Society. A representative collection of American music, Christian hymns, and original compositions with a Chinese quality were presented by the American singers. Buryl Red was struck by the similarity of the tonal quality of Chinese instrumentation and Appalachian music in the United States. He set Christian hymns to the instrumentation of the traditional Chinese music which proved appealing to the group's guests.

From Shanghai, the group travelled to Hangzhou for sightseeing and visiting a church in the city on Sunday. When the group spontaneously began singing at the conclusion of the service, their "nonauthorized" performance was reported to Beijing and the remainder of the itinerary was nearly cancelled. A prayer meeting into the night was credited for a change of heart by the Chinese leaders.

---

[30] Joe Justin Walters has written an unpublished history, "Adventures with the Centurymen," in which a chapter is devoted to this China trip. Several details of the trip are drawn from this source.

The highlight of the trip was a joint performance with the Beijing Philharmonic Chorus at the Central Conservatory in Beijing. A traditional Chinese orchestra accompanied the men as they sang two concerts—one for the faculty and staff and another for the public. A third event was a performance at the Radio Peking Music Hall recorded for national radio broadcast throughout the nation. This radio broadcast and the television recordings made for American broadcast meant the entire production was seen or heard by several million people. The group was officially recognized with a banquet celebration at the Great Hall of the People, becoming the first American group to perform on national radio and the first Christian group to be formally recognized as such. The final event of the trip was a concert at the Kowloon Baptist Church in Hong Kong to an overflow crowd as well as a public performance at the Tsuen Wan Town Hall in the New Territories.

Doors opened when a variety of Chinese officials created opportunities for even more ventures in China. Allen was invited by the head of the CCTV to return to Beijing for the dedication of a new imports building. During that visit, the invitation was extended for a second concert by the CenturyMen. Jimmy arranged for funding of $250,000 from ABC plus the use of ABC cameras for a documentary on the trip that included worship in Church of China congregations and interviews with local citizens in their homes and work as they explained their faith. A glimpse into daily Chinese life was seen by many Americans for the first time.

This was historic in that Chinese television and American television directors and film crews worked together for the first time. The Chinese edited the program for broadcast on CCCT and was later given the highest award in China, the Starlite Award. The program was of such quality, that in 1988–1989 Allen was awarded a Daytime Emmy Award as executive producer for the Outstanding Special Class Program Area: "China: Walls and Bridges." In what can only be an event of historical irony, he reported the award to the same board meeting of the RTVC trustees as the one in which he tendered his resignation.

The successes of these two ventures fueled Allen's imaginative visions of the potential for television in unifying groups of believers across the divides of geography and culture. After his previous visits in China, Allen attended the annual meeting of the National Association of Broadcasters in Los Vegas. He recalls:

> The head of CCTV wanted to talk to me. I went to that meeting usually and often did invocations. . . . so we had a session with him. His proposition was, "We have had good experience with you in China with the CenturyMen. We don't have anything we can do with the people of Taipei. We can't do any conversations with them, even economic or political conversations. The thing we have in common is music. I wondered if you might do a similar concert with the traditional orchestra of Taipei and the traditional orchestra of Beijing with The CenturyMen for a worldwide audience?" As we talked about it we decided we would do that on Chinese New Year in 1990.[31]

During 1989, Allen spent additional effort in putting together an international gathering of musicians in Singapore for simultaneous broadcasts throughout Asia and the United States. His plan was to bring an orchestral group from Beijing, another from Taipei, and the CenturyMen from the United States to perform in an auditorium in Singapore. A businessman he met in Fort Worth was from Taiwan and had numerous connections in the government there. So they travelled together where he met with a host of officials as well as a delegation of Christians led by Dr. Chou Lien Hua, the famous Baptist scholar,[32] in seeking to put together the concert.

The plan for the event was to broadcast the performance live to an international audience. He says, "Meanwhile I got the NBC president for international operations, who had just retired, as a consultant, and he worked on the clearances for this program in North Africa and Europe. The people in Beijing were working with India and Russia. We were going to have a worldwide broadcast of the CenturyMen, the Taipei orchestra, and the Beijing orchestra singing the gospel around the world in a broadcast that would have been the first cultural experience between the People's Republic and the Taipei government."[33]

Unfortunately, two events conspired to prevent such an event. The vortex of protests at Tiananmen Square and other cities of China occurred during the same time period in the spring 1989 as Allen announced his

---

[31] Allen, "President of RTVC," 169.

[32] A similar summary of this venture is describe in the Festschrift for Dr. Chou, Larry L. McSwain, "Jimmy R. Allen: Connecting American and Chinese Christians through Media," *Take Root Downward, Bear Fruit Upward*, ed. Johnson T. K. Lim, 229-43 (ABGTS Publications, 2008).

[33] McSwain, "Jimmy R. Allen: Connecting American and Chinese Christians through Media," 170.

resignation from the Television Commission. The grand hope of a truly international broadcast of an amazing cultural event did not happen.

Conclusions

An honest appraisal of the leadership of Jimmy Allen in fulfilling his vision of communicating the gospel to the world via radio and television requires a mixture of praise and questions. How could Christians committed to sharing the good news of Jesus Christ not employ every possible technology in making Him known to the world? Television was that medium in the 1980s. Baptists had a unique opportunity as a people to live out their theology of commitment to the Great Commission and the Great Commandment. But it required dedication to the dream: Christians had to have the vision of how to do that, the technical expertise to make it happen, and the willingness to find the resources to fund such efforts.

Southern Baptists, as one expression of the Christian family, succeeded in two of the three requirements for effectiveness in that mission. Jimmy Allen provided the vision of what could happen in a changing world where for the first time in human history the means of worldwide communication was possible. One cannot fault the scope of his vision for he dreamed beyond the possibilities of his time.

The technical skills were also available. The staff of the RTVC and other available personnel were uniquely qualified to develop programs for all age groups and demographic diversity of society with attractive communication of Christian faith. With the advent of satellite communication in the 1980s, the technology was available to delivering the vision Jimmy dreamed.

But it was a vision that failed in the broad scope of history. It did so for a number of reasons.

First, he was implementing a vision no denominational entity had ever achieved. To function as a nonprofit entity in a highly competitive, commercial television world was beyond realism. The changes in technology alone during his tenure were at the forefront of massive and expensive new possibilities. In reality, the RTVC was struggling when he arrived and it continued to struggle after he left. Richard T. McCartney was named interim president of the commission after Jimmy resigned. He was able to lead in the continuation of ACTS with a reduced staff and rigid budget constraints. He would not be considered for the permanent position because he was not publicly identified with the new fundamentalist leadership of the Convention.

Within three years of Allen's departure, the RTVC purchased Jerry Falwell's FamilyNet at a cost of one million dollars only to see losses mount to $10.8 million. Within five years of Allen's departure, the denomination folded the RTVC's mission into a merger with the SBC North American Mission Board, and in 2003 ACTS was terminated. The remaining shell of FamilyNet was sold in September 2007 to Charles Stanley's InTouch Ministries with no public disclosure of the purchase price. The Radio and Television Commission of the SBC is no more.[34]

Second, Jimmy Allen struggled to accomplish his vision of a Bold Mission enterprise amid the most-conflicted decade in the history of the SBC. The impetus for the ACTS satellite network was at its peak at the same time fundamentalist and moderate factions of the body politic were in warfare. The height of the conflict was in 1985 at the Dallas Convention just as ACTS was being established. But the Convention was focused elsewhere and the victory of the Patterson-Pressler forces in that Convention essentially sealed the future direction of the Convention. Though moderates pressed on each year until their final defeat in New Orleans in 1990, the outcome was sealed in 1985.

The results of such conflict for the RTVC were threefold. First, any impetus for Bold Mission Thrust was dissipated. By the end of the decade, little emphasis was made of the rhetoric that had been so central in the previous decade.

Second, the anticipated increase in CP funding on which the entire ACTS network had been organized never materialized. There was one year of significant BMT funding for the RTVC in 1982 in the amount of $1,309,900, but the regular allotment that year was reduced $502,900. The growth of the CP was modest during this decade of unprecedented effort to enlarge the media witness and the likelihood that Jimmy Allen as a clearly moderate denominational leader could secure a larger portion of the CP pie was untenable. A summary of the financial reports of the RTVC to the SBC is shown in table 1. It clearly reflects a situation in which the costs of

---

[34]Sam Hodges, "Baptists Sell Last of FamilyNet Broadcast Unit," *Dallas Morning News*, 7 September 2007 <www.dallasnews.com/sharedcontent/dws/news/localnews/stories/090507dnmetfamilynet-work> (accessed 18 September 2007).

fulfilling the ACTS dream were simply greater than SBC people, churches, or conventions were willing to support financially. When the marketplace realities did not generate enough income to cover the costs of the network, the experiment, grand as it was, was doomed.

Second, the denominational controversy took its toll with pressures on Allen to remain uninvolved in any moderate efforts to challenge the new Patterson-Pressler leadership within the Convention. Informal conversations within the RTVC became public in 1985 as an effort to ensure Allen's neutrality in the coming contest for SBC president between incumbent Charles Stanley and Winifred Moore, pastor of the FBC in Amarillo, Texas. John Roberts, chair of the Commission, asked Allen, "to refrain from overt politicking in the Baptists' fundamentalist-moderate controversy." Allen sought to dampen the importance of the conversation saying, "I'm going to stay low profile because that is my choice. But I'm not going to stop talking when people tell what they believe. There's been no threatened action of any kind."[35]

But if Allen were neutral, which he never was, the new leadership of the Convention was not. The kind of trustees being selected by the new Convention leadership had few of the skills needed for establishing policy, evaluating budgets, or making program judgments for an agency as complex and changing as the RTVC. It is difficult for the same people to build institutions who are committed to undoing them.

Trustees were chosen largely for their commitment to the Patterson-Pressler agenda of denominational change. Every year after 1985, trustees became more aggressive in pushing that agenda in all of the agencies of the SBC. A major push was made for replacing existing "moderate" leaders and most especially seminary presidents. Those forces caucused before each board meeting to plan their strategy, and the caucuses were successful in forcing the resignations of Randall Lolley at Southeastern Baptist Theological Seminary in 1987, and Roy Honeycutt at SBTS in 1993, with the termination of Russell Dilday at SWBTS in 1994.

The changes in trustee composition increased the pressure on Allen along with the financial challenges of the RTVC. At least one RTVC insider has indicated to me plans were underway to terminate Allen because of his

---

[35] Jim Jones, "Baptists Limit Church Politics of TV Official," *Fort Worth Star-Telegram*, 28 January 1985, 1, 15.

moderate leaning that had little to do with the financial crisis being faced. But he surprised them with his resignation. As he said in one interview, "I felt threatened for a long time but then I decided I had done all I could do there. I was not going to let them fire me."[36]

Finally, and most importantly, Baptist people did not rally to the financial challenges of this new technology. Baptists were an increasingly wealthy and influential people in the 1980s. They had the resources to make the ACTS network a successful reality. But it is far easier for a highly visible television personality to appeal directly to viewers for support than for a denomination to do so.

There may be a lesson for the readers of this story in that outcome. The lesson is this: institutions and organization that require resources may not be attractive to the typical Christian, but gifts to them may be far more effective in engaging in the work of God's kingdom than more popular causes.

Jimmy Allen's television dream failed ultimately. But it was a grand experiment in the use of the most important medium of the late twentieth century for communication of the gospel message across class, race, and culture. Television proved to be a major cultural invention that has shrunk the world dramatically and opened every corner of the world to international observation. No better indicator if its power can be imagined than the broadcast of the 2008 Olympic games from Beijing. What Allen imagined in the world of religion has been realized by the fascination of the world with sports.

If the twentieth century was the century of television, the early decades of the twenty-first century are the decades of the internet. Allen reflected philosophically on his accomplishments in 2005:

> I think the major accomplishment was we helped move the fellowship of our churches into a television mindset, the use of television for the forwarding of their message. I think it was a precursor of the new technology that allows us to do it through the internet. We made people in little churches able to do what is done in big churches and trying to access their people if they wanted to. The major frustration was so few were willing to put the time and energy into it to communicate on a regular basis to their homes and community. I felt it was so obvious that you could have a pastoral visit if you chose to do that. So I felt frustrated over that. We probably had a lot more impact in the

---

[36] Allen, "President of the RTVC," 159.

television experience with the churches in pathfinding than we did in production. That was the major accomplishment. That is where I get my satisfaction. We used the television and radio communication opportunity for a lot of things that were beyond the obvious. That is what God always does with us—when we have things here because of it you are able to accomplish things over there. A lot of the other impacts, the evangelism rallies that were televised, meant we were also nurturing people to be receptive to the gospel.[37]

Jimmy Allen resigned with no place of employment and limited income as interim pastor of Wilshire Baptist Church in Dallas at the time. Concurrently, his family was engaged in a saga of dealing with HIV/AIDS described in the next chapter. Soon he formed a new entity, Faith and Family Incorporated, which utilized the ACTS network by producing programs on moral issues and other religious resources to religious television stations from Carson Newman College in Jefferson City, Tennessee. He was successful in selling the concept to numerous stations across the country but the advertising revenue was too small. Within a matter of months he was bankrupt and used part of his retirement benefits to pay employees who were working with him. He says, "I went into a very deep psychological and spiritual agony over it. I once wrote an article on 'Learn to Fail before You Are Sixty.' I had never failed in my life on anything from my point of view. It totally failed and I was very burdened by that."[38]

He served as interim pastor of First Baptist Church, Amarillo in 1990, and then accepted a role with a New York development firm, Lawson and Associates, as a regional fund-raising consultant for a time. By 1993 Allen made a major change that would move him and Wanda to the mountains of North Georgia. There he found new fulfillment and renewed calling as chaplain of the Chapel at Big Canoe, Georgia. It was the beginning of a whole new chapter in his life.

---

[37] Allen, "President of the RTVC," 170-71.
[38] Allen, "President of the RTVC," 171-72.

Chapter 10

Loving beyond Your Theology: The Pain of a Prophetic Priest[1]

> Sensing Him through our pain
> Fine Tunes our radar, shriveling or expanding our souls.
> Sharing our pain frees Him to share His Pain with us.
> And we learn to call it Grace.[2]

Every person has a theology of some kind; that includes you as the reader of this book. Your theology is your value system—what you believe about the universe, whether you believe in God and God's relationship to it, the origin and nature of humans, and how we are to live life most fully. Some of us build our theology in a formal way on ideas, a worldview, or doctrines of faith. If you are a Christian the Bible will be the focus of that theology and it will center on Jesus Christ.[3]

Others of us are more informal in our theology. We may not think much about it, even have difficulty expressing it. We just do not know what we believe.

But let a crisis come our way and what happens? Whether we have a formal theology or an informal one, we immediately try to make sense of it. We may quote Scripture to explain it or say things we learned as children to describe it. We may sing a popular song or hum a hymn. When events of illness, accident, violence, and death happen to us, questions are usually more easily voiced than answers. "Why," we ask. "Why me? Why my family?"

Jimmy Allen struggled with those questions while seeking to communicate answers to people he encountered wherever he went, whether they were believers or unbelievers, whether churched or not. He was an evangelistic pastor who shared his faith, his theology, with ease with any who would listen. And listen many did. Several thousand persons have become followers of Jesus Christ, chosen to be baptized, and invested themselves

---

[1]This chapter draws from Larry L. McSwain, " 'Loving Past Our Theology:' Jimmy R. Allen and the HIV/AIDS Crisis," *Whitsett Journal* 13/1 (Spring 2005): 1, 3-9.

[2]Jimmy Allen, "No Frozen Images, (Exodus 20:4)" *Christian Ethics Today* 6/1 (February 2000): 19.

[3]Howard W. Stone and James O. Duke, *How to Think Theologically*, 2nd ed. (Minneapolis: Fortress Press, 2006) is a helpful resource for exploring your theology.

in learning the teachings of Christian faith in churches he led. Others who heard him preach or met him on a vacation or sat next to him on an airplane responded to his invitations to the faith journey in Jesus. Some asked him to pray for them. Some confessed their faith to him. He has a contagious ability to connect to people and share his faith with ease and honesty.

Yet, in the dark night of his soul, Jimmy struggles as much as any person with questions that do not have easy answers. The reason is that he experienced so many dark nights. His long-time friend and pastor of many years, James Cooper, summarizes what many who know his story would say, "I do not know any family that has had to endure so much trauma as this family has."[4]

Jimmy's life story thus far in this biography focused largely on success, effectiveness, and accomplishment. But the depth of his character is rooted in suffering and pain that even the most godly of prophets encounter. That pain forced him to reexamine how he understands God and God's work in our lives. It shapes which Scripture passages flood his consciousness and which doctrines of faith are emphasized most.

Darkness in the Allen Household

Jimmy Allen was "a man of sorrows, and acquainted with grief" (Isaiah 53:3b). Early in their marriage, Wanda began experiencing mood swings and periods of depression. The births of each of their sons were difficult for her and following each there were periods of migraine headaches and depression. By the late 1960s, she became severely depressed in reaction to medicines prescribed for her headaches and spent fourteen months in Timberlawn Hospital in Dallas. Only after more effective medications for depression became available was she able to resume a relatively normal life of activity with her family.[5]

Their first son, Michael Wayne, was born in 1953 when the family lived in Van Alstyne. Michael had a difficult birth and was overly active and difficult to control as a child. During his teen years he was diagnosed with paranoid/schizophrenia syndrome. Michael has great difficulty functioning with social expectations, the tasks of daily living, and struggles with all of

---

[4] James Cooper, interview with Jim Newton, Dallas, 5 July 2005, 9.
[5] Jimmy Allen, *Burden of a Secret* (Nashville: Moorings, 1995) 21-22, 31-32, describes forthrightly her medical issues and the effects on their family of her hospitalization and his frequent absences from home.

the effects of this mental illness. Medications help but do not cure. He is the father of Jimmy's only living grandchild, Diana. Jimmy writes, "Michael is a loving and caring human being. Most of all, he loves God."[6]

Their second son, Stephen Ray, better known as Skip, was born in 1954, in Wills Point. Skip is incredibly talented, has the verbal skills and memory of his father, and lives in a relationship of tension and love with his family. Skip is gay. He is a person of deep faith and profound care for people. He also lives outside the norms of conservative, Baptist expectations for the son of a Baptist preacher. He is comfortable with his identity and choices. Jimmy does not share his viewpoints on the issue of homosexuality. That difference has strained their relationship, sometimes to the breaking point. Yet, their differences have not severed their mutual recognition that they are family and love each other deeply.

Kenneth Scott was the third son born to the Allen's in 1956. Scott was born with a Rh blood factor. He barely survived the long ordeal of blood transfusions in Dallas. Jimmy was the primary caregiver of Scott during this time, spending many hours in the pediatric ward of Baylor Hospital in Dallas. Wanda was fully occupied with two other children and her own medical needs.

Unlike most ministers who live with the burdens of family struggle, Jimmy Allen has chosen to be quite public with his family's travail. Throughout his ministry he refused to hide Wanda's needs for privacy at times. Most of their ministry she was able to rise to the occasion for essential tasks while needing solitude when they were not so essential. She was his most ardent supporter and strongest critic. She often said, "My purpose in life is to keep Jimmy humble."[7]

He confessed quite openly in his preaching and speaking engagements the family's struggles with Wanda's illness and drug and alcohol use by his sons. Fortunately, a deep faith and the resources of Alcoholics Anonymous became gifts of grace for the sons and effective medications gave Wanda relief from the worst experiences of her depression.

How Jimmy was able to keep the pace of his incredible ministry while also seeking to be available to his family is a story in itself. In reality, both he and his family acknowledge how dysfunctional the family became with Wanda's illness and his constant absences, especially during the years of his

---

[6]Allen, *Burden of a Secret*, 204.
[7]Skip Allen, interview with Jim Newton, Dallas, 7 July 2007, 21.

elective Convention leadership. The problems were so severe during Scott's last year of high school that Jimmy cancelled most of his out-of-town commitments to be with Scott. To compensate for his frequent absences, he took each son with him on at least one annual trip that each got to plan. Lengthy family vacations were also a routine in the summers.[8] Yet, none of these challenges could compare with the heartache of this family that began with a telephone call on 25 September 1985.

HIV/AIDS in the Allen Family

Scott Allen married Lydia Williams, the daughter of Luke and Joyce Williams. Scott and Lydia were deeply committed Christians, graduates of Golden Gate Baptist Theological Seminary, and parents of Matthew and Bryan Caleb. During their seminary experience, Scott served as pastor of Pacifica Baptist Church and son Matthew was born in 1982. The birth was difficult, requiring transfusions of three units of blood for Lydia, of which one was later determined to have been donated by a gay man infected with the HIV virus. This was well before any standards of testing and screening had been adopted by the blood-donation industry.

Then they moved from California to Colorado where Bryan Caleb was born in 1985 with severe complications and continuing sickness. While serving as minister of education of the First Christian Church in Colorado Springs, Colorado, Scott called his father with the horrible news from Mt. Sinai hospital in San Francisco that the blood used in the earlier transfusion was HIV-positive. Lydia, Matthew, and Brian were tested, and each was positive for the virus. That fateful day when Scott called was 25 September 1985. It set in motion a continuing effort to deal with a crisis unlike any previously experienced in the Allen household.

The fuller story of the aftermath of that call is documented in Jimmy's 1995 book *Burden of a Secret*. Scott was terminated immediately by the church in Colorado Springs, Lydia resigned her job as a pediatric nurse to avoid contaminating patients, and the family moved in with Jimmy and Wanda in Fort Worth.

Scott and Lydia wanted their family involved in a local church but felt the pastors of the church needed awareness of the infection without any

---

[8]Allen, interview with Jim Newton, Dallas, 7 July 2007, 4-5, describes vividly some of the family's pain while communicating incredible love for his father.

public disclosure of it. Multiple pastors in the Fort Worth and Dallas area, several of whom were long-time family friends, were approached with the request their children be allowed to attend Sunday school. Each of the pastors offered pastoral condolences but confessed their laity could not accept an AIDS family into their fellowship with the terms of privacy they requested.

One has to understand something of the impact of this new disease in the social fabric to understand something of this reaction. HIV/AIDS became a public disease in the early 1980s as increasingly numbers of gay men and intravenous drug users began to die from previously unknown viral symptoms. Given the population affected, few church leaders expressed concern, and the more attention given to the spread of the virus, the greater the fear and unsubstantiated information began to flow through the popular media. Dread was the primary response from many and judgment was the response of most in the Christian conservative-evangelical community. HIV/AIDS became the new leprosy as contemporary Christians reacted to those with the disease. Few were able to model the acceptance demonstrated by Jesus in his willingness to touch the outcasts of his culture. After all, he was dining in the home of Simon the leper when anointed by expensive perfume (Mark 14:3).

Caution was the response of pastoral leaders because of this popular fear. Among the churches asked to accept Mathew and Bryan was FBC, Arlington. Charles Wade was the pastor and was one of Jimmy's most ardent admirers. They had worked together and Charles modeled much of his leadership of the church after what Jimmy did in San Antonio. First Baptist became a national model in community outreach and service through Mission Arlington with community ministries that serve over 5,000 people annually. Wade recalls:

> So I went over to visit with Scott and Lydia, and we talked, and I held the baby. This was in the middle 1980s, and people didn't know how to respond. . . . I tried to create a way in which we could have fellowship and hopefully the way to full involvement would open up; but it didn't work. So we failed them. We absolutely failed them. I regret that to this day.[9]

After these events, Wade led the congregation to adopt policies that would open their ministries to all children, with clear policies to ensure

---

[9]Charles Wade, interview with Jim Newton, Dallas, 6 July 2005, 5.

safety, whatever their illness or situation. That policy has been shared with more than 600 other churches, many of whom have adopted similar practices, including several that were not responsive to Scott and Lydia at the time of their need.[10]

The rejection of churches is among the most painful aspects of this story for a family whose identity was rooted in church. Finally, one Church of Christ congregation in Dallas accepted Matthew into its summer programs because of the care of the pastor toward Scott. In contrast, a public-school teacher proved to be a redemptive presence to Matthew and their family.

In a matter of months after the move to Ft. Worth, Bryan died on 2 February 1986. Lydia became involved in the formation of Bryan's House, an interfaith ministry in Dallas. Shortly after Bryan's death, Skip Allen announced to the family he too was infected by the disease.

Soon a house was found for Scott's family. He began working as a MSC volunteer with the Texas CLC, raising awareness of the AIDS crisis and offering ideas for creative church ministries to AIDS victims and their families. He helped form the AIDS Interfaith Task Force in Dallas and became a member of the Texas Study Commission on AIDS. The highlight of his work in this area was his selection as a member of the National AIDS Commission. The Commission was established as a part of the omnibus AIDS legislation passed by the Congress in 1988.[11] For the next four years the commission traveled to various cities exploring the needs for social policy changes and funding. Scott was often quoted in the press for his insights and perspectives on the issues, such as his observation in the first trip of the commission to Los Angeles that he was, " 'surprised at the lack of compassion here,' evidenced by the fact that the county Health Department provides only one twenty-two-bed AIDS inpatient clinic in an area with the nation's second-highest total of reported AIDS cases."[12]

The Commission did not finish its work until after the end of the first Bush administration and presented its report 28 June 1993 with heavy criticism of the lack of action on the issue and hopes of more attention and

---

[10]Wade, interview with Jim Newton, 5-6.
[11]"Cause for Optimism," *Los Angeles Times*, 26 July 1989, Metro Section, 6.
[12]Kenneth J. Garcia, "Disaster Relief Sought for Cities Hit Hard by AIDS," *Los Angeles Times*, 26 January 1990, Metro Section, 3.

funding from the administration of President Bill Clinton. Scott, who by this time had publically revealed the death of Caleb and Lydia and the infection of Skip, asked in response to inactivity on the issue, "Have we reached the point where an unacceptable epidemic becomes acceptable?"[13]

Skip continues to live with the virus, but Lydia and Matthew were not so fortunate. In July 1991, Luke Williams, suffered a massive stroke. Jimmy considers him another victim of AIDS as he internalized the stresses of the virus on his daughter's family. Private and inward, he never seemed to release his pain to others. He never recovered from the stroke and died 26 July 1991. As the family gathered for his funeral, Lydia talked openly for the first time with members of her extended family about her disease and impending death. Prior to that, her only public communication was an anonymous reflection of her experience "Wearing the Scarlet Letter 'A' " published in the *Baptist Standard* in 1987 in which she concluded:

> I wear the SCARLET A. I keep it well hidden. You may never see me cry or realize from my appearance that I have been infected by the virus. Nevertheless, I have been shattered. I need love, compassion, and community to help me make it from day to day. I have done nothing immoral or illegal to contract this disease, but those who HAVE hurt just as deeply as I. Their needs are as great or greater than mine for a compassionate and loving response to AIDS.[14]

She could become public only as the reality of crossing her own Jordan became clear. Lydia died in February, 1992.[15]

"Granddad! I don't have a secret anymore. I've gone public"[16]

Scott made the decision, in consultation with Matthew and his parents after Lydia's death, the time had come to "go public" with their story in the hope it would be helpful to others. While critical of the many churches that rejected the opportunity to minister to his family, Jimmy Allen is full of praise for the sensitivity of public-school leaders who accepted Matthew into their school and media persons who protected them from the public spotlight. Many in the media were aware of the story, but honored the

---

[13] "AIDS Panel Offers Critical Report: Group's Final Work Charges Government with 'Dogged Denial,' " *Washington Post*, 29 June 1993, A4.

[14] Allen, *Burden of a Secret*, 130.

[15] Allen, *Burden of a Secret*, 125-28.

[16] Matthew's report of the family decision in 1992 to report their experiences to the press. Allen, *Burden of a Secret*, 137.

family's request for privacy until they were ready to unburden the secret they all carried. The *New York Times* carried the family's story[17] followed by reports on NBC *Today*, a feature by *Dateline* and the *Texas Monthly*.[18]

By this time Jimmy had accepted the call as chaplain of the Chapel at Big Canoe, Georgia. The mountains of North Georgia became a place of renewal with their natural beauty, and this creative interfaith community became a base of support for Wanda and him as they experienced love and acceptance. Matthew became the focus of their efforts with frequent visits to the mountains to provide care and relief for Scott, who remarried after Lydia's death. Big Canoe also became a setting from which Jimmy could become more involved in public advocacy for the church to reach out to the untouchables who were affected by AIDS.

Jimmy Allen the Advocate for HIV/AIDS Ministry

People began to contact Jimmy for information and support in their own efforts to address the issue, especially in the churches of which they were a part. In 1994, he agreed to participate in a three-part interview with evangelist James Robison, the airing of which brought responses from those in a segment of church life most resistant to such ministries. Then he spoke to the T. B. Maston Foundation with an address entitled, "Echoes from the Valley." A videotape was produced from it and distributed by the Texas CLC, along with segments from health-care professionals and others on how best to minister to AIDS families. He also spoke to the national meeting of the SBC Woman's Missionary Union as they introduced the tape and distributed it with a workbook to key leaders interested in establishing AIDS ministries.[19] Soon *Burden of a Secret* was published, a moving account of the family's struggles with a profound theology of suffering, healing, and prayer. In the same year the book was published, Matthew entered the "peaceful place," as he called his death, on 11 November 1995.

Increasing numbers of churches developed programs and policies for ministries to infected children and others. First Christian Church in Colorado Springs invited Scott and Jimmy in 1996 to lead them in a three-day workshop on ministry with affected persons as the congregation

---

[17]Philip Hitts, "Touched by AIDS, Minister Finds Doors Shut," *New York Times*, 8 September 1992, A1.
[18]Allen, *Burden of a Secret*, 137-38.
[19]Allen, *Burden of a Secret*, 219-21.

established an HIV/AIDS ministry. This was a significant act of healing and reconciliation for Scott to return to the church from which he had been terminated.

Burden of a Secret resulted in even more invitations to speak on the topic. A publicity tour provided radio interviews in numerous cities, including Dallas and Chicago. Invitations were received to speak to the National Institute of Health Conference for AIDS professionals, the Texas Department of Public Health, annual AIDS Day Ceremonies on December 1 in numerous places, including a Baptist church in Memphis, Tennessee; Shorter College in Rome, Georgia; a community meeting near Savannah, Georgia focused on AIDS in rural communities; and speaking to Love in Action. Love in Action is an evangelical group with a national program of ministry involvement. Allen serves on their advisory board.

Bryan's House was one of the more innovative results of the family's attention to the issue. Jimmy's own words better describe how it developed:

> The Bryan's House began when Scott kept bringing home babies whose mothers had AIDS or who themselves had AIDS for Lydia to look after because he would be out working with the CLC in Texas. She decided that something needed to be done in daycare for children with AIDS. Lydia met with Stephanie Held from Temple Emmanu-El in Dallas, and they developed a plan for getting a house and putting together a board to create a daycare center. Lydia asked me to be on the board, but I felt her leadership would be more effective. Dr. Janet Squires [at Cook hospital in Ft. Worth] was our doctor and we were the first AIDS persons she dealt with. She became a major person in the field of pediatric AIDS. She joined the board with several other people in Dallas. . . . When it came to a name for the house, Dr. Squires suggested it be named after the first baby in Dallas to die of AIDS. Lydia was not present at that meeting, but was at the next meeting where it was revealed the baby was Bryan. She did not tell them it was her baby or that she had AIDS herself. That's how Bryan's House became a reality.
>
> The board began with volunteers and with support of six or seven people at first. Now they minister to about 800 persons per week they call either infected or affected by AIDS. It is a major facility and a major philanthropic purpose in Dallas.
>
> So I basically supported it, gave references for it, and encouraged people to support it. When Wanda died, we had a major music event at Big Canoe with René and Joseph Joubert who play with the CenturyMen in New York.

I went to Dallas recently and gave them that check. So it is a major ongoing concern.[20]

A group of women in Cincinnati read the book and decided to form a similar interfaith effort there. Lydia's House was formed and Jimmy has participated in fundraising efforts speaking there. Carolyn Weatherford Crumpler, retired leader of the national WMU, is a member of that board of directors.

Along with the speaking has come a multitude of contacts from individuals who seek his counsel as they face similar issues. He says:

> I have preached a lot of AIDS funerals in this area. I have a lot of people who come to the mountain (Big Canoe) to visit with me either because they have a homosexual child or have AIDS issues in their family and they want to be with somebody where they can unload. After the book, they know I am one of those somebodies. And a lot of telephone calls from people over the country who say, "I think you will understand."[21]

Among the more controversial of his actions was his decision to speak to the national convention of the Metropolitan Community Church (MCC) in California. He addressed a national meeting of leadership personnel on AIDS at the Carter Center in the late 1990s. Troy Perry, a former Southern Baptist pastor and elder and founder of the Metropolitan Community Church, was at the meeting and invited him to speak to their national convention in Los Angeles. He describes the experience:

> I went aside and prayed about it and talked to Skip and he said, "Dad, I can't tell you what to do but I can tell you there are a lot of hurting people out there who need to hear what someone like you can say about where you are, because they are hurting bad." So I prayed over that and then decided to do it. I went out and spoke to this convention of several thousand—people who are gay and are believers. I got standing ovations from them as I talked about the fact our problem is not the definition of sin; it is the understanding of grace....
> I had a feedback time with them and listened to all the anger they had to express. I found myself feeling like I was on a college campus in the 1960s

---

[20] Jimmy Allen, "Involvement in HIV/AIDS," interview no. 4 with Larry L. McSwain, McAfee School of Theology, Atlanta, 16 December 2004, 79. Ashley Cheshire, "Children of AIDS," *Fort Worth Star-Telegram*, 24 June 1990, sect. 1, 16-18, describes the needs of AIDS children and the work of Bryan's House.

[21] Allen, "Involvement in AIDS/HIV," 79.

listening to Black students as they vented their venom and anger and vindication about what I knew was truth. You know. I listened to it and had to respond to it and absorb it.[22]

When the original report of his visit[23] was carried in abbreviated form by the Associate Press, SBC leaders in Nashville quickly sought to clarify his decision with a *Baptist Press* interview. He defended his decision to speak to the group. He said:

> My decision to speak to the Metropolitan Church Churches' conference came on an appeal by [MCC founder] Dr. [Troy] Perry after he had heard me preach to a group of AIDS caregivers. I have stated clearly my beliefs about the issue of God's intention for our sexuality, both in my book, *Burden of a Secret*, and on platforms across the nation. However, he [Perry] pointed out to me that many of his people "need to know there are still parents in that [Baptist tradition] who love their children even if they don't agree theologically with them.
>
> I have a gay son with AIDS," Allen continued. "I love him and we do not agree. I believe it's time for us to talk *to* each other instead of *about* each other.[24]

Allen was not the only risk-taker in delivering his sermon to the MCC. Perry was criticized initially for inviting a conservative Baptist leader to the gathering. But when Allen declared tearfully, "I found out something about perfect love that casts out fear. . . . In our case, fear cast out perfect love. . . . We all felt the shaft of pain to be untouchable. Nobody should be untouchable," the crowd cheered and gave him a standing ovation as it broke into singing "On Christ, the Solid Rock I Stand."[25]

Theology from the Pain Down

If there is any impact this crisis seems to have made in the life of Jimmy Allen, it is a deepening of his sensitivity to his own grief and that of others. In an unpublished poem "Silent Songs of Sight," written after Matthew's death, he wrote:

---

[22]Allen, "Involvement in AIDS/HIV," 79.

[23]Larry Stammer, "Former Baptist Leader Seeks a Dialogue with Gay Church," *Los Angeles Times*, 17 July 1999, Metro Section, 1.

[24]Art Toalston, "Former SBC President Issues Statement about His Address to Homosexual Group," *Baptist Press*, 16 July 1999, 1.

[25]Stammer, *Los Angeles Times*, 2.

> The pain is like shards of glass slicing through my soul
> As I walk surrounded by the beauty of your mountain
> How can it be that such beauty is born of such pain . . .
> Upheavals of earth those centuries ago,
> > Tearing rocks and ripping soil
> > Shoving these rugged hills into such awesome shape.
> Sounds of a last remnant of cicadas singing their brief death songs
> > Pulse through the life of the mountain.
> Leaves dying and turning brilliant colors in sunlight's reflection
> > Produce Silent Songs of Sight.
> And I am dying with no strength to sing . . .
> The beauty of grieving over the rhythm of dying
> > Escapes me . . . because the death is not mine
> It is that of my innocent child.

Jimmy's biblical foundations still formed the framework of his theology. Part two of *Burden of a Secret* is an effort to make sense of the family story from the perspective of his theology. It can best be summarized as one in which trust in the wisdom of God is paramount, even when there is little or no human understanding of the "whys" of what has happened to us. He asks the question as frequently as any of us. But he suggests, there is another starting point. He writes, "To adequately address the *whys*, we must start with the pain and perplexity of God. It is not enough to start with our own pain. We feel it deeply; we may even be overwhelmed by it, but we can't understand it if we simply concern ourselves with our own lives."[26]

For Jimmy, a theology of pain must be rooted in the cross as the reality of the pain of God in the death of his son, "The One who loved, cared, and suffered like that is the God I serve. He loves and cares and suffers over me."[27]

His theology is one in which love toward the other, regardless of behavior, is the primary attitude for the Christian. But at the heart of it is the love of God who answers our prayers with wisdom more mysterious than the outcomes we desire. Consequently, the words mystery, grace, and love are now primary theological constructs of Allen's preaching and writing.

At the heart of his faith is the conviction that the core of the church is loving hurting people. He writes, "The church is at its best when it escapes

---

[26] Allen, *Burden of a Secret*, 190.
[27] Allen, *Burden of a Secret*, 192.

the captivity of its culture, and strips down to the basic task of loving, serving, and sharing the mystery of God's presence with hurting people."[28] Jimmy omits no one from this love, service, and caring, including those most alienated from the church. Addressing the responsibility of the church to minister to homosexuals, he concludes, "Can we Christians overcome our prejudices and *love past our theology* to help meet the needs of dying people? I pray so."[29]

Could that statement become a credo for the readers of this biography? What if each of us learned to "love past our theology" that is so often shaped more by culture than the reality of God in Scripture revealed in the ministry of Jesus? If that were to happen, the title of this book could become the experience of all of us: "Loving beyond Your Theology." What Jimmy Allen has done is to set forth a faithful understand of God that can be lived by all who claim Jesus Christ as Lord of their lives. When that happens, none of the people God created can be rejected from the circle of God's grace and the hopeful message of a prophet who knows the suffering of pain can declare, "We live in a pain-filled world; everybody hurts to some degree. Your pain can increase your capacity to be sensitive to someone else's pain—if you allow it to do so. Pain can cauterize you, creating scar tissue that makes you less sensitive. Or it can open you. But regardless of what you go through, God will meet you on the level of your understanding, and at the depth of your need."[30]

---

[28] Allen, *Burden of a Secret*, 210.
[29] Allen, *Burden of a Secret*, 226; emphasis added.
[30] Allen, *Burden of a Secret*, 247.

Chapter 11

Transitions:
New Geography, New Ministries, New Leadership

> The sun rises as I stagger lame and limp from battle,
> Can my new name really mean
> that God and I have grappled
> and in the Mystery
> Have I heard the VOICE of LIFE?[1]

The year 1989 marked a new chapter in the life of Jimmy. After nearly a decade of exhausting work at the Radio and Television Commission, he was without employment or steady income for the first time in his adult life. Skip describes the despair of that moment:

> Scotty called me saying "We need to go to Fort Worth and help Dad move out of his office." At the time, I didn't understand the gravity of what had taken place. We got over to Fort Worth and went into the building and there were all these boxes out in the hallway. . . . He was in there by himself, packing boxes. I asked, "What can we do?" He just stood there, looking around at all the things that needed to be done, and he couldn't even talk. So we just started picking things up randomly and putting them in boxes. If he said five words all afternoon, I'd probably be exaggerating.
>
> I've never seen him like this before or since. He was crushed, devastated. On the heels of having lost his grandson to AIDS, knowing he was going to lose his other grandson and Lydia, whom he had loved since she was a little girl, and then to find out that I too had AIDS—he was overwhelmed. And then everything he was working toward at the Radio-TV Commission and everything he had wanted it to be, had crumbled. Wow. I did not know until much, much later when my mother told me, when they were living well in Big Canoe, and we were talking about that dark, dark time in Dad's life she actually mouthed the words that she thought that "the bankruptcy was just going to take us under completely." She explained to me something that my father had never told me, and never has told me even to this day. He took their life savings and retirement funds and used it for severance pay for all the people who worked for him. And it wiped him out financially.[2]

Jimmy was depressed and sought help from a psychiatrist with little benefit. Now sixty-one, what would he do? Where would he go?

---

[1] Jimmy Allen, "Sunrise for Jacob at Jabbock," *Christian Ethics Today* (June 1999): 27.
[2] Skip Allen, interview with Jim Newton, Dallas, 6 July 2007, 10-11.

One of the great legacies of his life was a host of friends who continued to care about him and for him. By the beginning of 1990, a call came from the FBC, Amarillo, Texas, for him to serve as interim pastor. There he resumed his preaching to the same congregation on a consistent basis for the remainder of the year. This proved healing as he preached out of the pain of his experiences, taught the congregation new understandings of the controversy that had enveloped his beloved denomination, and prepared them for new pastoral leadership. The congregation called Ben Loring, longtime Allen friend and Texas CLC staff member, as its pastor in October of that year, beginning his service in January 1991.

After his interim in Amarillo, Jimmy got a call from a friend at Travis Avenue Baptist Church, where he had been a member while living in Fort Worth and serving as its interim pastor in 1983. He was introduced to Douglass Lawson, CEO of Douglas M. Lawson Associates, Inc., a New York-based fund-raising organization. Jimmy was employed by the organization and named a consulting associate. He preached on Sundays and spent his days consulting on fund-raising projects with a number of organizations. These included a Methodist and Episcopal Church in Houston, Texas, where he assisted in the raising of eight million dollars. He worked with the funding of the Absolom Center on the campus of the Interdenominational Theological Center in Atlanta. Religion in Life was another organization with which he worked.

Among his clients was Yonok College in Lampang, Thailand. He learned of the college and its president Nirund Jivasantikarn, a Ph.D. graduate of Baylor University, from Wayne Smith, executive director of Friendship Force, Inc. After contacting Baylor president Herb Reynolds about Nirund, and discovering he was also an associate member of the Chapel at Big Canoe, Jimmy became involved in fund-raising for the college. Jimmy agreed to serve on the board of the Yonok College American Foundation, travelled with Wanda to Lampang, assisted in fund-raising in the U.S. for the college, and established a long-term friendship with Nirund.[3] Incidentally, Scott spent a year working there after Matthew's death, a time of renewal and new direction for his life.

---

[3]Nirund Jivasantikarn, interview with Larry L. McSwain, Westminster SC, 21 September 2007, describes their friendship and many visits together.

The Chapel at Big Canoe

Among the fortuitous meetings of Jimmy's life was with Wayne Smith, the executive director of Friendship Force, Inc. During his travels for the ACTS Satellite Network, he visited Bert Lance, the Calhoun, Georgia banker who was part of Jimmy Carter's administration. Smith was in his office and Lance introduced them. Jimmy and Wayne developed a warm and enduring friendship during his years at the RTVC with frequent contact as Allen travelled to Georgia.

Wayne Smith was the founder of the international partnership organization; Roslynn Carter was a board member. As "soul brothers" in a common cause, Jimmy participated frequently in Friendship Force activities, and Smith introduced him to many people in his fund-raising efforts through the years.

Smith, an ordained Presbyterian minister, was a bigger-than-life figure who made a major impact in developing interfaith partnerships as he organized travel seminars to a variety of places in the world. He was also a member and associate chaplain of the Chapel at Big Canoe, Georgia. Following a meeting in Atlanta of the Yonok College American Foundation board in 1991, Wayne invited Jimmy to stay in his home in Big Canoe for the weekend in 1991. Smith was scheduled to preach at the Chapel the following day, but lost his voice and asked Allen to preach for him that Sunday. Jimmy Allen was introduced to the congregation of this creative, ecumenical, missional chapel in the resort community of Big Canoe in the mountains of North Georgia. The Chapel's founding Chaplain, Dr. Vernon Boyles, had announced his retirement; it was in search of a replacement. A dialogue was opened with the Chapel leadership about Allen succeeding him, a conversation that lasted the better part of a year.

The Chapel at Big Canoe called Jimmy Allen to be its chaplain in a congregational vote on 3 February 1992. He began his service there in March and was installed as chaplain in April.

The Chapel was founded to serve the entire Big Canoe community and to become a force for missions in the area.[4] Boyles's dream was for the chapel to give away fifty percent of its annual income, a goal that had not

---

[4]Charlene Terrell, *Church in the Wildwood: The Continuing Story of Big Canoe Chapel* (Big Canoe Chapel, 2007) is a descriptive account of the Chapel people, programs, and accomplishments from 1987 to 2006.

yet been met. Allen took it on as one of his first goals as the new leader. He determined that a thirteen percent increase in giving would allow it to achieve that goal. So, he and Wanda agreed to increase their giving to the Chapel by that amount, above their tithe. He wrote a personal letter to each of the major givers in the church challenging them to do the same. They responded and that pattern of giving was maintained throughout his service there.

Allen was able to translate his passion for the mission initiative of Bold Mission Thrust into a local application at Big Canoe. Chaplain Boyles had established an annual Missions Conference at the church which the new chaplain continued and enlarged. National groups such as Franklin Graham's Samaritan's Purse, Bill Glass with his prison ministry, and Jeanette Clift George's "Players" theatre group were among many invited to lead and encourage participation from Chapel participants. The missions committee of the Chapel would decide on contributions to each group and individuals were invited to help as well.

Local mission efforts dominated the use of these funds. When Allen learned of the needs for a place for juveniles and foster children at a Rotary meeting in Jasper, Georgia, the Chapel joined in building Hope House to provide services and support. They cooperated with the nearby Episcopal Church to support a Good Samaritan free medical clinic providing medicines, medical exams, and dental work.

Among the most enduring legacies of Dr. Boyles was a scholarship program for area high-school graduates to attend colleges and technical schools. The increase in resources allowed expanded giving to area youth. The Scholarship Committee interviews each applicant and provides $1,000 to those chosen to attend trade schools, colleges, and universities. Between the years 1982 and 2006, the Chapel provided awards to 1,283 students amounting to more than $1,241,400.[5]

At the time Allen began, there were only seven children living in the community. Residents decided their children should go to Pickens County Schools, so arrangements were made for school buses to pick them up and now more than 300 children attend public schools from the development. The youth minister of the Chapel has been involved in developing Young Life programs in the nearby communities of Jasper and Dawsonville.[6]

---

[5]Terrell, *Church in the Wildwood*, 51.
[6]Jimmy Allen, "Service at Big Canoe Chapel and Media Consulting,"

Equally creative has been the development of a strong Boy Scout program for the community by Chapel leadership. When a long-time scout leader joined the Chapel, Allen enlisted him to start a program. He said:

> We have had nine to ten Eagle scouts. We had some land and built a scout hut on it. Dr. Broyles had wanted to build a school on it. . . . He had seventeen acres he had reserved for that and next to it was the cemetery the Chapel had and next to that was a botanical area the naturalist, Robert Platt, had developed. We had to do something within two years or it would revert to the owner. So I got my people together to look at it and . . . we finally settled on an amphitheatre and meditation park. We could use the amphitheatre for summer events, so we did that. That whole project cost about $300,000 and we raised the money for it. So one day I said to the leaders, "We've got scouts without a hut and we have land with room for it, so let's build a scout hut there." One of our men asked what it would cost and I said $30-35,000 and he said he would do that. So then it became a big project for all of these retirees who went to Home Depot and other places and got things donated. I now call it the "Taj Mahut." They have a fireplace and all the equipment in the world. It is near the botanical area so we built a trail from it to the meditation area down along this beautiful creek. We had places where there would be a Bible in a box and people could walk the trail and read the Bible.[7]

As an interdenominational effort, the Chapel functions rather differently from denominational congregations. Allen described the structure of membership and involvement:

> We had three kinds of membership. We had regular membership which meant this was your only congregation to which you were related. We had an associate membership. I was an associate member. An associate member stayed connected to a home congregation, but was a full member in function. They have the right to teach, vote, and whatever else in the Chapel. Then we had a thing they had before I got there, which I was delighted to have, which was called a fellowship membership. If you don't agree with our statement of faith and you want to participate in activities and feel like you are one of us, you are a fellowship member. You don't teach and do those things, but you are considered a member of the Chapel with full fellowship. So in the process the Chapel increasingly became the center of the community. There was no auditorium so the Chapel was the center of meetings. We have writers groups,

---

interview no. 9 with Larry L. McSwain, Atlanta, 22 June 2007, 215.
[7]Allen, "Service at Big Canoe Chapel and Media Consulting," 216-17.

craft groups, women's guild with a tour of homes, and benevolent work, etc. We had membership and support. We had almost 500 members when I got there. It was almost double when I retired. The money the first year I was there was $416,000 and was over $1 million when I left.[8]

Allen maintained his membership at the First Baptist Church in Arlington, Texas through his tenure as chaplain. He retired from his role at the end of 2002 in order to care for Wanda, who was quite ill. A special event honoring their ministry was provided by the Chapel on 1 February 2003.

Wanda died after a struggle with cancer 13 November 2003 at the age of seventy-three. Her life was celebrated in a service of memorial at the Chapel on 17 November 2003 with participation by James McCormick, Jimmy's successor at the Chapel; Charles Wade; James Dunn; Phil Strickland; and Foy Valentine. A special fund-raising event with performances by René and Joseph Joubert from the CenturyMen provided funds in her honor given to support Bryan's house in Dallas.

Big Canoe provided another renewing experience for Jimmy Allen in the person of Linda Greer. Linda is a retired educator and attorney who was a part of the ministry of the Chapel as she and her husband, Jack, came under the influence of Allen's ministry.

Linda is also a major leader in the Big Canoe community. While serving as chair of the property owner's board, a role that earned her the title of "mayor" of Big Canoe from Jimmy, she led in the transition of governance from the developer to the homeowners association. She also developed Leadership Big Canoe, creating the first course for executive leaders in community processes in a gated community in the country.

Jimmy was a significant pastor to her husband, a retired professor from Georgia State University, during an extended illness. When he died, Linda became a fast friend and frequent caregiver to Wanda in her illness. She was a close friend of the Allen family and it was natural that she and Jimmy would find love and companionship with each other. They were married in Big Canoe, 21 December 2004, in a private ceremony at the Chapel led by William Self, pastor of the Johns Creek Baptist Church in the north Atlanta suburbs. Since his retirement, Jimmy and Linda continue their associate

---

[8]Allen, "Service at Big Canoe Chapel and Media Consulting," 214-15.

membership of the Chapel while maintaining active membership and involvement at Johns Creek Baptist Church.

Religion and the News Media

Jimmy Allen's rich experience in dealing with media through most of his ministry was also put to good use after his move to Georgia. The Chapel was not able to pay its chaplain at the time of his call a level of salary that was adequate for his needs. Allen negotiated for sixty percent of his time there with the freedom to pursue other income options for the remaining forty percent. He had established the Faith and Family Corporation which he maintained for consulting work.

A call from Charles Overby at the Freedom Forum offered a new opportunity to use his skills and contacts in the media industry. Overby is a Pulitzer Prize-winning editor and a Mississippi Baptist with a long career in journalism who serves as chairman and chief executive officer of the Freedom Forum. It is a foundation established by *USA Today* to maintain First Amendment freedoms, with initial leadership from Al Neuhart, its publisher. The forum had established a First Amendment Center at Vanderbilt University. John Seigenthaler, former publisher of the *Nashville Tennessean* and editorial editor of *USA Today*, led education projects at the First Amendment Center. Overby and Seigenthaler invited Allen to participate in the work of the center on one of several research projects on media and medicine, media and business, and media and religion. Jimmy and John Dart, former religion writer for the *Los Angeles Times* and now with the *Christian Century*, worked on the media and religion project. He described the arrangement:

> So they paid my way, gave me an apartment and staff and I became a visiting scholar in their First Amendment Center for the relationship between religion and the news media of the country. I did that for a whole year. I went up every week and was there for four days and spent the weekends at the chapel. . . . So, in the process of that it filled out my income. It also gave me access to a whole new world. They asked me because of my radio and television background and what I did in San Antonio. What we did was design a study in which we found out about religion and media at that time.[9]

---

[9] Allen, "Service at Big Canoe Chapel and Media Consulting," 221.

The research for the project was first published in 1993 and then updated in 2000 as *Bridging the Gap: Religion and the News Media*, winning a Wilbur award. The 1993 study was distributed free to 25,000 people.[10] The 2000 update added to the original research a description of changes in the media since its publication. The original study was an extensive analysis from interviews, development of a bibliography on religion and the media, and a survey of pastors and media leaders. The survey was designed and analyzed by Robert O. Wyatt, professor of journalism and director of the Office of Communication Research at Middle Tennessee State University. The five-page questionnaire was mailed to 988 clergy, 550 members of the Associated Press managing editors organization, and 151 members of the Religious Newswriters Association. The response rate was unusually high and provided a substantive overview of the view and attitudes of these target audiences.[11]

Following the publication of the research, Oeita Bottorff Chancellor organized a series of conversations for Allen with local news outlets in Dallas, San Antonio, Phoenix, Seattle, and Cleveland, designed to foster communication between news media and local religious leaders. Several, especially the *Dallas Morning News*, enlarged their religious coverage as a result of his work. Allen reported progress on the impact of the study:

> Since publication of the original report, at least nine of these newspapers [of the 21 percent responding to the survey] have for the first time assigned a full-time editor to religion coverage, and 30 have assigned new part-time editors. The number of full-time religion reporters among these papers has increased from 57 to 92, with the number of part-time religion reporters increasing from 95 to 163.
>
> Coverage of religious stories also has increased. Newspapers reporting one-to-ten religion stories a week increased from 188 to 248, and those reporting more than ten stories a week increased from fourteen to thirty-one.

---

[10]John Dart, "Gap Narrows and Religion Coverage Expands," *Bridging the Gap: Religion and the News Media* (Nashville: First Amendment Center, 2000 update) iv.

[11]A visual presentation of the findings are found on pp. 87-91 of the published report. The most important finding of the survey was a significantly more negative appraisal of the work of the media in reporting on religion by clergy than either the editors or writers of the reported material in virtually all media forms.

The number reporting no religion stories in an average week declined from seventy-four to fourteen. While 190 newspapers say their coverage of religion has increased during this period and eighty-three remain about the same, only four say their coverage has "decreased somewhat."[12]

As a result of his work on the advisory board of the First Amendment Center, Overby invited Jimmy to membership on the board of directors of the Freedom Forum, the national body. There he was able to meet a host of national leaders such as Caroline Kennedy, Paul Simon, astronaut Alan Shephard, and former Canadian Prime Minister Brian Mulrooney. He summarized:

> So, I had seven very pleasant years with them. They were trying to solve the problem of trying to enhance the ethical and practical performance of journalism in the country. They did a best-practices study and I was very pleased to be a part of that. It was also very lucrative because sitting on those boards is a way people in that area make their living. As the chapel got larger I negotiated a little more time, but it never got more than eighty-five percent because I wanted to be free to pursue what I knew was my sense of calling.[13]

Work at the First Amendment Center and the Freedom Forum expanded Allen's circle of influence, for everywhere he went there were people to pastor. He often engaged in pastoral conversations with fellow board members, editors, and others he met in the course of his work. Allen is a man with a network of connections and much of his work has been a ministry of introduction as he offered suggestions and names for persons to implement a program. One example was encouraging the Freedom Forum to become engaged in religious liberty and public schools, and Allen offered the names of Charles Haynes and Oliver Thomas for a program that was funded by the group. The primary focus of the Freedom Forum is now on the operation of a Newseum in Washington, D.C., celebrating the role of media in promoting liberty. It was Allen's suggestion that led to including an emphasis on religion in the development of liberty with a display of the Gutenberg Bible as an early example of religion in media.[14]

---

[12] Jimmy Allen, " 'Snapshot' Shows Gap Closing," *Bridging the Gap: Religion and the News Media* (Nashville: First Amendment Center, 2000 update) ii.

[13] Allen, "Service at Big Canoe Chapel," 223.

[14] Allen, "Service at Big Canoe Chapel," 226.

Organizing the Cooperative Baptist Fellowship

Throughout his career, Jimmy Allen was clearly identified with the progressive wing of the SBC. While he steadfastly attempted to keep a low profile in the denominational fight of the 1980s, he was initially involved in the work of the *Baptist Laity Journal, Inc.*, a Texas publication formed by John Baugh and others dedicated to the election of denominational loyaltists in the BGCT and SBC. During the political efforts in the SBC, its name was changed to Baptists Committed to the SBC (BC) on 1 January 1989. The mission of the organization was

> Baptists Committed to the SBC is an organization committed to returning our convention to its historic basis of cooperation in missions, evangelism, and education, thus ending this ten-year period of disunity.[15]

When Jimmy was criticized for his involvement during his tenure at the RTVC, he resigned for a time from the organization. But after his resignation as president of the RTVC, he resumed his role in the organization and became the chairman of the group in November 1989. At that time his political judgment on the "controversy" was clear. He said upon his election to this role, "[T]he struggle may have started with theological concerns but the 'so-called cure' turned out to be worse than the disease. 'Presslerism' is the use of secular political methods and power tactics sowing seeds of distrust within a family of faith."[16]

For the next year he worked diligently with networks of state organizations to turn the tide of fundamentalism in the SBC at the national conventions. When Daniel Vestal was defeated for president of the SBC in New Orleans in 1990, the mood of the moderates shifted from continuing the fight within to organizing for a new future outside the politics of the old SBC.

Daniel Vestal, now the Coordinator for the Cooperative Baptist Fellowship describes the idea that formed late in the night after his defeat in New Orleans.

---

[15]Jimmy Allen, "The History of Baptists Committed," *The Struggle for the Soul of the SBC: Moderate Responses to the Fundamentalist Movement*, ed. Walter B. Shurden, 96 (Macon GA: Mercer University Press, 1993).

[16]"Baptists Committed Taps Jimmy Allen," *Western Recorder*, 28 November 1989, 1.

After the New Orleans Convention, Tuesday night, I had some folks up in my suite from FBC, Midland, and Dunwoody Baptist Church, and Jim Denison was there [Denison was his successor in Midland and nominated him for the SBC post].... So, after the folks left my suite, I turned to Jim Denison, and I said, "Jim, let's go up and see Jimmy Allen." I remember we went to his bedroom. He was in bed, pajamas on, and Jim and Jimmy and I, we looked at each other and said, "Well what are we going to do now?"

And I really don't know who suggested it, but we decided that I would call for a meeting of concerned Baptists in Atlanta sometime that fall, and that we would ask BC to plan the meeting, and Jimmy Allen in particular, as chair, to plan that meeting.[17]

Baptists Committed had planned a breakfast meeting for the next morning and Vestal was scheduled to speak. He stayed up until 3:00 a.m. that morning preparing what he would say. He assessed the moderate Baptist movement and its lack of a future in the SBC. He called for a gathering in Atlanta in August to chart a new future. More than 700 people were in that meeting and new energy for a different future was ignited.

Allen gathered the Baptist Committed leadership to plan an "invitation only" meeting of key leaders to be called "Consultation I" in Atlanta in August. Twenty board members representing several states were enlisted to recruit attendees. Oeita Bottorff Chancellor was the primary staff support for BC and managed many of the details of the meeting. When the interest grew beyond the size of the Airport Sheraton Hotel, conference space originally reserved for the meeting, it was moved to the Inforum in downtown Atlanta. More than 3,000 Baptists gathered there on 23-25 August 1990 to seek guidance on the future of moderate Baptists. Jimmy brought the opening welcome, presided at the meeting, and Daniel brought the message calling for action by the group.

A hopeful analysis of the meeting by Walter Shurden identified the emergence of new leadership along with the stable of traditional SBC leaders. He identified key names and key themes from the meeting and said of Allen, "Scratch him and he cries Southern Baptist piety. Impeccable. Credible. Believable." Allen was credited with giving the group a name:

Jimmy Allen gave us another word: "The Fellowship." It is a word akin to "solidarity." It is a dynamic rather than static word. It is a personal rather than

---

[17]Daniel Vestal, interview with Larry L. McSwain, Atlanta, 16 July 2008, 6.

organizational word. "The Fellowship" refers to the movement, the momentum, the energy which is now swirling among moderates.[18]

The meeting resulted in the formation of a Steering Committee for the Fellowship, chaired by Allen and involving some sixty individuals. Jimmy was one of seven at-large members. A new giving mechanism, incorporated by Duke K. McCall, the Cooperative Baptist Missions Program, Inc., was affirmed at the meeting. At McCall's request, Allen recruited thirteen recognized SBC leaders to form its board of directors.

Soon plans were underway for another gathering and the first formal convocation of what by then became known as the Cooperative Baptist Fellowship (CBF) was underway. More than 4,000 people gathered in Atlanta in May 1991; Jimmy presided. John Hewitt, pastor of FBC, Asheville, North Carolina, was elected the first moderator of the group. Patricia Ayres was elected moderator-elect and presided at the 1993 and 1994 annual meetings of the group.

By 1991, the CBF was becoming a viable organization. Allen and Jeanne Bond were cochairs of the Global Missions Ministry Group. They immediately began developing processes for engaging in mission initiatives. When the FMB defunded the Ruschlikon Theological Seminary in Switzerland, the missions group immediately supported replacing as much funding as possible. Fellowship leaders travelled to Europe and committed to the appointment of SBC missionaries in Europe who resigned from the FMB in protest. Thus, the pattern of SBC missions was being quickly replicated, much to the chagrin of some in the Baptist Alliance who were attending fellowship meetings.

Cecil Sherman was elected the first coordinator in spring 1992 and the fellowship took on more structure and purpose. It needed help in the growing mission arena as hundreds of SBC missionaries inquired about CBF appointment. If there were ever a statesman of missions in the era of BMT, it was Keith Parks.

Jimmy Allen made the first telephone call on behalf of the Global Missions Ministry Group to Keith Parks in February 1992 encouraging him to assume missions leadership of CBF. Keith was denied the opportunity by

---

[18]Walter B. Shurden, "Noted Baptist Historian Gives Reflections on Historic 'Fellowship' Meet in Atlanta," *SBC Today* (October 1990): 4.

the FMB trustees to extend for three years his retirement beyond the age of 65. He completed his service as president of the FMB in October 1992.

After months of conversation with Sherman and the missions group, Parks became the Global Missions Coordinator of CBF in February 1993. A staff was emerging of trusted leadership in Sherman and Parks, appointment of missionaries was occurring at a rapid rate, budget receipts were growing, and CBF was on its way.[19]

In recognition of emerging new leadership and the limitations of his new role at Big Canoe, Jimmy resigned in March 1992 from the leadership of Baptists Committed. In time, it would develop into Mainstream Baptists under the leadership of David Currie. It continues to work for the election of moderate Baptists within the Texas convention and has state organizations in a number of other states.

Celebration of a New Baptist Covenant

The opening paragraph of this biography described the development of the New Baptist Covenant. It was the brain child of the consummate peacemaker, Jimmy Carter, who enlisted the new president of Mercer University, William D. Underwood, to assist in putting together the effort. Carter had attempted a reconciliation of competing SBC leaders in a meeting at the Carter Center in the late 1980s without success. He withdrew his own participation from the Convention with the passage in 1987 of a negative SBC resolution toward the role of women in church leadership.

The New Baptist Covenant was an effort to bring together any Baptists who could focus their agenda on ministries of reconciliation without regard for theological agreement. Representatives of the North American Baptist Fellowship (NABF), a subgroup of the BWA, met at the Carter Center on 10 April 2006 to fashion a statement of commitment:

> They specifically committed themselves to their obligation as Christians to promote peace with justice, to feed the hungry, clothe the naked, shelter the homeless, care for the sick and the marginalized, welcome the strangers among us, and promote religious liberty and respect for religious diversity.[20]

---

[19]Cecil Sherman, *By My Own Reckoning* (Macon GA: Smyth & Helwys Publishing, 2008) 214-50, tells the fuller story of CBF.

[20]<http://Newbaptistcovenant.org/history> (accessed 25 July 2008).

Underwood enlisted Jimmy Allen to bring together another larger gathering to continue the discussion. The enlarged meeting of eighty representatives of thirty Baptist groups met on 9 January 2007, again at the Carter Center. Plans were made for a celebration event for January 2008 that would unite the supporting groups in a mass meeting of representatives of all of these groups in a time of worship, study, and brainstorming for the future. Jimmy was involved in each of these meetings and a major source of connection with a number of the representative groups, especially National Baptist leaders.

Bill Underwood accepted the task of supporting the logistics of what was a massive effort. After the January meeting, Bill called Allen from his car on the way home from the meeting:

> I remember calling Jimmy right after the news conference when we announced this. I was driving back to Macon when I called Jimmy on my cell phone, and I said, "Jimmy, what have you done?" I said, "I feel like I've just jumped off a cliff with you." And he laughed, and he said, "Well, at least we've jumped off together."[21]

They worked together the next twelve months putting together the event. Mercer University provided an office, lodging in Atlanta, a full-time executive assistant, and travel funds for Jimmy. He worked with his usual intensity without salary. Together they travelled to raise the funds to support the costs of the event—one and one-half million dollars for publicity, rental space, event consultants, sound, and music leadership. Neither honoraria nor expenses were provided for any of the plenary speakers or the approximately 100 small group leaders. Jimmy and Diane Warren, his executive assistant at Mercer, organized the program with the assistance of a program committee, and other Mercer staff managed contract and business details.

Space does not allow a full description of the event. Needless to say, it was met with a euphoric response from participants. The Celebration for a New Baptist Covenant clearly was the most inclusive, positive, and significant meeting of North American Baptists in their history. It generated its own controversy with accusations from some of a "liberal' bias and no SBC leader participated, though invited to do so.

---

[21]William D. Underwood, interview with Larry L. McSwain, Macon GA, 10 July 2008, 2.

The future impact of the event will require the passage of time before a meaningful assessment can be made of it. A follow-up meeting of seventy leaders of the event was held at the Carter Center on 12 March 2008. Hundreds of suggestions from the Celebration were reviewed and the group identified eleven areas of consensus for cooperative Baptist ministry. It was also agreed that another celebration event would be planned in three years.[22]

The event seems to have generated energy of its own. At the time of this writing five regional events are in the planning stages to move the impact of the gathering to a local level. One might think Jimmy Allen would be ready to rest awhile and bask in the bright light of his many accomplishments. But if you think that, you would be wrong. Jimmy is hard at work helping the regional groups experience their own celebration of a New Baptist Covenant.

Jimmy Allen has never retired from his calling "to make a difference for the Father," his classic language for the leadership of God in doing kingdom ministry in the world. He maintains an active ministry of networking, telephoning, encouraging, travel, and speaking for the causes to which he is committed. He continues his involvement on the board of directors of *Baptists Today*. He delivered one of the inaugural addresses, "Evangelism and Ethics," at the newly established Currie-Strickland Distinguished Lectures in Christian Ethics at Howard Payne University, 28 April 2008. He is still a man with a misson.

---

[22]"Statement on March 12 New Baptist Covenant Follow-Up Meeting," e-mail to registrants for the celebration, 8 April 2008.

Chapter 12
Postscript
The Measure of the Man and His Ministry

> He is an absolutely incredible person to be married to. He is bright, funny, keeps me laughing. He is warm, and caring, and loving. I am never bored. It has been a terrific experience.
>
> —Linda Greer Allen

Describing the life and work of any person of the complexity in personality, significance of accomplishment, and variety of connections and experiences of a Jimmy Allen is difficult, if not impossible. Reading the facts and stories of a life without reflection is as sterile as viewing a masterpiece of art with no reaction to its symbolism and meaning.

This saga is in many ways a metaphor for the larger currents of change that swept across the global, national, and regional landscape since the birth of Jimmy Allen. An examination of the poverty, provincialism, and limitations of the culture of his childhood were no more restrictive of his capacities to dream and contribute to a different world than they were for the culture itself to change. One cannot look at the man today and see more than an outline of the perspectives bred by a Texas ethos in the 1940s and 1950s. So much has changed for the demographic, economic, political, and religious soil that nurtured his life. And as it changed, he changed with it. The values of honesty, hard work, basic commitments to Jesus Christ, and love for the kingdom of God are still intact. But the certainty with which they can be applied have shifted into a more postmodern flexibility of application that is more generous than Southern Baptist theological orthodoxy allowed or denominational structuralism contained. His world is a global world that stretches from Hope, Arkansas to Beijing, Tel Aviv, Tehran, Dublin, and points between. It is a world that includes a cell phone as his constant companion and the latest Apple computer to maintain his database of friends and contacts for continuing his work of kingdom activity. His is a networked world vis-à-vis an institutional one. His is a postdenominational world vis-à-vis a denominational one. His is a pragmatic more than ideological one. His is a world in which Jesus is primary, the individual is central, and the church is important. But the work of the state is sometimes more able to accomplish the ideals of the primary than either the individual or the church. Jimmy Allen is ever the adaptive prophet/priest.

Yet for all of the change in both his context and life, there is an amazing consistency in his identity. There are some things about him that have not changed.

The first word one must use in describing this dynamo from the Southwest is *transparency*. There is little about the man that has been hidden by either himself or his multitude of friends. I have interviewed him ten times over the course of four years and there has never been a question I have asked he did not answer openly and forthrightly. No subject was off limits, though the focus of each interview was on his feelings, work, relationships, connections, and accomplishments. No effort was made to engage in a search for secrets or create of this work an *exposé* of the man.

He is aware of his failures and perceptions of others around him. He knows of the driving ambition others perceive as the force of his efforts, yet he interprets his drive as a part of his call from a God with whom he lives in a feeling of intimacy and direction. All he does he ascribes to the work of the Father in his many sermons and conversations.

The transparency is a product of his integrity. The man knows he has been and is a public figure. There is an attention in the press and in the buzz of conversation by mutual acquaintances of any public figure that uncovers hubris, greed, and scandal in the best of persons. Knowing this, Jimmy Allen has chosen to say what he believes, act on the basis of conviction, live with the consequences of conflict and disagreement from others, and sleep easily at night. His transparency has been such as to open to me his personal files with every scrap of paper he has collected, photographs of family and friends, clippings of news articles that were both critical and complementary, and even the occasional strongly worded letter written to a critic. Twenty-five formal interviews and multiple informal conversations by Jim Newton and me with friends and coworkers who know him best uncovered not even a hint of scandal or moral failure in his long life. While he may exaggerate a financial goal or numerical fact, most can be attributed to the fading memory of a long life than deception or dishonesty. I have attempted to confirm as many of his personal reflections with written records and recollections of others and find an amazing consistency between his memory and reality. Jimmy's public disclosure of his family's pathos and development of a deeper sense of the presence of God in such pain is consistent with his transparency. His life is an open book.

Jimmy Allen is a strong *extrovert*. Seldom has he shown shyness in calling, writing, visiting, or connecting with people of every imaginable status, belief system, ethnicity, race, nationality, or political perspective. "Stanger" is not a word in his vocabulary. On one occasion, he saw Jimmy Durante smoking a cigarette outside a club in the French Quarter in New Orleans where Allen was visiting Bob Harrington, the "Chaplain of Bourbon Street." He walked to him, introduced himself, and struck up a conversation. He laughed as he told the story, "I went home and said, 'I met Jimmy Durante.' Wanda said, 'Everywhere you go!' "[1]

He offered Bob Hope a quarter to use when he observed him making a telephone call at Love Field airport in Dallas years ago, just to strike up a conversation with him. He has met with presidents and peasants, world leaders and neighborhood outcasts, corporate and university CEOs and janitors who work for them, visited executives and dying grandmothers in hospitals, and shared his faith with terrorists and the terrorized. He is a man able to connect because at the heart of who he is, Jimmy Allen loves people.

Yet for all of his extroversion, he is amazingly inward in his decision-making processes. As an RA leader, a pastor, a denominational leader, an administrator, and a prophet of the social gospel, he acted largely on the basis of intuitive responses to the moment. While not immune to the opinions of others, he has always shaped his decisions of what to do as an act of inward obedience to his understanding of the "will of the Father." Sometimes his actions did not make much sense to those around him, whether family members who experienced too much of his absence in their lives, church members who read in local news accounts with amazement of travel to Iran, board members who considered his ideas too expensive, or friends who thought he was seeking the limelight of public attention. Every major decision of his life grew out of an inward and prayerful searching after the heart of God.

Closely related to this inwardness is the fact Jimmy is a *whistler*. Once he has acted, reactions seldom ruffle him. Coworkers describe a man who walked the halls of his work place whistling, because he was relaxed in the tasks he was doing and direction he was leading. Disagreements could come his way, but he seemed never to take them too seriously. Whistlers sleep well at night, and he seemed to manage his usual four hours of sleep at night with little restlessness or anxiety. The most difficult questions for him

---

[1]Jimmy Allen, "Service at Big Canoe Chapel and Media Consulting," interview no. 9 with Larry L. McSwain, Omni Hotel, Atlanta, 22 June 2006, 227.

to answer in my frequent interviews were related to enemies, detractors, persons with whom he had conflict, or opponents. He managed differences with a minimum of internal *angst*.

Jimmy Allen is an exciting *preacher*. He should be. He has been doing it for more than sixty-five years. The content of his preaching is usually a unique blend of biblical text with an interpretation that applies to the world today, the identification of problems or issues to which the text can speak, and illustrations of the major points of the sermon from current news, literature, movies, television, or other entertainment venues. His listeners connect at multiple levels to the sermon.

This preacher's style probably explains more of his attractiveness than its content. Many preachers bring solid content to the pulpit. But Jimmy Allen's preaching has about it an energy and excitement that are contagious. His father had a speech difficulty in that he was a heavy stutterer. Jimmy Allen does not stutter, but there is a unique pattern of staccato-like intensity that borders on it when he preaches. He ascends the pulpit as though he is assaulting the gates of hell and speaks with the intensity and enthusiasm of a mass evangelist, but with a message that balances the call to discipleship with that of a social prophet. If his theology were different, he could have been a Pentecostal preacher—his emotion is nearly that strong! James Dunn described it to me in a note as "high energy, sometimes breathless." That is to say, there is a feeling dimension to his preaching and his listeners are moved as much by the emotion of the sermon as its content. Because he has lived so long on the edge of personal pain, there is a confessional quality in preaching that brings laughter, grief, breaks in the voice, and tears. Anyone who could hear his sermon, "Echoes from the Valley of Darkness" and not shed tears has little feeling.

Jimmy Allen is the *networker of all networkers*.[2] He developed the practice early in his ministry of keeping detailed information on the people he met in his travels. In addition to his prodigious memory, he kept a rolodex and now a computer file of names and contact information for hundreds of people. Stories emerged throughout this study of literally thousands of telephone calls, letters, conference meetings, conversations, travel encounters, connections made, and assistance provided. To this day,

---

[2]This is the description of his long-time friend and former personal attorney P. Oswin Chrisman, interview excerpts with Jim Newton, Dallas, 2 July 2005, 2. He said, "He seemed to know everyone."

one can secure the information needed to contact people he knows; the files are up-to-date. He remains a source people contact if they want a recommendation for a pastor, teacher, or denominational/fellowship worker. Especially important are his contacts with leaders of Baptist African American churches, a level of trust and experience few other white Baptists in the South can claim. This skill enabled him to organize large collections of Baptists in mass meetings at Houston when president of the BGCT and later the SBC. More recently his service as program chair of the Celebration for a New Baptist Covenant demonstrated his skills in connecting with a wide variety of leaders across the spectrum of white moderate and black Baptist life in North America.

Jimmy Allen is a *survivor*. He has never been a participant of the popular television program by that name, but his ability to maintain a strong sense of providence, to keep on serving when life was crashing in within the family, to organize new alliances when the denomination he loved was falling apart, and to seek new life with a new partner after the death of his beloved are all testimony to an unusual endurance.

I have been privileged to share in both the public and private life of this unusual man. In one of our interview sessions, I asked him to reflect on his life with a pointed question: "What if you were twenty-two in 2006 and you had your life ahead of you. What would you dream to do, to become?"

> You know, one of the things I learned back there and I wasn't twenty two when I learned it, I learned it when I was twenty-six or -seven. I learned that it's more important to do the next thing God has for you than to think about what you want to do with the rest of your life. I've been accused of being very ambitious. I have never consciously been ambitious. I am sure I am. I think if I were twenty-two I would want to look around and find what vehicle God is using and I would want to attach myself to it for God to use me. I don't know where that would be right now. . . . I would try to find some place where I could serve him more than trying to save the world's ecology, but include that, more than try to do the racial justice, but include that. When you get down to it, there is nothing better than being a Baptist preacher doing the gospel and being alert to try to figure out how to apply it. So, I don't know that I would do anything radically different. I would probably find a congregation that would listen to me and preach the gospel and try to make that work.[3]

---

[3] Allen, "Service at Big Canoe Chapel and Media Consulting," 229.

One thing is clear. The thirteen-year-old lad who heard George W. Truett declare, "I would rather be a Baptist pastor than the president of the United States" learned a lesson he never forgot. Jimmy Allen had a higher destiny than just serving the world or the people within it. He had a calling. That calling and the nurture of loving parents were decisive for his life. His explanation for his chosen paths is clear:

> My explanation comes down to John 15:16 which is the theme of my life: "You are chosen. I have chosen you and ordained you that you go and bring forth fruit. And that you abide in me and whatever you ask in my name I will give you." I discovered that is the theme of my life basically when I was in seminary. . . . Everything I have touched comes of a sense of calling and an alertness I feel to do whatever the Father opens at that time. . . . And those things open up. They open up because the feeling that if you have a sense of calling and that calling is pastoral and good news sharing you just pastor folks wherever they are. You don't just pastor the people on your roll. You don't make your judgment on how well the structure is doing at that moment. The gospel is bigger than that.[4]

The accomplishments of this life did not come without some regrets. I asked again at the conclusion of our interview process, "As you look back, what do you wish you hadn't done?" There was no hesitation in his response:

> There is lots of that. Oh me. What I wish I had not done? Vocationally, I don't think there is any move that I felt I made a mistake in the move. . . . I think I wasn't as aware and useful as a husband and father as I wanted to be. . . . I wish I not been on the road as much as I was when Wanda was going through her emotional traumas and her illnesses. Because that meant that my children, whom I was affirming as best I could, were doing things I should have known about and dealt with in a different way. I think those are the things I regret. . . . I think life hits you in the solar plexis with things like AIDS and all you can do is plough through it the best you can. The things I wish I hadn't done? There aren't many of them vocationally. I don't think of anything right now that I would go through the agony of trying to redo.[5]

Few Baptist leaders have received the honors and accolades as has Jimmy. Appendix A lists the most important of the honors and awards he

---

[4] Allen, "Service at Big Canoe Chapel and Media Consulting," 226-27.
[5] Allen, "Service at Big Canoe Chapel and Media Consulting," 228-29.

has received. He is the only Baptist minister I know to receive a Golden Halo award from the Southern California Motion Picture Council and an Emmy for programming at the Radio and Television Commission. Added to it is a Wilbur award from the Religious Public Relations Council, Inc. for his work as co-author of *Bridging the Gap*. He is the recipient of honorary doctorates from Howard Payne University, California Baptist College (now University), University of Richmond, Southwest Baptist College, and Mercer University. He has received at least a dozen distinguished service awards including distinguished alumni awards from his high school, college and seminary. It is altogether appropriate he would be identified as among the ten most influential Baptists in Texas in the twentieth century.

The word I would ascribe to Jimmy Allen is *friend*. When Wanda died in 2003, Jimmy made a nostalgic journey connecting with friends across the country to remember, grieve, and heal. He had to make a lot of stops between Georgia and Texas to touch a small percentage of the many people who have known him, admired his leadership, and loved him for his passion and commitments. I first heard him in a seminary classroom in 1964 and have heard him preach, read his writings, and listened to his life story. Many across the years of his ministry could echo the judgment made by Charles Wade, who at the time of this interview was executive director of the BGCT:

> Bottom line, I would say that Jimmy Allen was as close to being a mentor to me as any other person in the world, except perhaps my own father. I saw in Jimmy Allen the strengths that I wanted to develop in my own life. Here's an interesting little story that I told Jimmy, and he appreciated it. When I came to First Baptist Church, Arlington, Texas, and we started Mission Arlington, I told Jimmy that our ministry is a direct outgrowth of all that I saw in the life and ministry of Jimmy Allen and First Baptist Church of San Antonio; and what God was doing in my life to help me to see that the work of the church is to be the presence of Christ as the Body of Christ to do what Jesus did. So we got involved in Mission Arlington and developed a ministry to the least and the last and the left out across our city. God blessed it. I had Jimmy Allen come and preach a revival; he told me that we [FBC Arlington] were doing what he had hoped to be able to do [at FBC San Antonio]. That's as fine affirmation as I've ever had from anyone.[6]

---

[6]Charles Wade, interview with Jim Newton, Dallas, 6 July 2005, 3.

Learning the story of one of God's servants has been a blessing to me as well. It is my hope and prayer that this journey with him will enrich your life as much as it has mine.

Appendix
Jimmy R. Allen Honors and Awards

Distinguished Alumnus Award, Howard Payne College, 31 October 1969.

Distinguished Service Award for Outstanding Leadership in Christian Ethics, Christian Life Commission, Southern Baptist Convention, 12 September 1972.

Diploma de Honor de Merito, El Ministerio de Salud Publica e Asistencia Social, Tegucigapa, DC by Enrico Aguilar Paz, 20 April 1975.

Doctor of Divinity, Howard Payne University, Brownwood Texas, 13 May 1978.

Citation and Recognition of Leadership for Service as President of the SBC, City Council, City of San Antonio, 19 January 1979.

Doctor of Humanities, California Baptist College, Riverside, California, May 1979.

Doctor of Divinity, University of Richmond, 13 May 1979. Also Baccalaureate speaker.

Commencement Address, San Marcos Baptist Academy, San Marcos, Texas, 21 May 1979.

Doctor of Humanities, Southwest Baptist College, Bolivar, Missouri, 3 March 1980. Also Commencement Speaker.

Distinguished Service Award, Christian Life Commission, Baptist General Convention of Texas, 1980.

Distinguished Alumnus Award, Southwestern Baptist Theological Seminary, presented by Foy Valentine, St. Louis, Missouri, 11 June 1980.

Golden Halo Award, Southern California Motion Picture Council recognizing the need for substantive, people-centered TV programming. Presented by David Soul, star of "Starsky and Hutch," Los Angeles, California, March 1985.

Daytime Emmy Awards, Outstanding Special Class Program Area, "China: Walls and Bridges," shown on ABC, Jimmy R. Allen, Executive Producer, 1988–1989.

Wilbur Award from the Religious Public Relations Council, Inc. to John Dart and Jimmy Allen for "Bridging the Gap: Religion and the News Media, Birmingham, Alabama, 1994.

T. B. Maston Christian Ethics Award, T. B. Maston Foundation, Ft. Worth, Texas, 21 November 1997.

National Service Award, Love In Action, Bethesda, Maryland, to Jimmy Allen and Family, October 1998.

Vocational Excellence Award, Rotary Club of Jasper, 1998.

Brooks Hays Christian Citizenship Award, Second Baptist Church, Little Rock, Arkansas, November 7, 1999.

Named one of the 10 most influential Texas Baptists in the Twentieth Century by the *Baptist Standard*, 8 December 1999.

Inaugural Judson-Rice Award by *Baptists Today*, Big Canoe, Georgia, 17 September 2001.

One of thirty-seven in inaugural class of the Baptist Hall of Fame, Mainstream Network, Charlotte, North Carolina, 15 February 2002.

Expression of Appreciation, Property Owners Association of Big Canoe, Big Canoe, Georgia, 20 November 2002.

T. B. Maston/Jimmy R. Allen Scholarship at Wake Forest University Divinity School, 2003.

Doctor of Humanities, Mercer University, Macon, Georgia, 17 May 2003.

Distinguished Alumnus Award for Outstanding Achievements, Forrest High School Alumni Association, May 2004.

Whitsitt Courage Award, William H. Whitsitt Baptist Heritage Society, Dallas, Texas, 30 June 2005.

Bibliography

Dissertations

Allen, Jimmy R. "A Comparative Study of the Concept of the Kingdom of God in the Writings of Walter Rauschenbusch and Reinhold Niebuhr." Th.D. Dissertation, Southwestern Baptist Theological Seminary, 1958.

Stricklin, Billy David. "An Interpretive History of the Christian Life Commission of the Baptist General Convention of Texas, 1950–1977." Ph.D. Dissertation, Baylor University, 1981.

Books and Book Chapters

Allen, Jimmy. *Burden of a Secret: A Story of Truth and Mercy in the Face of AIDS*. Nashville: Moorings, 1995.

_____. "The Bible Speaks on War and Peace," *Peace! Peace!* edited by Foy Valentine, 26-47. Waco TX: Word Books, 1967.

_____. "The History of Baptists Committed," *The Struggle for the Soul of the SBC: Moderate Responses to the Fundamentalist Movement*, edited by Walter B. Shurden, 93-100. Macon GA: Mercer University Press, 1993.

Annual(s) of the Southern Baptist Convention, 1975–1990.

Baker, Robert A. *A History of Southwestern Baptist Theological Seminary, 1908–1983*. Nashville: Broadman Press, 1983.

Bennis, Warren G. and Robert J. Thomas. *Geeks and Geezers: How Era, Values, and Defining Moments Shape Leaders*. Cambridge MA: Harvard Business School Press, 2002.

Bowden, Mark. *Guests of the Ayatollah: The First Battle in America's War with Militant Islam*. New York: Atlantic Monthly Press, 2006.

Brokaw, Tom. *The Greatest Generation*. New York: Random House, 2004.

Carroll, Jackson W., Douglas W. Johnson, and Martin E. Marty. *Religion in America: 1950 to the Present*. San Francisco: Harper & Row, 1979.

Christian Life Commission, Baptist General Convention of Texas, 1950–1970. Dallas: Christian Life Commission of Texas, n.d. (Cited in Storey, 140.)

Dart, John and Jimmy Allen. *Bridging the Gap: Religion and the News Media*. Nashville: First Amendment Center, 2000.

Dawson, J. M. *Christ and Social Change*. Boston: Judson Press, 1937.

Hankins, Barry. *Unease in Babylon: Southern Baptist Conservatives and American Culture*. Tuscaloosa: University of Alabama Press, 2002.

In the Shadow of His Hand, First Baptist Church of San Antonio, Texas, Supplement 1, 1961–1981. Austin, Texas: Hart Graphics, 1981.

Lewis, Paul. "Walter Rauschenbusch (1861–1918): Pioneer of Baptist Social Ethics." *Twentieth-Century Shapers of Baptist Social Ethics*, edited by Larry L. McSwain, 3-22, 335-36. Macon GA: Mercer University Press, 2008.

Lindsell, Harold. *The Battle for the Bible*. Grand Rapids MI: Zondervan, 1978.

McBeth, Harry Leon. *Texas Baptists: A Sesquicentennial History*. Dallas: Baptistway Press, 1998.

McIver, Bruce. *Riding the Wind of God: A Personal History of the Youth Revival Movement*. Macon GA: Smyth & Helwys, 2002.

McSwain, Larry L. "Jimmy R. Allen: Connecting American and Chinese Christians Through Media," *Take Root Downward, Bear Fruit Upward, A Festschrift for Chou Lien Hua*, edited by Johnson T. K. Lim, 229-43. ABGTS Publications, 2008.

Pinson, William M., Jr. *An Approach to Christian Ethics: The Life, Contribution, and Thought of T. B. Maston.* Nashville: Broadman Press, 1979.

Pressler, Paul. *A Hill on Which to Die: One Southern Baptist's Journey.* Nashville: B and H Publishing Group, 1999.

Richardson, Ronald W. *Becoming a Healthier Pastor.* Minneapolis: Fortress Press, 2005.

_____. *Family Ties That Bind.* Third edition. North Vancouver BC: International Self-Counsel Press, 2007.

Sapp, David. "Foy Valentine (1923-2006): Helping Changed People Change the World." *Twentieth-Century Shapers of Baptist Social Ethics*, edited by Larry L. McSwain, 296-310, 342-43. Macon GA: Mercer University Press, 2008.

Schweitzer, Albert. *Out of My Life and Thought: An Autobiography.* Translated by C. T. Campion. Reprint: New York: Holt, Rinehart & Winston, 1961 [1933].

Sherman, Cecil. *By My Own Reckoning.* Macon GA: Smyth & Helwys, 2008.

Shurden, Walter B., editor. *The Struggle for the Soul of the SBC.* Macon GA: Mercer University Press, 1993.

Skinner, Tom. *How Black Is the Gospel?* Philadelphia: Lippincott, 1970.

_____. *Black and Free.* Grand Rapids MI: Zondervan, 1971.

_____. *Words of Revolution.* Grand Rapids MI: Zondervan, 1971.

_____. *If Christ Is the Answer, What Are the Questions?* Grand Rapids MI: Zondervan, 1974.

Smith, Timothy L. *Revivalism and Social Reform: American Protestantism on the Eve of the Civil War.* New York: Harper Torchbooks, 1957.

Stone, Howard W., and James O. Duke, *How to Think Theologically.* Second edition. Minneapolis: Fortress Press, 2006.

Storey, John W. *Texas Baptist Leadership and Social Christianity, 1900–1980.* College Station TX: Texas A&M University Press, 1986.

Strickland, David. *A Genealogy of Dissent: Southern Baptist Protest in the Twentieth Century.* Lexington: University Press of Kentucky, 1999.

_____. "Koinonia Farm: Epicenter for Social Change, Clarence Jordan (1912–1969), Jasper Martin England (1901–1989), and Millard Fuller (1935–   )." *Twentieth Century Shapers of Baptist Social Ethics*, edited by Larry L. McSwain, 163-87, 328-29. Macon GA: Mercer University Press, 2008.

Suter, Carr M., Jr. *O Zion, Haste: The Story of the Dallas Baptist Association.* Dallas: Dallas Baptist Association, 1978.

Sweet, William Warren. *Revivalism in America: Its Origin, Growth and Decline.* Gloucester MA: Peter Smith, 1965.

Terrell, Charlene. *Church in the Wildwood: The Continuing Story of Big Canoe Chapel.* Big Canoe Chapel, 2007.

Tillman, William M., Jr. "T. B. Maston (1897–1988): Mentor to Southern Baptist Prophets." *Twentieth-Century Shapers of Baptist Social Ethics*, edited by Larry L. McSwain, 61-80, 334-35. Macon GA: Mercer University Press, 2008.

Towery, Britt. *Churches of China: Taking Root Downward, Bearing Fruit Upward*. Third edition. Waco TX: Baylor University Press, 1990.

Walker, J. Brent. "Religious Libertarians: J. M. Dawson (1879–1973) and James M. Dunn (1932–)." *Twentieth Century Shapers of Baptist Social Ethics*, edited by Larry L. McSwain, 277-95, 323-26. Macon GA: Mercer University Press, 2008.

Walker, J. Brent Walker, editor. *James Dunn: Champion for Religious Liberty*. Macon GA: Smyth & Helwys, 1999.

Interviews

Oral Memoirs of Jimmy Raymond Allen. Religion and Culture Project, Program for Oral History. Waco TX: Baylor University, 1973.

 Allen interview no. 1, by Thomas L. Charlton, San Antonio TX: First Baptist Church, 15 September 1972.

 Allen interview no. 2, by Thomas L. Charlton, Waco TX: Baylor University, 1 May 1973.

 Allen interview no. 3, by Daniel B. McGee, San Antonio TX: First Baptist Church, 9 June 1973.

 Allen interview no. 4, by Daniel B. McGee, San Antonio TX: First Baptist Church, 27 August 1973.

 Allen interview no. 5, by Daniel B. McGee, San Antonio TX: First Baptist Church, 28 August, 1973.

Oral Memories of Jimmy Raymond Allen. Waco: Baylor University Institute for Oral History, 2007. A Series of interviews Conducted by Susie Valentine and Robert Parham, Fort Worth TX: Radio and Television Commission, 13 March 1980–24 June 1983.

Allen, Jimmy. "Early Life Experiences," Interview Number 1 with Larry L. McSwain. Big Canoe GA, 1 November 2004.

_____. "Faith and Education Journey" Interview Number 2 with Larry L. McSwain. Alpharetta GA, 13 November 2004.

_____. "The Christian Life Commission and Texas Baptist Life," Interview Number 3 with Jim Newton and Larry L. McSwain. Big Canoe GA, 14 November 2004.

_____. "Involvement in HIV/AIDS," Interview Number 4 with Larry L. McSwain. McAfee School of Theology, Atlanta GA, 16 December 2004.

_____. "Service as Pastor of First Baptist Church, San Antonio," Interview Number 5 with Larry L. McSwain. Big Canoe GA, 7 March 2005.

_____. "President of the SBC," Interview Number 6 with Larry L. McSwain. Cumming GA, 20 September 2005.

_____. "President of the Radio and Television Commission, SBC," Interview Number 7 with Larry L. McSwain. Big Canoe GA, 12 December 2005.

_____. "Visits to Israel and Iran," Interview Number 8 with Larry L. McSwain. Big Canoe GA, 2 March 2006.

_____. "Service at Big Canoe Chapel and Media Consulting," Interview Number 9 with Larry L. McSwain. Omni Hotel, Atlanta GA, 22 June 2006.

_____. "Life, Ministry and Friendships," Interview with Jim Newton. Dallas TX, 31 July 2005.

Allen, Linda Greer, "Interview with Larry McSwain." Big Canoe GA, 16 July 2008.

Allen, Stephen "Skip." "Interview with Jim Newton." Dallas TX, 1 July 2007.

Ayers, Patricia. "Interview with Larry L. McSwain." Atlanta GA, 11 November 2004.

Brake, Janice. "E-mail Interview with Larry L. McSwain." Atlanta GA, 9 September 2007.

Carter, Jimmy. "Interview with Larry L. McSwain." Carter Center, Atlanta GA, 19 May 2006.

Chancellor, Oeita Bottorff. "Interview with Jim Newton," Dallas TX, 2 July 2005.

Chrismon, P. Oswin. "Interview with Jim Newton." Dallas TX, 2 July 2005.

Cooper, James. "Interview with Jim Newton." Dallas TX, 5 July 2005.

Dixon, Ron, "Telephone Interview with Larry L. McSwain." Atlanta GA, 11 August 2008.

Dunn, James. "Inteview with Jim Newton." Dallas TX, 1 July 2005.

Gray, Nadine "Pinky." "Telephone Interview with Larry L. McSwain." Atlanta GA, 12 August 2008.

Jivasantikarn, Nirund. "Interview with Larry L. McSwain." Westminster SC, 21 September 2007.

Jones, Jim. "Interview with Jim Newton." Dallas TX, 1 July 2005.

McCartney, Richard T. "E-mail Correspondence with Larry L. McSwain." Gentry, AR, 18 July 2008.

Newton, Jim. "Telephone Interview with Larry L. McSwain." Atlanta GA, 2 July 2008.

Parks, Keith. "Interview with Jim Newton." Dallas TX, 30 June 2005.

Pinson, William M., Jr. "Interview with Jim Newton." Dallas TX, 30 June 2005.

Stinson, Roddy. "E-mail Interview with Larry L. McSwain." San Antonio TX, 28 August 2007.

Strickland, Phil. "Interview with Jim Newton." Dallas TX, 4 July 2005.

Towrey, Britt. "E-mail Correspondence with Larry L. McSwain." San Angelo TX, 15 August 2008.

Underwood, William D. "Interview with Larry L. McSwain." Macon GA. 10 July 2008.

Vestal, Daniel. "Interview with Larry L. McSwain." Atlanta GA. 11 July 2008.

Wade, Charles. "Interview with Jim Newton." Dallas TX. 6 July 2005.

Articles, News Accounts, and Unpublished Materials

"AIDS Panel Offers Critical Report: Group's Final Work Charges Government with 'Dogged Denial.'" *Washington Post*, 29 June 1993, A4.

"Allen Supports Carter Call for American Unity," *San Antonio Express-News*, 18 July 1979, n.p.

Allen, Jimmy. "Distrust Cited between Press and Church Leaders." *Western Recorder*, 21 September 1993, 8.

_____. Editorial. *Christian Index*, 15 June 1978.

_____. "Eulogy for Foy Valentine." *Christian Ethics Today* 12/1 (Winter 2006): 6-8.

_____. "Georgi Vins is Voice to Conscience." *San Antonio Express-News*, 5 May 1979, B3.

_____. "Lay Religion Being Revived in Japan." *San Antonio Express-News*, 7 August 1976, C12.

_____. "Media Violence in America." *Christian Ethics Today* 1/3 (October 1995): 21-25.

_____. "No Frozen Images, (Exodus 20:4)." *Christian Ethics Today* 6/1 (February 2000): 19.

_____. "Our Troubled Baptist Conscience in Separation of Church and State." *Christianity and Political Action*, Messages from the Christian Life Conference on Christianity and Political Action, Glorietta and Ridgecrest, August 11-17 and August 25-31, 1960. N.p.

_____. "Star Maker/Sparrow Watcher." *Christian Ethics Today* 5/3 (June 1999): 27.

_____. "Studies Differ on Media's Coverage of Religion." *Western Recorder*, 29 March 1994, 7.

_____. "Sunrise for Jacob at Jabbock." *Christian Ethics Today* 5/3 (June 1999): 27.

_____. "The Tears of God." *Christian Ethics Today* 8/1 (February 2002): 4-7.

_____. "Thomas Buford Maston: Baptist Apostle of Biblical Ethics." *Christian Ethics Today* 9/5 (December 2003): 6-10.

_____. "Where There Is Vision . . . the People Flourish." *Baptist Standard*, 14 June 1978, 5.

"ACTS Network Given Boost with $2.8 Million Pledged." *Baptist Standard*, 18 April 1984, 5.

"Allen Attacks 'New Right' Evangelicals." *San Antonio Express-News*, 7 October 1980, 7-A.

Ammerman, Nancy T. "SBC Moderates and the Making of a Postmodern Denomination." *Christian Century* (22-29 September 1993): 896-99.

"Anita Bryant Beaten in Baptist Balloting: 'Messengers' May Spend $12 Million." *The Atlanta Constitution*, 14 June 1978, A1, A24.

Annual(s) of the Southern Baptist Convention, 1975–1990.

"As Baptist Convention Grows, Cities Available Are Scarcer." *Atlanta Journal and Constitution*, 17 June 1978, B8.

"Baptists Get Dynamo by Electing Allen." *San Antonio Express-News*, 17 June 1977, editorials, A14.

Baptists Close by Condemning Racism, Rapping ERA Extension." *The Atlanta Journal*, 16 June 1978, A1, A22.

"Baptists in State Entering Satellite Age of Television." *The Baptist Record*, 9 September 1982, 1-2.

Beck, Rosalie, "Jimmy Allen." *Baptist Standard*, 8 December 1999, 4.

"Bishop Allin Press Faith Appeal to Iran." *Diocesan Press Service*, 20 December 1979, 2.

Bishop, Amelia. "Eula Mae Henderson." *Baptist Standard*, 8 December 1999, 8.

Bowden, Mark. "Among the Hostages Takers." *Atlantic Monthly* 294/95 (December 2004): 77-96.

_____. "Captivity Pageant." *Atlantic Monthly* 295 (December 2005) <http://www.theatlantic.com/doc/200512/december-1979/3> (accessed 18 April 2008).

_____. "The Desert One Debacle." *Atlantic Monthly* 296 (May 2006): 62-77.

Bunch, David T. "Mission Service Corps History." An unpublished paper, n.d.

"Cable Stats." *Cablevision*, 1 February 1988, 64.

"The Camp David Guest List." *Time*, 23 July 1979, 30-31.

"Carter Challenge Brings $750,000 Response." *Baptist Standard*, 10 May 1978, 3.

"Carter's Test: 'I Want Our Country to Be Strong.'" *Atlanta Journal and Constitution*, 17 June 1978, A5.

"Cause for Optimism." *Los Angeles Times*, 26 July 1989, Metro Section, 6.

Cheshire, Ashley. "Children of AIDS." *Fort Worth Star-Telegram*, 24 June 1990, sect. 1, 16-18.

Chesser, Larry. "Baptists Collide over Prayer Amendment." *Baptist Standard*, 4 August 1982, 5.

Chuvala, Bob. "Television Preachers Who *Don't* Ask for Money," *Christian Herald* (October 1987): 18-22.

"Clerical Group Urges Americans to support Carter 'Call to Action.' " *New York Times*, 17 July 1979.

Coleman, Lucien. "The Southern Baptist Convention and the Media," *Review and Expositor* 81/1 (Winter 1984): 19-29.

Demarko, Sharon. "Two Jimmys Lead Parade of Southern Baptists." *Pensacola Journal*, 20 June 1978, 1.

Disraeli, Benjamin. *Contarina Fleming*, 1832. <http://www.quotationsbook.com/quote/4266> (accessed 4 April 2009).

"Down to Earth." Weekly series of commentaries on moral and spiritual issues published in the *San Antonio Express-News*.

"Evangelical Christians and the New Right." *USA Today*, February 1981, 13.

"Evangelism Is Losing that Old-Time Religion." *New York Times*, 5 August 1970, 29.

Garcia, Kenneth J. "Disaster Relief Sought for Cities Hit Hard by AIDS." *Los Angeles Times*, 26 January 1990, Metro Section, 3.

Gibson, Campbell. "Population of the 100 Largest Cities and Other Urban Places in the United State: 1790 to 1990." Population Division Working Paper No. 27. Washington DC, June 1998. <http://www.census.gov/population/www/documentation/twps0027.html> (accessed 22 August 2007).

_____, and Kay Jung. "Historical Census Statistics on Population Totals by Race, 1790 to 1990, and By Hispanic Origin, 1970 to 1990, For Large Cities and Other Urban Places in the United States." Working Paper No. 76. Washington DC: U.S. Census Bureau, February 2005. <http://www.census.gov/population/www/documentation/twps0076.html> (accessed 22 August 2007).

Gordon, Pat. "Tune in to Tranquility: Baptist Broadcasters See End to Rocky Road." *Dallas Morning News*, 13 July 1980, 1, 4.

Goldman, Peter, et al. "To Lift a Nation's Spirit." *Newsweek*, 23 July 1979, 20-26.

Harwell, Jack. Editorial. *Christian Index*, 25 May 1978.

"The Haystack Prayer Meeting" and "America's First Protestant Missionaries," <http:/wso.williams.edu/dchu/MissionPark/meeting.htm> (accessed 2 October 2007).

Hastings, Robert J. "Jimmy's Never Been Afraid to Ask." *The Baptist Program*, April 1987, 12-14.

Hendricks, David. "Allen Leads 'Church That Cares.' " *San Antonio Express-News*, 26 January 1978, 9-A.

_____. "Allen Supports Carter Call for American Unity." *San Antonio Express-News*. 18 July 1979, A2.

Hitts, Philip. "Touched by AIDS, Minister Finds Doors Shut." *New York Times*, 8 September 1992, A1.

Hodges, Sam. "Baptists Sell Last of FamilyNet Broadcast Unit." *Dallas Morning News*, 7 September 2007 <www.dallasnews.com/sharedcontent/dws/news/localnews/stories/090507dnmetfamilynet-work> (accessed 18 September 2007).

"Hollywood Group Honors ACTS for Excellence." *Florida Baptist Witness*, 14 March 1985.

"Hyman Jedidiah Appleman, 1902–1983." <http://www.believerweb.org> (accessed 28 May 2007).

"Independence Is All History." *San Antonio Express-News*, 15 April 1978, 1-8.

"Interfaith Panel Questions 'Christian Right' Politics." *Baptists and Reflector*, 15 October 1980.

Irwin, Julie. "Safe Haven for Children Affected by AIDS: One Christian Family's Struggle with the Disease Inspired Lydia's House." *The Cincinnati Inquirer*, 6 May 1999.

Jarboe, Jan. "Dr. Jimmy Allen: A Light Profile." *San Antonio Light*, 29 January 1979, A2.

"Jimmy Allen Announces Premiere of TV Network." *Western Recorder*, 6 February 1990, 5.

"Jimmy Allen Talks about the Southern Baptist TV Strategy." *Religious Broadcasting* 12/6 (September 1980): 45, 50.

Jones, Jim. "Baptist Leader Taking on Another Challenge." *Fort Worth Star-Telegram*, 16 August 1981, 1-3.

_____. "Baptist Network on Air with Wing'n'Prayer." *Fort Worth Star-Telegram*, 16 May 1984, 13-14.

_____. "Baptist Official Sees Rejoicing if Hostages Freed Soon." *Fort Worth Star-Telegram*, 3 November 1989, 3.

_____. "Baptist TV Network Seeks to Raise Funds: Officials Hope $12.5 Million Will Help ACTS Become Self-Sufficient." *Fort Worth Star-Telegram*, 23 January 1985, A1, A15.

_____. "Baptists Hire FW Firm for $6 Million TV Fund Campaign." *Fort Worth Star-Telegram*, 17 April 1985, n.p.

_____. "Baptists Limit Church Politics of TV Official." *Fort Worth Star-Telegram*, 28 January 1985, 1, 15.

_____. "Baptists Marshal Forces for 'Duel at Dallas.'" *Fort Worth Star-Telegram*, 7 June 1985, 1, 6.

_____. "Baptists Move Toward Network Sale." *Fort Worth Star-Telegram*, 13 April 1988, 15, 18.

_____. "Christian Television Network to Lay Off 18." *Fort Worth Star-Telegram*, 18 March 1989, 12.

_____. "Critics Can't Keep Baptist Network Down." *Fort Worth Star-Telegram*, 12 March 1988, sect. 4, 9.

_____. "Former President of Baptist Network Forms Company." *Fort Worth Star-Telegram*, 25 July 1989, 4-1, 4-3.

_____. "Minister Resigns as Head of TV Network." *Fort Worth Star-Telegram*, 12 April 1989, sect. 1, 13-14.

_____. "Southern Baptist TV Network Set for Large Start." *Fort Worth Star-Telegram*, 16 December 1983, 1, 3.

Jordan, Hamilton. "Carter: The Final Hostage." *San Antonio Express-News*, 28 December 1980, C1.

Kenyon, Bill. "New President Feels Baptist Faith Maturing." *Dallas Morning News*, 16 June 1977, A12.

Kimball, Charles A. "Listening to the Voices of Iran." *Boston Sunday Globe*, 27 January 1980, A4.

_____. "Perspective: Mission to Iran." *Harvard Divinity Bulletin* (December-January 1980): 15-16.

_____. "Iran's Agony—An Eyewitness Report," *Inquiry Magazine* 3/6 (3 March 1980): 6-8.

Knox, Marv. "Leaders of '40s Youth Revivals Gather to Reminisce, Kindle New 'Fires.'" *Baptist Standard*, 24 October 2006; *Baptists Today*, December 2006, 15.

_____. "New Baptist Covenant: Unity, Harmony. Now, What Comes Next?" <http://www.newbaptistcelebration.org/news> (accessed 7 July 2008).

_____. "SBC Presidents: Study of 12 Reveals Trends over 20 Years." *SBC Today*, May 1983, 4-7, 23.

Leonard, Bill J. "When the Denominational Center Doesn't Hold: The Baptist Experience." *Christian Century* (22-29 September 1993): 905-10.

Livingston, Victor. "Acting on Faith: The Southern Baptist Convention Plans to Launch ACTS in May with an Evangelical Bent and a Funding Twist." *CableVision*, 30 January 1984, n.p.

Lord, Lewis J., et al. "An Unholy War in the TV Pulpits." *U.S. News and World Report*, 6 April 1987, 58-65.

McSwain, Larry L. " 'Loving Past Our Theology': Jimmy R. Allen and the HIV/AIDS Crisis." *Whitsett Journal*, 13/1 (Spring 2005): 1, 3-9.

Mangrum, Robert G. "A Brief History of Howard Payne University." 2 November 2006 <hppt://www.hputx.edu/history> (accessed 15 June 2007).

_____. "Dr. Thomas H. Taylor, 1929–1955." 24 January 2005 <hppt://www.hputx.edu/history/presidents> (accessed 15 June 2007).

_____. "Historical Vignettes." 24 April 2006 <hppt://www.hputx.edu/historical vignettes> (accessed15 June 2006).

Mann, James. " 'Soft Sell' Is New Password for Churches." *U.S. News and World Report*, 22 August 1983, 32.

Mayer, Caroline E. "Religious Broadcasters: Beyond Pray TV." *Washington Post*, 5 February 1984, F1, 8-9;

Mohler, Al, and Dan Martin, "Meeting Recounts History of Moderate Movement." *Western Recorder*, 27 October 1992, 8.

Moore, Louis. "ACTS to Keep Dallas Base." San Antonio Light, 17 June 1988, n.p. Also distributed by Religious News Service and published in *The National Christian Reporter* (15 July 1988).

_____. "Baptists Trying to Find Crowd for Carter Speech." *Houston Chronicle*, 14 June 1978.

_____ and Tommy Miller. "Polarized Political Views Evident as Baptists Meet." *Houston Chronicle*, 12 June 1979, 1, 8.

Murray, Alice, "Schism Over Scepticism Shakes Southern Baptist Meeting," *The Atlanta Constitution*, 14 June 1978, B1.

"New Baptist Chief Asks Social Push." *San Antonio Express-News*, 6 November 1969, G6.

Newton, Jim. "Into All the World: Or at Least Those Homes with TV Sets." *MissionsUSA*, July–Aug 82, 3-8.

_____. "The Competitors." *MissionsUSA*. July–Aug 1990.

_____. "Vestal Urges Dialogue on Future of Denomination." *Baptist Message*, 21 June 1990, 19.

Parker, J. Michael, "Ex-S.A. Pastor's Book Conveys Gethsemane Agony of AIDS." *San Antonio Express-News*, 30 September 1995, A1, A12.

Parmley, Helen. "Baptist Radio-TV Commission Lays Off 35 Workers." *Dallas Morning News*, 1 September 1984, A37.

Perrigo, Dalene. "Christian TV Ready to Air in Anchorage." *Anchorage Times*, 7 January 1984, C8.

Pierce, John. "Baptists Remember Word Entertainment's Humble Roots in Texas." *Baptists Today*, 17 December 2001.

Rutledge, John. "Layman Acts as Pilot, Inspiration to Allen." *Baptist Standard*, 27 July 1977, 6.
Sawyers, Susan. "Mainline Religions Plugging Into the Power of Cable." *Greensboro News & Record*, 25 September 1988, C1-C2.
"Schoolboy's Triumph", *Time*, September 3, 1934. <http://www.time.com/time/magazine/article/0,9171,747859,00.html> (accessed 28 May 2007).
Shackleford, Al. "Radio-TV Commission Trustees Vote to Sell ACTS Network." *Baptist Press*, 15 April 1988, 1-2.
_____ and Dan Martin, "Network Sale Fails: RTVC to Continue ACTS." *Baptist Press*, 15 March 1989, 1-2.
Shurden, Walter B. "Noted Baptist Historian Gives Reflections on Historic 'Fellowship' Meet in Atlanta." *SBC Today*, October 1990, 4.
Smith, Elizabeth F. "Religious Freedom Essential Allen Tells Israeli Committee." *Foreign Mission News*, 20 May 1980, 2.
Speed, Billie Cheney. "Baptist Delegates Back Human Rights, Justice." *The Atlanta Journal*, 15 June 1978, A1, A24.
Stammer, Larry. "Former Baptist Leader Seeks a Dialogue with Gay Church." *Los Angeles Times*, 17 July 1999, Metro Section, 1.
"'Strong Can Be Generous:' President Talks to Baptists, Protesters Try to Interrupt." *The Atlanta Journal*, 16 June 1978, A1, A22.
"Southern Baptists Reject Anita Bryant for Office." *The Wall Street Journal*, 12 June 1978, 32.
"To Lift a Nation's Spirit." *Newsweek*, 23 July 1979, 20-30.
Toalston, Art. "Former SBC President Issues Statement about His Address to Homosexual Group." *Baptist Press*, 16 July 1999, 1.
Thompson, C. Lacy. "ACTS Sale Represents Move Forward, Leader Insists." *Baptist Message*, 26 May 1988, 5-6.
Tomoso, Bruce. "Amid the Turmoil: Ex-minister at Peace after Going Public on Family AIDS Crisis." *The Dallas Morning News*, 13 September 1992, A1, A40.
Tucker, Bert. "Independence Church Still Making History." *Baptist Standard*, 15 March 1967, 8-9.
"Vins Says Protests Help Soviet Prisoners." *Baptist Standard*, 9 May 1979, 3.
"Vins Chooses to Speak Rather than Meet Family." *Baptist Standard*, 20 June 1979, 11.
"Visionary: He Wants to Preach to Entire World." *The* (Raleigh NC) *News and Observer*, 18 June 1978, 1, 8.
Warner, Greg, Sarah Zimmerman and David Winfrey, "Fellowship Will Chart Future at Fort Worth Meeting." *Western Recorder*, 24 March 1992, 2.
Waters, Joe Justin. "Adventures with the Centurymen." Unpublished manuscript.
White, Gayle, "Do Reporters Hate Religion?" *Atlanta Journal and Constitution*, 6 March 1994, F2.
Winston, Diane. "ACTS Network Still Struggling." *The National Christian Reporter* 5/52 (28 February 1986): 1.

_____. "Baptist Cable-TV Chief Resigns." *Dallas Times Herald*, 12 April 1989, B3.

_____. "Christians Spar for Upper Hand Over Cable TV." *Dallas Times Herald*, 5 June 1988, A1, A18-19.

_____. "Southern Baptists' Sale of ACTS Cable Collapses." *Dallas Times Herald*, 15 March 1989, B3.

Woodward, Kenneth L., with Jerry Buckley and Eloise Salholz. "If You Can't Beat 'Em . . ." *Newsweek*, 9 February 1981, 103.

Index

Abe Lincoln Awards, 20, 179
ACTS Satellite Network, 27, 113, 177, 180-81
Agah, Ali, 167
AIDS Interfaith Task Force, Dallas, 205
Alex Spence School, Dallas, 45
Allen, Bryan Caleb, 203-206
Allen, Charles, 33
Allen, Diana, 202
Allen, Earl, 4, 15, 32-34, 42
Allen, Edna Ray, 14-15, 32-34
Allen, Lanny, 114
Allen, Linda Greer, 21, 30, 218
Allen, Lydia Williams, 29, 202-206
Allen, Kenneth Scott, 29, 202-207, 213-14
Allen, Matthew, 203-207
Allen, Michael Wayne, 29, 159, 201
Allen, Steven Ray (Skip), 29, 32, 94, 98, 205-206, 209, 213
Allen Temple Baptist Church, Oakland CA, 98
Allen, Wanda Massey, 13, 29, 71-73, 79, 134, 141, 159, 162, 199, 201-202, 208, 214, 216, 218, 234
Allen, William O., 33, 44, 52
Americans United for Separation of Church and State, 28, 85
Amity Foundation, 191
Anderson, Don, 108
Anderson, Earl, 38, 47
Anglin, Gene, 153
Appleman, Hyman, 45
Ascher Silberstein Elementary School, 43, Dallas, 46
Astrodome, Houston, 21, 27, 136, 155
Atkins, Center (Chip), 189
Ayres, Patricia, 112, 144, 159, 224

Baergen, Darrell, 179
Bailey, James, 111
Baines, George Washington, 40
Baker, Bo, 61
Baker, Robert, 75, 77
Bakker, Jim, 178, 188
Baldwin, Charles, 119
Baptists Committed to the SBC, 29, 222-25
Baptist General Convention of Texas, 25, 40, 58, 66, 85, 102, 132
    Christian Life Commission, 25, 80, 83, 85-105, 112, 207
    Department of Ministry with Minorities, 86
    Royal Ambassadors, 49, 50, 66-70
    Texas Baptist Historical Center of Independence, 40
    Urban Strategy Council, 134-135, 137
    Woman's Missionary Union, 49, 67-68
Baptist Joint Committee, 28, 85, 103, 158
Baptist Laity Journal, Inc., 222
BaptistNet, 182, 184
Baptist Press, 123, 161, 209
Baptist Standard, 27, 91- 92, 96, 102, 108, 123
Baptist Temple Baptist Church, San Antonio, 108
Baptists Today, 28, 30, 227
Barnette, Henlee, 25
Basden, Harold, 88
Bassett, Wallace, 56
Baugh, John, 222
Baylor University, 52
Baylor University Medical Center, Dallas, 202
Baylor University Oral History Project, 22
Begin, Menachem, 17, 150, 158-60, 163
Behesht Zahra Cemetery, Tehran, 169
Beijing Central Conservatory, 192-93
Bishop College, 98
Bishop, J. Ivyloy, 67
Black, Claude, 100, 108
Boggs, Frank, 63
Bond, Jeanne, 224
Botts, Laura, 22
Bowden, Mark, 164
Bowles, Chester, 107-109, 125
Boyles, Vernon, 215-17
Brake, Janice, 128-29, 176
Brannon, Clifton W., 140
Brown vs. Board of Education, 78-79
Bryan's House, 205
Bryant, Anita, 146, 148
Buckner Homes, 41
Buryl, Red, 190-92
Butt, Howard, 61

Cai, Dorothy, 192
Calhoun, Royce, 114
Cambodian Baptist Church, San Antonio, 118
Campbell, Will, 25

Camp David Peace Accords, 150, 159, 160
Cargill and Associates, 185
Carroll, B. H., 74
Carroll, Jack, 120
Carson Newman College, 82, 199
Carter Center, 12
Carter, Jimmy, 11-12, 17- 18, 24, 27, 28, 95, 139, 140-41, 143-44, 148, 150, 159, 164-65, 168, 170, 179, 190, 225
Carter, Rosalynn, 11, 18, 144, 215
CenturyMen, 190, 208
Cauthen, Baker James, 161
Central Baptist Church, Lawton, OK, 46
Cesaretti, Charles A., 167
Chambers, Tim, 98
Chancellor, John, 179
Chancellor, Oeita Bottorff, 220-25
Chapel at Big Canoe, 30, 83, 199, 207, 215-19
Cheng, Jean, 191
Chinese Baptist Church, San Antonio, 116
Chou Lien Hua, 194
Chrisman, P. Oswin, 231
Christian Century, 93
Christian Index, 144
Clarke, Chelsea, 22
Clinton, Bill, 206
Clawson, Cynthia, 179
Cockerell Hill Baptist Church, Ft. Worth, 80, 88
Coffin, William Sloan, 169, 174
Collins, Carr, 98-99
Colson, Charles, 179
Community Welfare Council, San Antonio, 111-12
Connally, John, 92, 100
Conner, W. T., 82
"Controversy" TV Program, 121
Cook, Verna, 46
Cooper, James, 50, 51, 56, 71, 94, 201
Cooper, Owen, 138-39, 143-44
Cooper, R. B., 52
Cooper, R. B., Jr., 114-15
Cooperative Baptist Fellowship, 112, 222-25
    Cooperative Baptist Missions Program, Inc., 224
    Global Missions Ministry Group, 224
Cooperative Services International, 191
Courtney, Ragan, 179

Craig, Marshall, 38
Criswell, W. A., 90
Cronkite, Walter, 179
Crook, William, 111
Cothen, Grady, 182
Crouch, Cleo, 110
Crumpler, Carolyn Weatherford, 209
Culpepper, Alan, 23
Currie, M. K., 98
Currie, David, 225

Dallas Baptist Association, 38
Dart, John, 219-220
Davey Crockett Elementary School, 44
Davis, M. E., 51
Dauphin Way Baptist Church, Mobile AL, 140
Dawson, J. M, 103-105
Dehoney, Wayne, 153
Deng Xiaoping, 190
Denison, James, 223
Dilday, Russell, 132, 197
Dinitz, Simcha, 158
Disraeli, Benjamin, 66
Dixon, Ron, 176
Down to Earth, 123
Duke University Divinity School, 74
Duffau Baptist Church, Hico, 57
Dunn, James, 16, 23, 25, 68, 83, 94-105, 138, 167, 218
Dunn, Marylyn, 103
Dunaway, John, 23

Edwards, James, 188
Elder, Lloyd, 183
Emmett, Arkansas, 41
Emmy Award, 20, 27, 193
English Language Institute, 117-18
Evans Avenue Baptist Church, Ft. Worth, 68, 102

Fairview Baptist Church, Evant, 57
Faith and Family, Inc., 199, 219
Falk, Richard, 166, 173
Falwell, Jerry, 172, 196
Family Net, 196
Fanning, Buckner, 108
Farhand, Mansour, 167
Farrar, C. W., 67
Finlator, W. W., 25

FBC, Amarillo, 199, 214
FBC, Arlington, 204, 218
FBC, Ashville, NC, 224
FBC, Beaumont, 89
FBC, Celeste, 40
FBC, Columbia, SC, 140
FBC, Dublin, 58, 66
FBC, Gonzalez, 87
FBC, McKinney, 92
FBC, Marshall, 70
FBC, Midland, 140
FBC, New Orleans, 155
FBC, Pleasant Grove, 52
FBC, Richardson, 137
FBC, San Antonio, 11, 25, 29, 80, 89, 104-131
FBC, Tulsa, OK, 139
FBC, Tyler, 101
FBC, Van Alstyne, 70, 76
FBC, Wichita Falls, 102
FBC, Wills Point, 78, 88
First Christian Church, Colorado Springs CO, 203, 207
First Missionary Baptist Church, Los Angeles, 99
Fletcher, Jesse, 147
Florida Baptist Convention, 90
Flowers, Amanda Jane, 33
Fooshe, Joanne, 70
Forrest High School, Dallas, 47, 71
Fort Worth Star-Telegram, 93
Fourth Street Inn, 118, 120
Fox, Arthur, 34
Freedom Forum, 30, 219, 221
Freeman, C. Wade, 136
Freezor, Forest, 90
Friends of ACTS, Inc., 189
Friendship Force, 11, 215
Fuller, J. Woodrow, 90

Gambrell Street Baptist Church, Ft. Worth, 82
Garrett, James Leo, 77
Gaston Avenue Baptist Church, Dallas, TX, 25, 88
George, Jeanette Clift, 216
Geshun Ma, 190
Ghotbzedeh, Sadegh, 168, 170
Gilmore, Herbert, 25

Girl's Auxiliary, 49
Glass, Bill, 119, 216
Glass, David, 160-162
Golden Gate Baptist Theological Seminary, 29, 102, 203
Goldstein Women's Hat Factory, 53
Good News TV Program, 120
Good Street Baptist Church, Dallas, 98
Graham, Billy, 59, 145, 155
Graham, Ruth Bell, 145, 147
Grant, Marian, 145
Griffin, Marvin, 93
Griffin, Otho, 118
Gumbelton, Thomas, 169, 174

Hagee, John, 189
Hall, Tammy, 22
Hardin-Simons Baptist College, 54, 86
Harvard University Divinity School, 74
Hard Rock Café, 39
Harwell, Jack, 144
Haselden, Kyle, 93
Hastey, Stan, 168
Hatfield, Mark, 179
Haynes, Charles, 221
Held, Stephanie, 208
Henderson, Eula Mae, 67
Hewitt, John, 224
Hightower, Jack, 159
Hillis, Marvin, 101
Hinson, William, 155
Hollis, Harry, 147
Holmes, Thomas, 25
Houston Chronicle, 22
House, William, 75
Houston, Sam, 40
Howard, William, 124-25
Howard, Rev. William, 169, 174
Howard, W. F., 62
Howard Payne College, 52, 53, 58, 66, 71, 124
Huff, Z. D., 59
Hughey, J. D., 158
Hultgren, Warren, 139, 140
Humphries, Barbara, 89
Honeycutt, Roy, 197
Hunter Street Baptist Church, Birmingham, 108
Hurt, John, 138

Independence Baptist Church, Dresdan, 40, 41
International Covenant on Civil and Political Rights, 163
InTouch Ministries, 196

Jacobsen, David and Helen, 111
Jackson, Richard, 140
James, E. S., 91-92, 102, 108
James, Rhett, 99
Jarkowski, Gene F., 179
Jinling Union Theological Seminary, 191
Jivasantikarn, Nirund, 214
Johns Creek Baptist Church, Alpharetta GA, 218
Johnson, Lyndon B., 40, 85, 100, 102, 111
Johnson, Walter Nathan, 25
Jolley, Marc. 23
Jones, Jim, 93, 101
Jordan, Clarence, 25, 57
Joske's Department Store, San Antonio, 100, 108
Joubert, René and Joseph, 208, 218

Kimball, Charles Anthony, 167, 172
Kennedy, John F., 92, 100-101
Kennedy, Bobby, 101
Kerrigan, Herbert, 162
Khomeini, Ayatollah, 164, 166, 169-171
King, Coretta Scott, 145, 147
King, Martin Luther, Jr., 97
Kirby, William, 166- 167
Kollach, Teddy, 159
Kuralt, Charles, 179

Lackland Air Force Base, San Antonio, 107, 117-19
Laingen, Bruce, 169-170
Laotian Baptist Church, San Antonio, 118
Landis, James, 137
Langley, Ralph, 61
Latham Springs Baptist Assembly, 50
Lawson, Douglass, 199, 214
Lindsay, Harold, Sr., 154
Lindsey, Robert, 158-62
Lolley, Randall, 197
Loring, Ben, 214
Love in Action, 208
Lundy, Emily "Rusty" Nail, 63

Martin, Tom, 162
McCall, Abner, 92, 154
McCall, Duke K., 224
McCartney, Richard T., 23, 188-89, 195
McClellen, Albert, 144
McCormick, James, 218
McGlamery, M. E., 79
McKinney Avenue Baptist Church, Dallas, 38, 42, 64
McCracken, Jerrell, 63
McCullough, Glendon, 139, 148
McIver, Bruce, 61
Mahoney, William, 114
Mainstream Baptists, 225
Malone, John, 177
Manor Baptist Church, San Antonio, 108
Marcus, Sidney, 98
Marney, Carlyle, 25
Martin Springs Baptist Church, 40
Maston, Essie Mae MacDonald, 81
Maston, T. B., 25, 27, 75-77, 81-83, 86-87, 127, 152
Massey, Bill, 71
Massey, Luther, 72
Mayflower Hotel, Washington, D.C., 11, 144
Merrit, Jack, 79
Metro House, San Antonio, 115, 125
Metropolitan Community Church, 209-210
Mexican Baptist Institute, San Antonio, 117
Miles, Olan, 55
Miller, Acker C., 86-88, 92, 105
Miller, Laurania, 49
Mission Arlington, 204
Mitchell, Henry, 98
Montazari, Ayatollah Husayn-ali, 171
Moody, Broadus, 149
Moody, Jess, 61
Moore, Guy, 93
Moore, Winifred, 197
Moral Side of the News, 121
Moyers, Bill, 92, 100-101
Mt. Lebenon Baptist Assembly, 89
Mt. Sinai Hospital, San Francisco, 203
Mountview Baptist Church, 57
Mulholland, Bob, 179
Munger Place Baptist Church, Dallas, 38-39, 45
Myers, Charles, 92
Myers, Lewis, 191

Navon, Yitzhak, 159
Naylor, Robert, 154
National AIDS Commission, 205
National Baptist Convention, USA, Inc., 98
National Conference on Broadcast Ministries, 182, 190
Neibuhr, H. Richard, 82
Neibuhr, Reinhold, 81
Neuhart, Al, 219
Nelson, Dotson, 140
New Baptist Covenant, 24, 98, 137, 225-27
Newman, Stuart, 75
New Orleans Baptist Theological Seminary, 74
Newport, Russell, 144
Newton, Jim, 22, 130, 143
Newton, Louie B., 37
New York Times, The, 102, 131, 149, 207
Nixon, Richard, 92
Norris, J. Frank, 38
Northcutt, Jesse, 75-77
North American Baptist Fellowship, 225
North Dallas High School, 49
North Phoenix Baptist Church, Phoenix AZ, 140

Oakcliff Baptist Church, 56
Office of Economic Opportunity, 111
Oldenberg, Bob, 114, 120
Overby, Charles, 219

Pacifica Baptist Church, San Francisco, 203
Pahlavi, Shah of Iran, 118, 164-165
Palmer, Gerald, 138
Parham, Robert, 173
Park Cities Baptist Church, Dallas, 98, 152
Parks, Keith, 58, 224-25
Patterson, Paige, 22, 152-53, 196-97
Patterson, Thomas Armour, 89-93, 101, 108, 132, 154
Paxon, Tom, 177
Payntner, Suzii, 96, 105
Peace Corp, 100
Perry, Beth, 22
Perry, Troy, 209-10
Phelps, Ralph, 75-76, 103
Pine Street Baptist Church, 40, 47, 51, 53, 71

Pinson, William M., Jr., 83, 85, 87-89, 94, 95, 97, 100, 102, 132, 134, 137, 142
Pleitz, James, 152
Porter, Jack, 92
Precht, Henry, 167-168
Pressler, Paul, 28, 152-53, 196-97
Price, Ed, 153
Price, J. M, 75, 82
Providence, Arkansas, 32, 44
Providence Baptist Church, Lufkin, 40

Ramsey, Bob N., 79
Rauschenbusch, Walter, 25, 81-82, 86
Ray, Billy, 48
Ray, Ida, 44
Ray, J. W., 34, 44
Ray, Leo, 34
Reinhart Baptist Church, Detroit, MI, 37
Reflections . . . by the Pastor, 122
Resource Development, Inc., 185, 188
Revolutionary Communist Youth Brigade, 149
Reynolds, Herb, 214
Richardson, Lonnie, 55
Ricks, Thomas M., 168-170, 172
Riley, James, 79
Ringle, Al, 114-115
Roberts, John, 197
Robertson, Pat, 177-178
Robison, James, 178, 207
Robison, Olin, 151
Rogers, Adrian, 153, 154
Routh, Porter, 142, 144
Rowe, Lynwood "Schoolboy", 44
Rowell, Edd, 23
Royal Lane Baptist Church, Dallas, 105
Rutledge, Arthur, 70

Sadat, Anwar, 150, 159
Sagamore Hills Baptist Church, Ft. Worth, 93
Sandole, Bob, 119-120
Satellite Network Services, 189
Scales, John, 179
Scarborough, L. R., 74, 82
Scott, Manuel, 155
Scudder, C. W., 77
Second Baptist Church, Houston, 140
Seigenthaler, John, 219

Self, William L., 147, 218
Shaiot-Madari, Ayatollah, 171
Shamberger, William, 101, 133-34
Shanghai University, 190, 192
Shaw, William, 98
Sherman, Cecil, 30, 224-25
Shriver, Sargent, 100
Shurden, Walter, 24, 223
Skinner, Tom, 109
Smith, Bailey, 146
Smith, David and Gloria, 144, 162
Smith, Estelle, 59
Smith, J. Alfred, 98
Smith, Wayne, 214-15
Southern Baptist Convention, 19, 21, 25, 26, 81
   Baptist Sunday School Board, 142, 182
   Bold Mission Thrust, 26, 138-42, 147, 155, 176, 178
   Brotherhood Commission, 11, 139, 142
   Christian Life Commission, 87-88, 112, 147
   Cooperative Program, 139, 140, 178, 179
   Executive Committee, 183
   Foreign Mission Board, 139, 142, 155
   Home Mission Board, 116, 138, 142, 155
   Mission Service Corp, 13, 26, 142-45, 155
   Radio and Television Commission, 26, 27, 28, 29, 131, 166, 175-99
   Ridgecrest Baptist Assembly, 50
   Volunteers in Missions, 139, 142
SBC Pastor's Conference, 146
Southern Baptist Theological Seminary, 74, 79, 86
Southwestern Baptist Theological Seminary, 45, 46, 65, 67, 73-83, 87, 92
Squires, Janet, M.D., 208
Stanley, Charles, 196, 197
Starlite Award, 193
Stevens, Paul, 175, 179
Stinson, Roddy, 122, 127
Strickland, Phil, 16, 25, 94-105, 218
Stroud, Margille S., 123
Sullivan, James, 138
Summers, Ray, 75, 77
Sumner, Bill, 22
Swaggart, Jimmy, 188

Swank, Fred, 93

Tacker, Ralph, 190-191
Timberlawn Hospital, Dallas, 201
Tamir, Shmuel, 158-59, 161
Tanner, William, 143
Tapcott, L. H., 67
Taylor, Bob, 179
Taylor, Thomas H., 53-54
Tebbets, Gary, 154
Temple Emmanue-El, Dallas, 208
Tennison, Clifton, 138, 190
Texas Christian University, 76, 82
Texas Study Commission on AIDS, 205
Texas Wesleyan University, 76, 103
Thomas, Oliver, 221
Thornton, Robert, 98, 179
Ting, Bishop T. H., 191
Todd, W. A., 59
Touchton, Don, 154
Towery, Britt, 191
Travis Avenue Baptist Church, Ft. Worth, 214
Trentham, Charles, 151
Trinity Baptist Church, San Antonio, 107, 108, 144
Trueblood, Elton, 147
Truett, George W., 64, 73, 83
Trull, Joe, 25
Turner, Paul, 25
Turner, Ted, 177
Tyler Street United Methodist Church, Dallas, 101-102

Underwood, William, 24, 225-26
Union Seminary of New York, 74
United Christian Council in Israel, 158, 163
USA Today, 30
UN Declaration on Universal Human Rights, 147, 149, 160, 163
United States Services Organization Service Center, 115, 125
University of Chicago Divinity School, 74, 82
University of North Carolina, 82

Valentine, Foy, 16, 25, 87, 92, 94, 105, 138, 218
Vanderbilt University, 30
   Divinity School, 74

First Amendment Center, 28, 219-21
Veeco Group, 189
Vestal, Daniel, 24, 30, 140, 222-25
Vines, Jerry, 140-41
Vins, Georgi, 151, 155

W. Tyler Associates, 185
Wade, Charles, 204, 234
Waldheim, Kurt, 179
Walsh, John, 166-68, 172
Ware, Browning, 50, 52
Ware, Martha, 52
Ware, Weston, 52, 96, 102
Warren, Diane, 226
Washington Post, 150
Watterson, A. Douglas, 138, 147, 154
Wayland Baptist College, 67
Webb, Perry F., Sr., 107
Wellborn, Grace, 59, 71
Wells, Charles, 93
Werblowsky, Zwi, 163
West Texas State College, 102
White, C. Dale, 168, 173
White House Conference on Children and Youth, 103
White House Conference on Civil Rights, 100
White Rock Baptist Church, Philadelphia, 98
Wilbur Award, 220
Wilkes, Chester, 124-15
William B. Travis Elementary School, 45
Williams, J. Howard, 67, 79, 86
Williams, Luke, 108, 113, 152, 176, 178, 206
Willis, Ron, 114
Wilshire Baptist Church, Dallas, 199
Winter, Jimmie, 114-15
Witherspoon, J. B., 79
Woman's Missionary Union, SBC, 113, 142, 207
Wong, David, 192
World Evangelism Foundation, 133
World Mission Journal, 143
Wyatt, Robert, 220

Yale University Divinity School, 74, 82
Yonok College American Foundation, 214
Young, Andrew, 173
Young, Edwin, 140
Youth Revival Movement, 59-63